# THE HISTORY OF
# WESTERN AFRICA

# THE BRITANNICA GUIDE TO AFRICA

# THE HISTORY OF
# WESTERN AFRICA

EDITED BY AMY MCKENNA, SENIOR EDITOR, GEOGRAPHY AND HISTORY

Britannica®
Educational Publishing

IN ASSOCIATION WITH

ROSEN
EDUCATIONAL SERVICES

Published in 2011 by Britannica Educational Publishing
(a trademark of Encyclopædia Britannica, Inc.)
in association with Rosen Educational Services, LLC
29 East 21st Street, New York, NY 10010.

First Edition

Britannica Educational Publishing
**Michael I. Levy: Executive Editor**
J.E. Luebering: Senior Manager
Marilyn L. Barton: Senior Coordinator, Production Control
Steven Bosco: Director, Editorial Technologies
Lisa S. Braucher: Senior Producer and Data Editor
Yvette Charboneau: Senior Copy Editor
Kathy Nakamura: Manager, Media Acquisition
Amy McKenna: Senior Editor, Geography and History

Rosen Educational Services
Shalini Saxena: Editor
Nelson Sá: Art Director
Cindy Reiman: Photography Manager
Nicole Russo: Designer
Matthew Cauli: Cover Design
Introduction by Monique Vescia

**Library of Congress Cataloging-in-Publication Data**

The history of western Africa / edited by Amy McKenna.—1st ed.
    p. cm.—(The Britannica guide to Africa)
"In association with Britannica Educational Publishing, Rosen Educational Services."
Includes bibliographical references and index.
ISBN 978-1-61530-316-8 (library binding)
1. Africa, West--History. I. McKenna, Amy, 1969-
DT475.H577 2011
966—dc22

2010021500

*Manufactured in the United States of America*

**On the cover:** A Tuareg herder rests with his camels in Timbuktu, once a thriving centre of
trade and Islamic scholarship in Mali. © *www.istockphoto.com / Alan Tobey*

**On pages 1, 17, 39, 57, 81, 86, 91, 99, 103, 108, 114, 119, 124, 134, 139, 146, 153, 162, 167,
173, 194, 200, 207:** Partial view of Elmina Castle (formerly called São Jorge da Mina) in
present-day Ghana. *Issouf Sanogo/AFP/Getty Images*

# CONTENTS

6

12

31

62

85

94

110

115

126

137

147

154

210

INTRODUCTION

## AFRICA,
### NORTH-WEST PART.

Scale, 188 English Statue Miles to One Inch.

Importance of places is indicated by style of type, approximately, as follows:

TUNIS, Freetown, Timbuktu,
Kamerun, El-Harib.

Native States: MANDINGO
Native Tribes: *MANDINGOES*

Volcanoes, active during 19th century, thus: ●

Capitals of Countries
Capitals of smaller divisions and of native States
Railroads, finished
Railroads, projected
Steamship Lines
Caravan Routes
Submarine and Overland Telegraph Lines
Lights & Lighthouses
Forts
Battlefields
Wells
Sandy Desert
Wady
Unexplored Rivers
Falls and Rapids
Salt Lakes
Elevations in English Feet
Depths in English Feet

NOTE.—Algeria, Tunis, nearly all of the Sahara, and the Niger Basin above the State of Gando belong to France or are within the French sphere of influence.

Morocco is an independent sultanate.

The coast country south of Morocco, including the Guinea coast, is divided up between Spain, Portugal, France, England and Germany by international agreements. The kingdom of Sokoto and the lower part of the Niger Basin are English. The boundaries between the possessions of England, Germany and France in the "hinterlands" of Togo, Ashanti, etc., are being settled in Europe.

Kamerun is German, the Canary Islands Spanish and the Madeira Islands Portuguese.

Liberia is an independent Negro Republic. Descendants of freedmen removed from the United States constitute the dominant class.

M.-N. WORKS.

Translations:

Adrar, Uplands or Mountains; Aïn, Spring; Areg, Desert or Waste Region; Beni, Son; Bir, Well; Birat, Capital; Erg, Hammada, Desert or Waste Region; Jebel, Mountain; Ras, Cape or Point; Sebkha, Shott, Salt Lake; Ulad, Progeny; Wady, Riverbed.

COPYRIGHT, 1897 AND 1900, BY THE CENTURY CO.

The many terrains of western Africa—including deserts, grasslands, equatorial forests, river basins, and thousands of miles of coastline—are perhaps as diverse as the various peoples who have called the region home over the centuries. Although the countries of the area have faced innumerable hardships, they are also home to cultures that have drawn strength from their past and incorporated traditions from a wide range of influences. This volume examines the rich history of western African kingdoms and countries as they have variously struggled against invasions by other kingdoms, slavery, colonialism, and corruption, and emerged as independent states striving to secure economic growth and stability into the 21st century.

Human civilization in western Africa can be traced back many thousands of years. Archaeologists have found evidence in the Sahara of agricultural practices and cattle herding that date to 4000 BCE, before that region had turned into desert. These cultural developments mirror those that occurred in Egypt's Nile Valley around the same time. Systems of trade evolved between the ancient population centres of western Africa and peoples to the north early on as well, and they persisted even after the desert emerged, as trans-Saharan trade routes linked northern and western Africa. Amazigh (Berber) tradesmen from Morocco and other lands to the north crisscrossed the desert sands to exchange cloth and salt for gold, ivory, and slaves. The domestication of the camel early in the 1st millennium CE furthered the expansion of trade across this region. Along with trade of goods and slaves, Islamic religious beliefs and practices eventually made their way across the Sahara.

During a period sometimes called the Golden Age of West Africa, a series of powerful empires developed in the western Sudan, an area of grassland plains that stretched roughly from Lake Chad to the Atlantic Coast of Africa, the northern reaches of which formed the southernmost border of the Sahara Desert. The ancient kingdom of Ghana (actually centred on the border of the modern-day countries of Mauritania and Mali and not in modern-day Ghana) was a wealthy centre of trade in the western Sudan with a sophisticated system of political and social organization. Ghana acquired its wealth by trading gold—which it procured from other sources—for salt, as well as through farming and raising livestock. The people of Ghana possessed the advanced technologies of ironworking, and the kingdom commanded an impressive military. A system of import and export taxes helped enrich Ghana, and by the 9th century, it had become a rich and powerful empire.

In the mid-13th century, the wealthy kingdom of Mali with its abundant

*Map of northwest Africa, from the 10th edition of* Encyclopædia Britannica, *published in 1902.*

goldfields succeeded Ghana as the dominant power in the western Sudan. Under a king named Sundiata, the kings of Mali, who were members of the Keita clan, took over what was left of ancient Ghana, creating a more extensive empire. While the society of the western Sudan was largely pagan before this time, Islam had since spread among the traders and merchants.

The earliest firsthand account of the region was likely the one written by Ibn Baṭṭuṭah (born in 1304), the famous Arab world traveler whose journals chronicle his many explorations and provide fascinating glimpses of medieval western Africa. Ibn Baṭṭuṭah visited Mali between 1352 and 1353 CE after the reign of Mansa Mūsā, who had been king of the Mali Empire from 1307 to 1332 and had taken a legendary pilgrimage, or hajj, from Mali via Egypt to Mecca. Mansa Mūsā's hajj reflected the increasing prevalence of Islam in the region, and the extravagant nature of his journey was a testament to the incredible wealth of his kingdom. After his hajj, Mansa Mūsā built a great mosque (Djinguereber) in Timbuktu, a great city that was home to madrasas, or Islamic schools, such as the Sankore University. Timbuktu was an intellectual and spiritual centre of Islam throughout Africa during the 15th and 16th centuries and had a history as an important trading centre. Founded by Tuareg nomads in the 11th century CE and later incorporated into the Mali Empire, Timbuktu is situated just north of the Niger, one of the longest rivers in Africa and a natural avenue of communication and trade. The might of

the Mali Empire eventually receded, and it was absorbed by the nearby Songhai Empire, which ruled much of western Africa during the 15th and 16th centuries. Under the leadership of Sonni 'Alī, the Songhai conquered several cities, including Timbuktu, and expanded the empire. The capital of the kingdom was Gao, situated along the Niger River in what would become present-day Mali. Founded in the 7th century, Gao became a major terminus for caravans crossing the Sahara.

The first Europeans to reach western Africa were Portuguese sea traders looking to divert some of the gold trade from North Africa. In 1471 they landed along the coast of what would be modern-day Ghana between the mouths of the Ankobra and Volta rivers, a stretch that became known as the Gold Coast, though the Portuguese called it Mina ("the mine"). The Akan people who lived there had access to gold, which they were willing to trade for cloth, base metals, and other manufactured goods. The Dutch followed the Portuguese and established trading posts . Between 1652 and 1713, the Netherlands, France, and Britain fought one another to maintain trading footholds in western Africa.

In a land with too few people to cultivate its resources, human beings represented a valuable commodity long before the arrival of Europeans. Conquered peoples were often enslaved and kept in western Africa or sent to the Mediterranean and the Middle East. When the Europeans began landing along the western coast of the continent and trading with the people there, they were able to exploit this practice. They sought slaves to work on newly established plantations in Brazil, the Caribbean, and the Americas. By the 1520s, a small slave trade had sprung up between Europeans and Africans to supply field workers for Caribbean plantations. The majority of African slaves were taken from western Africa, and part of the coastal area adjacent to the Gold Coast became known as the Slave Coast. In the 18th century, the number of indigenous people from all of Africa who were landing in the "New World" as slaves was approximately 5.2 million; an additional one million died en route. Eventually, changing attitudes about the buying and selling of human beings lead to the abolition of slavery in Britain, the United States, and other countries and brought an end to the Atlantic slave trade in the second half of the 19th century.

However, Africa meant more to Europeans than just a source of labour. Beginning in the mid-1800s, European countries with designs on Africa's rich natural resources began competing again for control over the continent. After the Berlin West Africa Conference (1884–1885), a new period of colonial expansion parcelled out the western region among the French, British, and Germans (Spain and Portugal already controlled certain areas), leaving only the Republic of Liberia, which was colonized by freed American slaves, as an independent territory. Subduing the indigenous people in those territories proved extremely difficult, time-consuming, and costly for the colonial powers.

The scramble for possession of Africa was rationalized, in part, by a belief that European civilization was far superior to African culture. The terrible carnage of World War I forced many people to re-evaluate that notion. Changing European attitudes toward Africa coincided with increasing efforts among Africans to shake off colonial rule. Organizations such as the African Democratic Rally began to form and attract support among politicians of French colonies. Under the leadership of Kwame Nkrumah, in 1957, the British colony of the Gold Coast was the first colony in sub-Saharan Africa to gain its independence when it became the country of Ghana. Other countries quickly followed, bringing to power African leaders such as Léopold Sédar Senghor in Senegal and Sékou Touré in Guinea. By 1976, all former European colonies in western Africa had been recognized as independent states.

As this volume makes clear, western Africa has long been home to a diverse array of peoples, each with its own distinct histories, cultures, and traditions. However, the map of western Africa had been divided by the colonizing powers without respect for geographic or ethnic boundaries, which has affected numerous aspects of the cultures of each country. For example, many citizens in western African countries still speak the language of the former colonial power: French is the official language in former French colonies such as Côte d'Ivoire and Burkina Faso, and English is the official language in countries such as Ghana and Nigeria, which once were under British rule.

Still, many pre-colonial traditions are apparent throughout the region. For example, most people in western Africa communicate in indigenous African languages that fall into three major language families, evidence of the deep cultural connections that predate the colonial period. Additionally, in the 17–19th centuries, a series of jihads, or holy wars, contributed to the spread of Islam in the western Sudan. In countries such as Guinea, Mali, Mauritania, Niger, and Senegal, Islam is currently the dominant religion.

Despite possessing rich natural resources, many western African countries have struggled economically since gaining their independence. One of the most crippling legacies of colonialism, during which many colonies produced only select exports, is that today many African countries must import most manufactured goods. Having to rely on imported goods for many basic necessities has put these countries at an economic disadvantage, resulting in poverty and heavy burdens of debt. Some countries have suffered devastating civil wars and political upheaval. The brutal regimes of some dictators have prompted other countries to impose economic sanctions and various means of pressuring governments to comply with international laws.

Despite these challenges, western Africa appears poised for economic growth, which may, if well managed, improve the quality of life for its peoples in the 21st century. The region still boasts a wealth of natural resources, including diamonds, uranium, petroleum, and bauxite (used to produce aluminium), avidly sought by other countries. International investment has allowed for greater development in a number of areas. The region has seen a growing number of stable governments, and in 2005, Liberia elected president Ellen Johnson Sirleaf, the first woman head of state in Africa. The future of the region's economic health will depend, to a large degree, on whether its individual states can achieve political stability.

The world's understanding of African history has often been compromised by the fact that many accounts of this region were written by Europeans and were thus shaped by European attitudes about race and lack of knowledge of African culture. Archaeological evidence, oral histories, art objects, and artifacts all prove western Africa was home to a series of richly developed civilizations, which were long established by the time the Europeans arrived. Today, there is still much we can learn by examining the past.

# CHAPTER 1

## EARLY HISTORY

W estern Africa is a term used in this book to designate a
geographic region within the continent of Africa and
includes the countries of Benin, Burkina Faso, Cameroon,
Cape Verde, Chad, Côte d'Ivoire, Equatorial Guinea, The
Gambia, Ghana, Guinea, Guinea-Bissau, Liberia, Mali,
Mauritania, Niger, Nigeria, Senegal, Sierra Leone, and Togo.
The term West Africa is also often used to refer to this part of
the continent. As conventionally understood, however, West
Africa is primarily a political and economic designation and
comprises all the areas considered here except Cameroon,
Chad, Equatorial Guinea, and the Saharan parts of Mali,
Mauritania, and Niger.

A reasonable body of sources for the writing of western
African history begins to be available about 1000 CE. Three
centuries earlier the Arabs had completed their conquest of
Africa north of the Sahara and so came into possession of the
northern termini of trade routes reaching across the desert to
western Africa. The lively school of geographers and historians that flourished in the Muslim world from about the 9th
to the 14th century thus secured access to growing amounts
of information about what they called the bilād al-sūdān, the
territory of the black peoples south of the Sahara.

This information has its limitations. The Muslim writers, contemptuous of non-Islamic societies, passed on little
of what they must have known about the organization of

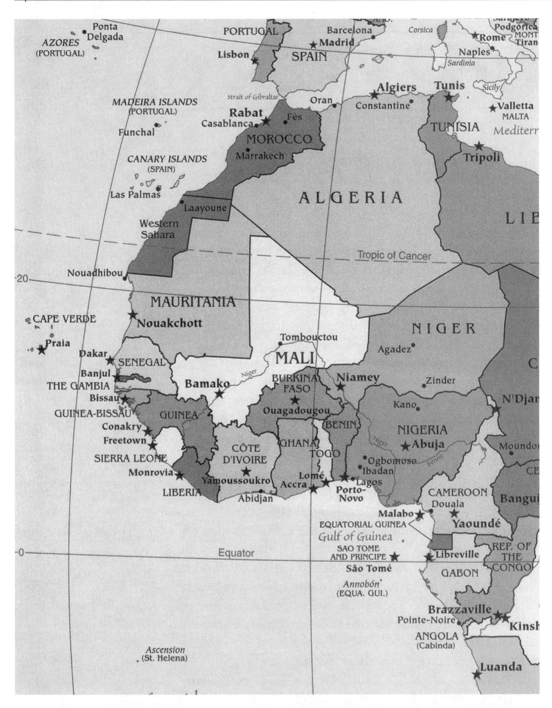

*The countries of western Africa include a number of coastal states as well as island and land-locked regions.* Courtesy of the University of Texas Libraries, The University of Texas at Austin

pagan black societies and tended to concentrate on and condemn what struck them as their more monstrous aberrations. Conversely, they doubtless exaggerated the importance of the Islamization that entered western Africa with the Muslim traders crossing the Sahara. The earliest firsthand account of western Africa is probably that of the world traveler Ibn Baṭṭūṭah, who visited the western Sudan in 1352–53. Finally, the North African merchants did not penetrate into western Africa beyond the urban centres of trade and government that existed or came to develop on the northern fringes of the cultivable savannas fronting the Sahara. Their *bilād al-sūdān* was in fact only the northern marches. Nevertheless, the picture of western Africa given in the early Muslim writings is of major interest.

## MUSLIMS IN WESTERN AFRICA

It is apparent that, right from the beginnings of Arab contact, the organization of the more northerly western African peoples was not solely on the basis of small groups. They had considerable towns and cities that were supported by a developed agriculture. They had organized networks of markets and trade and a developed system of monarchical government. Kings, whose claim to power was based on descent from the mythical divine founding ancestors of their ethnic groups, taxed trade and levied tribute on the agricultural villages through their possession of bodies of retainers who provided them both with military force and with a hierarchy of officials.

It seems likely that there was an increase in the volume of trans-Saharan trade following the organization of North Africa under Muslim dynasties and that this growth of international trade with western Africa stimulated the growth there of internal trade, urbanization, and monarchical government. Certainly the control of trade, towns, and government in western Africa became increasingly Islamic in form. But it is quite clear that the foundations for the economic and political development of the western Sudan were in existence before the time of contact with Muslim traders or authors.

## THE SUDAN

*When presented with the term* Sudan, *most people think of the large country of that name in northeastern Africa that became independent in 1956. The Sudan, however, is also the name of the vast tract of open savanna plains extending across the African continent between the southern limits of the Sahara and the northern limits of the equatorial rain forests. It extends for more than 3,500 miles (5,500 km) across Africa, from Senegal's Cape Verde peninsula on the Atlantic to the highlands of Ethiopia and the Red Sea. The Sudan geographical region is mentioned frequently when discussing the history of western Africa.*

Early Muslim interest was concentrated on two major western African kingdoms: Kanem, in the east, north of Lake Chad; and Ghana, in the extreme west, on the borders of modern Mauritania and Mali. The Muslim sources, which are broadly confirmed by local tradition, indicate that the kingdom of Kanem was being formed during the 9th and 10th centuries through an interaction between Saharan nomads and agricultural village communities. But ancient Ghana (not to be confused with its modern namesake, considerably farther to the south and east) had already reached levels of organization that presuppose several centuries of continuing development.

The earliest extant Arabic reference to a kingdom of Ghana dates from the early 9th century. In the middle of the 11th century, the Córdoban geographer Abū U'bayd al-Bakrī described its capital, court, and trade in some detail. The capital was made up of two towns, a stone-built town inhabited by the Muslim traders and a mud-built one of the local Mande in which the king had his walled palace. Their centres were six miles apart, and the whole of the intervening country was more or less built up. The considerable population was supported by the produce of surrounding farms, which were watered from wells. The court displayed many signs of wealth and power, and the king had under him a considerable number of satellite rulers. A principal part of his revenue was derived from regular taxes on trade. The mainstay of this trade was the exchange of gold, which Ghana's

own merchants brought from lands to the south, for salt, which the northern traders brought in from salt deposits in the Sahara.

Al-Bakrī's description is broadly confirmed by archaeology. The region in which ancient Ghana was situated contains the ruins of a considerable number of stone-built towns that must have been supported by extensive agricultural and commercial activity; those at Koumbi Saleh are generally identified with the capital described by al-Bakrī.

The relatively extensive Muslim interest in Ghana was undoubtedly due to its importance as a source of gold. Kanem seems to have been less important commercially; the main interest of the Muslim authors seems to have been in the quasi-divine status of its kings, which offended their Muslim principles. Other western African kingdoms undoubtedly existed at this time, but the Muslim sources record little of them beyond their names and approximate locations. Thus between Ghana and Kanem was Kawkaw, perhaps the nucleus of the later Songhai kingdom of Gao. Malel, to the south of Ghana, may similarly have been a prototype of the later Mande kingdom of Mali, which ultimately was to eclipse and absorb Ghana itself.

There are perhaps three possible—and not mutually exclusive—explanations for the origins and development of the kingdoms that Arab trade and scholarship had revealed by about 1000 CE. The first is that they were the result of the invasion of agricultural territory by pastoralists from the Sahara who belonged to the Libyan Amazigh (plural: Imazighen) groups who spoke a non-Semitic language and were dominant in North Africa before its conquest by the Arabs.

This is the explanation often given in western Sudanese traditions and chronicles. From roughly the 15th century onward, many of these were preserved by local authors who wrote in Arabic and were Muslims, and who thus had some incentive to link the history of their peoples with that of North Africa and with the adjacent Middle East. It was also the explanation favoured by European historians of the later 19th and earlier 20th centuries when Europeans were themselves conquering and colonizing black Africa. There thus evolved the so-called "Hamitic hypothesis," by which it was generally supposed that any progress and development among agricultural blacks was the result of conquest or infiltration by pastoralists from northern or northeastern Africa. Specifically, it was supposed that many of the ideas and institutions of monarchy had spread through Africa by diffusion from the ancient civilization of Egypt and the Nile valley.

There can be no doubt that over the centuries pastoralists from the Sahara have indeed advanced and conquered southward. But not all of these were Libyan Imazighen; some, such as the dynasts of Kanem, were black African in language and culture. Nor is it easy to understand how mobile desert pastoral groups could be effective transmitters of ideas and institutions from the settled civilization of the Nile valley to other agricultural lands in western Africa. It would seem more probable that conquering pastoralists who did succeed in establishing new kingdoms and dynasties in western Africa should do so by taking over existing monarchies, perhaps city-states or even "village-states," and amalgamating these into larger units. Some early western African traditions can certainly be interpreted in this sense.

This leads to the second explanation for the origins and development of monarchical statehood among the western African groups. There is archaeological evidence for the evolution of a cattle-herding and agricultural economy among a mixed population of Libyan Imazighen and black agricultural peoples (now called Ḥarāṭīn) in the Sahara by at least 4000 BCE—i.e., more or less contemporary with similar developments in the Nile valley. The desiccation of the Sahara and the evolution of its present desert between about 8000 and 2000 BCE must have occasioned an outflowing of population in which the blacks concentrated in the savannas to the south of it. There, in favourable riverine or lacustrine environments, it seems reasonable to suppose that the same desire to avoid conflicts over land and water rights and to control and exploit agricultural surpluses, which had led in the exceptionally fertile but extremely constricted environment of the Nile valley to the dramatic kingship and civilization of the pharaohs, should have occasioned the evolution of similar if less spectacular monarchies.

It should be noted, however, that the major western African monarchies known to the Arabs by approximately 1000 CE were situated not in the well-watered lands along the Sénégal and Niger valleys nor around Lake Chad but north of these, in the less favoured agricultural territory between them and the southern edges of the Sahara. This suggests that a third factor in the evolution of these northern monarchies was the influence of long-distance trade. The western African kingdoms had their own resources of iron, which in some cases were being worked by about 500 BCE, but they imported other metals, notably copper, together with horses, luxury manufactures, and—above all—salt, a vital commodity that was scarce in all of western Africa except the coastlands. In exchange they could offer gold, ivory, certain agricultural commodities, and slaves.

The exchange across the Sahara of such commodities probably goes back to times before the establishment of the modern desert. The emergence of the

*A salt caravan travels through the Sahara Desert in the Ténéré region of Niger. Historically, salt deposits in the Sahara and along the coasts provided vital resources for much of western Africa where access to salt was limited.* Philippe Bourseiller/The Image Bank/Getty Images

desert did not lead to the cessation of the trade but meant that its surviving pastoralists were encouraged to organize regular trans-Saharan expeditions for trade and plunder. It is known from Herodotus and other classical authors and from surviving rock engravings in the desert that horse-drawn chariots were in use in the Sahara by about 500 BCE. Chariots would have been used for short raids rather than for trans-Saharan trade. But the fact that the engravings are deployed along two principal lines, from the Fezzan and southern Morocco toward the upper Niger and Sénégal rivers, suggests a North African interest in the alluvial gold of these rivers. This could well have occasioned the 6th-century Carthaginian expedition led by Hanno to explore the possibility of direct sea trade with western Africa along the Atlantic coast. Despite this expedition, the Carthaginians do not seem to have been capable of opening up a regular sea trade with western Africa. The links with western Africa remained firmly in the hands of the Saharan groups, although, at about the beginning of the Common Era, camels and other pack animals came into use to supplant the horse-drawn vehicles.

The profits to be obtained by distributing Saharan and Mediterranean produce in western Africa, and by controlling the collection and export of the western African commodities that were exchanged for them, must have been a powerful factor in encouraging the kings of communities on the southern fringes of the Sahara to extend their rule by conquest over adjacent similar communities. Control over more extensive territories meant that by tribute and taxation they could acquire greater stocks of goods for exchange with North Africa and the Sahara and more clients and slaves to extend their power at the expense of their neighbours. Some of their increased human power could be mounted on horses, obtained from the Saharan trade, to increase the mobility and power of their armed forces over the open savannas. It is tolerably certain that the power of the kings of ancient Ghana, controlling the export of gold from the Sénégal and Niger valleys, was built up in this way.

## THE STATES OF THE SUDAN

There were several states that emerged in the Sudan. Through their interactions with other states and peoples, many of them had an impact on the wider region.

### THE EARLY KINGDOMS AND EMPIRES OF THE WESTERN SUDAN

In the 10th century the kings of Ghana extended their sway over the Ṣanhājah, the congeries of Amazigh nomadic groups living around Audaghost, just north of their kingdom, who supplied them with salt and North African goods.

This move must have upset the economic balance between agricultural Ghana and the pastoral Ṣanhājah, and ultimately it provoked a reaction.

Like the North African Imazighen, the Ṣanhājah groups were already to some extent Islamized, and they shortly found in a militant, puritanical version of Islam the means to eliminate their differences and to unite in the movement known to history as the Almoravids. In the middle of the 11th century they began to expand into the productive lands on either side of the western Sahara, and it would seem that later in the century Ghana became dominated by them.

One important result of this domination, following as it did upon some centuries of trading contact by Muslims, was that the ruling and merchant classes of the western Sudan became converted to Islam—though in the case of the rulers the conversion was for many centuries not wholehearted. The justification for a king's claim to enforce his rule over his subjects, who remained pagan, was his descent from the original ancestor who had first settled the land and, by accommodation with its deities and spirits, had developed and controlled it for agriculture. If he were not to be rejected and replaced as king by a rival member of its royal family, he had to continue to observe the ancestral and land cult rites in which he was the principal figure.

However, the depredations of the Almoravids' herds and their internecine quarrels must have undermined the prosperity of agriculture in a marginal environment and would have accelerated the decay of Ghana. More southerly Mande groups, many of which had formed satellite kingdoms of the Ghana empire,

began to act independently and to compete among themselves for primacy. Eventually about 1235, in the time of a king called Sundiata, the Keita kings of Mali, in the well-watered and gold-bearing lands of the uppermost Niger valley, gained ascendancy and incorporated what was left of ancient Ghana into their own considerably more extensive empire.

The Keita clan seem originally to have been traders from lower down the Niger, and the strategy of their empire was to extend their power down river to the Niger Bend and to its trading cities of Timbuktu and Gao, which lay at the foot of the shortest trans-Saharan routes. The initial success of the Almoravids and their subsequent rapid decline had upset the stability of the more westerly caravan roads leading to Ghana, while by the 13th century Ifrīqīyah (Tunisia and eastern Algeria) and Egypt provided more stable bases for trans-Saharan trade than did Morocco. The Niger River provided a natural means of communication from Mali and its goldfields to Timbuktu and to Gao and also provided Mali's merchants with the possibility of opening up trade elsewhere in black western Africa. By the 14th century, Mande merchants, the Dyula, were trading as far east as the city-states of the Hausa, between Lake Chad and the Niger. By about the same time they had also begun to develop a new trade route southeastward from Jenne (modern Djenné, Mali), on a southerly tributary of the Niger, toward goldfields that were being opened up along the Black Volta and further south still, in what is now modern Ghana.

These Mande merchants were Muslims, and their activities led to a considerable expansion of Islam among the trading classes of western Africa and, with the qualification mentioned earlier, also among its kings. Thus the first conversions of Hausa monarchs seem to date from the 14th or 15th centuries. The Mali kings themselves valued Islam for the commercial and diplomatic advantages it gave them, and some of them, of whom the best known is Mansa Mūsā (1307–32), made notable pilgrimages to Mecca via Egypt. As may be seen from Ibn Baṭṭuṭah's account of his travels in 1352–53, the essentially pagan society of the western Sudan became open to a considerable degree of Islamic influence, and literacy and even scholarship became firmly established in its major cities.

The success of the Mali empire depended, however, on its rulers maintaining firm control of the Niger waterway. This in its turn depended on their maintaining control over a non-Mande people, the Songhai, who monopolized the fishing

*The tomb of al-Ḥājj Muḥammad Askia is located in Gao, Mali, once the seat of power of the Songhai empire.* lpiphotos/Newscom

and canoe transport of the middle Niger. The Songhai had an independent monarchical tradition of their own, and Mande control of their capital, Gao, proved somewhat fitful. During the 15th century it was lost altogether, and eventually a Songhai king arose, Sonni 'Alī (1464–92), who, appealing to traditional Songhai paganism against the Islamic universalism of the Mande system, destroyed the Mali empire by ceaseless military campaigning and erected in its place a new empire ruled from Gao. But if this empire were to be profitable and strong, the Songhai needed the Mande as much as the Mande had needed the Songhai. After Sonni 'Alī's death, power passed to one of his former generals, al-Ḥājj Muḥammad Askia (1493–1528), who was both a Mande and a Muslim, and thereafter there was a continual struggle for power between the two groups.

The Songhai empire was never strong in the west, where a number of Mande kingdoms remained in the tradition of Ghana and Mali, but was more effective to the east. There the kingdom of Kanem, whose kings had become Islamized in the 11th century, had declined during the 14th and 15th centuries following quarrels among its aristocracy when it was subject to pressure from new nomad invasions. Eventually, however, the Kanem kings reestablished their state in the former province of Bornu in the southwest, close by the Hausa kingdoms. But in the 16th century, Songhai was the most important external influence over the latter, which began to grow in power and importance. South of the Niger Bend the kingdoms of

the Mossi-Dagomba peoples were emerging, founded by bands of cavaliers who may have been in some way connected with the ruling families to the northeast.

Songhai was strong enough to extend its sway northward across the Sahara to as far as the salt mines of Taghaza, close to the Moroccan borders. This upset the balance of trans-Saharan trade, as Ghana's attempt to control the Ṣanhājah had done, and in 1591 finally provoked effective retaliation from the Sa'dī dynasty of Morocco. An expeditionary force of some 4,000 soldiers was sent across the Sahara and took the important cities of Gao, Timbuktu, and Jenne. The Moroccans had firearms, but their success against the much larger numbers of the Songhai army was also facilitated by the internal divisions of the Songhai state. For a time the profits of this enterprise were considerable, but the Moroccans were not strong enough to control the network of trade routes within western Africa that brought gold and other produce to the Niger cities. Ultimately the main gainers from their conquest were the Saharan groups, essentially Amazigh in origin (such as the Tuareg) but now increasingly Muslim and even Arabized, who finally levied tribute on the descendants of the Moroccan soldiers who formed the military caste (Arma) of Gao, Timbuktu, and Jenne.

Firearms also came to the central Sudan about the same time through the trading relations that existed between Bornu and the Ottoman Turks in North Africa. Together with Muslim cavalry, they enabled Idris Alawma of Bornu (end of 16th century) to impose a Muslim bureaucracy on his pagan subjects and to reconquer Kanem. This revival of the Kanem-Bornu dynasty, however, was relatively short-lived. By the 18th century it was the much smaller Hausa kingdoms, especially Kano and Katsina—which had learned much from Mande commercial and industrial experience and had developed a trading network to the south to rival that of the Mande themselves—that took the leading role in western Africa's external trade with North Africa across the Sahara.

## THE WIDER INFLUENCE OF THE SUDANIC KINGDOMS

The development of such major Sudanic kingdoms and empires as Ghana, Mali, Songhai, the Hausa states, and Kanem-Bornu along the southern fringes of the Sahara had a number of important consequences for the history of western Africa as a whole. For example, it provided the background for the expansion of the Fulani, the only pastoral western African people (also variously known as Fulbe, Fula, Fellata, and Peul).

The fact that, uniquely in western Africa, the Fulani are pastoralists has led to suggestions that they were originally a Saharan people. The Fulani language, however, is classified as part of the Niger-Congo family of languages spoken by black Africans, and the earliest historical documentation reports that the Fulani were living in the westernmost Sudan close to ancient Ghana. The development of this organized kingdom thrust pastoral peoples outward, and the ancestors of the modern Fulani seem to have chosen to settle to the southwest, toward the middle Sénégal valley. But there another settled, and (from the 11th century) an Islamized, black kingdom evolved, that of Tekrur. Some Fulani participated in this kingdom and became Tukulor—the Tukulor and Fulani languages being practically identical. Some, however, chose not to accept the settled way of life and, to preserve their traditional pastoral and religious customs, migrated eastward over the savanna grasslands. Grazing land was available between the agricultural villages, and the growing towns provided the Fulani with markets where they could exchange their pastoral produce for agricultural and manufactured goods. Eventually some Fulani settled in these towns, no doubt initially as trading agents for their fellows in the countryside, where the bulk of the Fulani continued to live under their own leaders, aloof from the social and political life of the cultivators, though increasingly paying rent for their grazing and rendering military services to the settled authorities.

In this way, by the 15th century large numbers of Fulani had settled in the Fouta Djallon and in and around Macina, the inland delta country of the Niger upstream of Timbuktu, and they were beginning to appear as far east as Hausaland, where today many millions of their descendants live. By the 16th century the Fulani were appearing in Bornu,

# FULANI

Fulani chieftain riding up to salute the emir of Katsina at the end of the Muslim holy month of Ramadan in northern Nigeria. Ken Heyman—Rapho/Photo Researchers

The Fulani—also variously known as Fulbe, Fula, Fellata, and Peul—are a primarily Muslim people scattered throughout many parts of western Africa, from Lake Chad, in the east, to the Atlantic coast. They are concentrated principally in Nigeria, Mali, Guinea, Cameroon, Senegal, and Niger. The Fulani language, known as Fula, is classified within the Atlantic branch of the Niger-Congo language family.

Interaction of the widely dispersed Fulani with disparate other groups has produced a variety of socioeconomic patterns. The Fulani were originally a pastoral people, and their lives and organization were dominated by the needs of their herds. The pastoral Fulani today enjoy greater prestige than town and sedentary agricultural Fulani as the most truly representative of Fulani culture. Interaction with other groups has sometimes resulted in a considerable degree of cultural absorption. This is most notably the case in northern Nigeria, where perhaps half of the Fulani have adopted the Hausa language and culture and where, as a result of a series of holy wars (1804–10) purporting to purify Islam, they established an empire, instituting themselves as a ruling aristocracy. The urban Fulani are the most ardently Muslim; pastoral Fulani are frequently lax and sometimes even nonpracticing. The pastoralists also exhibit a much greater variation of physical traits. They wander in nomadic groups, making temporary camps of portable huts. Some of their dairy products are exchanged at markets for cereal foods; cattle are rarely killed for meat. Many sedentary Fulani, who frequently have become sedentary as a result of the depletion of their herds, also own cattle, but they rely principally on cultivation.

The social structure of the pastoral Fulani is egalitarian, in marked contrast to that of other Muslim groups, such as the Hausa, and to most sedentary Fulani. The influence of Islam on kinship patterns is evident in the general preference for cousin and other intralineage marriages. Most men are polygynous, the typical household unit comprising the family head, his wives, and his unmarried children.

and by the 18th century large numbers of them were settling in the grassy uplands of the Cameroons. Although the bulk of the Fulani remained animists, gradually significant numbers of them became Muslims and indeed provided some of the leaders of Islam in western Africa.

The growth of organized statehood in the western African savannas also had important consequences for more southerly lands and peoples. Unsuccessful contestants for power in the major savanna states sometimes moved off toward the south. Traders from these states, especially from Mali and, later, from the Hausa kingdoms, also settled in the south as their trading networks developed, and they often had important political, as well as economic, influences on the groups with whom they came to live. The consequences of these two kinds of movement, which were sometimes interlinked, can best be considered in two sections—firstly, those deriving from developments originating in the Mande sphere in the western savannas, and secondly, those deriving from the Hausa-Bornu region in the east.

In the west one notable emigration was that of the Susu, a Mande group that had lost out to the Keita in the 13th-century struggle for the inheritance of ancient Ghana. This emigration created a wedge of Mande-speaking people close to the Atlantic in the modern Republic of Guinea and in northern Sierra Leone among peoples who had not advanced politically beyond the village level. With the subsequent growth of Mali's power, other smaller groups—sometimes traders, sometimes conquerors, often both—also infiltrated these West Atlantic coastlands. They began to organize their people into petty kingdoms that tended to owe a nominal allegiance to Mali. Major incentives for these migratory movements seem to have been the desire to gain access to coastal supplies of salt and, from the 15th century onward, to the foreign merchandise brought by European sea traders.

In the 16th century the West Atlantic coastlands were invaded by yet another Mande group, the Mane, who advanced westward parallel to the coast from Liberia onward. These were military bands that systematically attacked and overcame the villages of each group they came across. Some of them would stay behind to organize these conquests into small kingdoms, while others, reinforced by auxiliaries recruited from among their victims, would proceed farther west to repeat the pattern. Their advance was halted only when they came up against the Susu. South and east of the Susu, however, the West Atlantic social and ethnic patterns were considerably altered by the actions of the Mane. New Mande-speaking groups emerged, such as the Mende and Loko, while some West Atlantic peoples who retained their original language, such as the Temne, accepted a new aristocracy of Mane provenance.

The Mane advance into the West Atlantic coastlands from the east may have been connected with the growth of Mande influence in the Ivory Coast (modern Côte d'Ivoire) and in modern Ghana. This was commercial in origin; Dyula merchants developed trade routes in search of gold, slaves, and kola nuts, in exchange for which they offered salt, cloth, and other Sudanic or North African goods. It is known that by 1500 the Dyula were trading as far south as the coast of modern Ghana, and their first contact with the Akan peoples who populate almost all the southern half of this territory was probably one or two centuries earlier than this.

This development of trade by the Dyula in modern Ghana and in the adjacent Ivory Coast had important political consequences, and sometimes military implications as well. Ambitious Akan chiefs began to develop and expand their political power to secure the maximum profit from the exploitation of the resources of as much territory and as many people as possible. On the northern fringes of the forest, astride the routes along which gold and kola nuts were brought for exchange with the Dyula, important new kingdoms emerged such as Bono and Banda, both of which were probably in existence by about 1400. As the economic value of gold and kola became appreciated, the forest to the south of these states—which had hitherto been little inhabited because it was less favourable for agriculture than were the savannas—became more thickly populated, and the same principles of political and military mobilization began to be applied there. Village communities became tributaries of ruling groups, with some of their members becoming the clients and slaves needed for the support of the royal households, armies, and trading enterprises. By 1500 most of the Akan territory seems to have been organized in this way and, as trade increased, so the political units—initially very small—tended to increase in size.

Sometimes these political changes were not to the advantage of the Dyula, who employed Mande warriors to guard their caravans and, if necessary, could call in larger contingents from the Sudanic kingdoms. Tensions between the Dyula and the increasingly powerful animist monarchy of Banda erupted in the 17th century into a civil war that destroyed the kingdom and led its Dyula merchants to establish a new trading base of their own farther to the west at Bonduku (Bondoukou). In the following centuries there were at least two major examples of the Dyula taking political authority for themselves at strategic points on the trade routes running through the eastern Ivory Coast.

But the most interesting Mande political initiative along the trade routes south of Jenne was the creation in the early 17th century, just north of the Akan lands, of the new Dyula state of Gonja. This seems to have been inspired by a general worsening of the competitive position of the Mande traders, and it was occasioned by three factors: (1) the near monopoly in the control of the export of forest produce achieved by the Akan kingdom of Bono, (2) the rise to power farther north of the Dagomba kingdom, which controlled local salt pans, and (3) the arrival in the region about 1500 of rival long-distance traders from Hausaland. The Dyula seem to have tried to combat these developments by erecting a major kingdom of their own in Gonja—the territory that the northern traders had to cross to reach the Akan forestlands. But much of Gonja was barren, and its kings lacked the resource base to withstand the growth of Akan power.

Rather less is known about the nature of Sudanic influences in the more easterly zone south of Hausaland and of Bornu. However, it has already been suggested that Dagomba (and a number of similar kingdoms in the Volta basin, including Mamprusi) and the Mossi kingdoms—such as Wagadugu (Ouagadougou) and Yatenga (or Wahiguya), north of Dagomba and closer to the Niger Bend—were founded by conquerors coming from the east. The structures of these kingdoms, which were extant into the beginning of the colonial era, seem to have been erected about the 15th century by relatively small bands of immigrants who eventually merged with the autochthonous Gur-speaking inhabitants of the Volta basin. Their success in conquering and organizing the Gur villages into kingdoms seems to have been due to their possession of cavalry, which subsequently remained a badge of royalty and of aristocracy.

Somewhat earlier, and farther to the east, astride the Niger and closer to

Hausaland, similar kingdoms seem to have been developed through the same kind of process by invaders who may well have been ancestral to the Mossi-Dagomba state builders. Examples of these survived in Borgu into colonial times. An interesting corpus of legends—such as that of Kisra, a character derived from the Sāsānian conqueror of Egypt, Khosrow II, who is supposed to have migrated southwestward from the Nile valley founding various kingdoms—suggests that state-building invaders also proceeded south of Borgu and Hausaland through Nupe, Jukun, Igala, Yoruba, and Benin territory (all in modern Nigeria) to as far as southern Dahomey and to the southeasternmost tip of modern Ghana. Much of this territory, however, was subjugated in the 19th century by Muslim Fulani and Hausa, and the legends as they survive often have an Islamic colouring, which makes it difficult to assess their historicity. It could well be that the traditions of the autochthonous pagans had become coloured by the folklore of incoming Muslim traders. But if the legends are really evidence of conquest, there can be no doubt that the conquered peoples had already achieved a high degree of cultural, economic, and—probably—political sophistication.

The archaeological evidence of the Nok culture shows that the inhabitants of central Nigeria engaged in agriculture and were using iron and other metals by about 500 BCE. It is moreover generally accepted that the terra-cotta sculptures associated with Nok are precursors of the later court sculpture of southwestern Nigeria, in bronze or brass and stone as well as terra-cotta. The bronze or brass sculpture of Yoruba and of the kingdom of Benin is especially famous for its naturalism and for the high degree of metallurgical skill used to cast the figures by the lost-wax process.

Tradition asserts that the Yoruba town of Ife (Ile-Ife) was the centre from which this art, and the type of monarchy that supported it, spread to other parts of the region. Modern archaeologists have found nothing to contradict this and have moreover provided evidence for the existence in Yorubaland of a high degree of urbanization by at least the 11th century. Thus in southwestern Nigeria urban civilization seems at least contemporary with the same development in Hausaland and in Kanem-Bornu, the point of departure for Kisra-type conquerors. The probability, therefore, is that if the Kisra and similar legends are evidence of conquering cavaliers, they were—like the Saharan invaders in the Sudan—exploiting rather than creating urban civilizations, though no doubt they may have welded smaller units into larger kingdoms.

It should be pointed out that the territory southwest of Hausaland toward Dahomey is often open country suited to the deployment of cavalry. The effectiveness of cavalry decreased southeastward toward the forest; in the Benin kingdom, horses were little more than residual symbols of monarchical and aristocratic power. Still farther east, in the forest on the other side of the Niger, where there are no traditions of invasion or of developed monarchical government, the archaeological finds at Igbo Ukwu revealed that ancestors of the modern Igbo (Ibo) had, as early as the 9th century, a sophisticated society with surpluses of wealth supporting considerable craft specialization, including a highly developed bronze art with a distinctive style of its own. Recent thinking suggests that the origins of the small, competitive city-states of the eastern Niger delta south of Igboland, with which Europeans were to develop flourishing commerce from the 17th century, may well be associated with earlier, purely indigenous trading activities of which very little is at present known.

On the available evidence, the establishment in eastern Guinea of the network of Hausa trade and trade routes in the form in which it has been known in modern times, essentially similar to the Mande system farther west, can hardly be dated earlier than about the 16th century. Yet the European traders arriving at Benin, in the Yoruba coastlands, and in the Niger delta, from the end of the 15th century, were able to secure regular supplies of goods, some of which (e.g., cloth and beads) clearly originated in the hinterland and seem to have had an already extant market among the Akan peoples of southern Ghana. This presupposes appreciable indigenous commercial development in eastern Guinea before the emergence of the Hausa system.

# CHAPTER 2

## THE BEGINNINGS OF EUROPEAN ACTIVITY

T he arrival of European sea traders at the Guinea coast-lands in the 15th century clearly marks a new epoch in their history and in the history of all of western Africa. The pioneers were the Portuguese, southwestern Europeans with the necessary knowledge, experience, and national purpose to embark on the enterprise of developing oceanic trade routes with Africa and Asia. Their main goals were in Asia, but to reach Asia it was necessary to circumnavigate Africa, in the process of which they hoped, among other things, to make contact with Mali and to divert some of the trans-Saharan gold trade from Muslim North Africa to Christian Europe.

The colonization of the Cape Verde Islands, from the 1460s onward, provided bases for trade with the fringes of the Mali empire. The most momentous discovery in west-ern Africa, however, came in 1471, when Portuguese captains first reached the coast of modern Ghana between the mouths of the Ankobra and Volta rivers. It was quickly appreciated that the Akan peoples of this coast had access to supplies of gold, which were plentiful by contemporary European standards, and that they were willing and organized to trade some of this gold for base metals, cloth, and other manu-factures. The Portuguese called this coast Mina, "the mine," while in European languages generally it became known as the Gold Coast.

The wealth obtainable from trade with the Gold Coast was so important for the completion of the Portuguese design to establish regular commerce with Asia by circumnavigating Africa that the Portuguese crown quickly took steps to exclude foreign rivals from the western African trade and to bring it under its direct control. Portugal was not a naturally wealthy nation, however, and its overseas interests had become very widely extended by the beginning of the 16th century. The western African coastlands and their trade were only one element in a system that also embraced the Congo region and Angola, Brazil, the East African littoral, and India and the East Indies. By and large it was the trade of the latter that was regarded as the major prize, and elsewhere activities tended to be restricted to those which might strengthen the prosperity of the overseas enterprise as a whole without unduly straining the limited resources, especially perhaps of labour, available for its control and exploitation.

The general strategy in western Africa—as elsewhere in the Portuguese trading empire—was to keep territorial and administrative commitments to the minimum necessary to develop and benefit Portuguese commercial activities that were already in existence. The main interest in western Africa was the gold trade of Mina, and it was there—and virtually there alone—that the Portuguese endeavoured to maintain a positive presence on the mainland. In 1482 they built the strong fort that they called São Jorge da Mina (the modern Elmina Castle) on the shores of the Gold Coast, on land leased from the local Akan, and in subsequent years this was supplemented by the construction of three additional forts, at Axim, Shama, and Accra. The purpose of these forts and their garrisons was to try to ensure that the local people sold their gold only to agents of the Portuguese crown. No other Europeans succeeded in establishing lasting footholds on the Gold Coast before the close of the 16th century, and the Portuguese purpose was largely achieved. The surviving records suggest that up to about 1550 the Portuguese were securing from the Gold Coast on average at least 12,400 ounces (352 kilograms) of gold each year, a sizable proportion of the production then available to Europe.

In exchange, the Gold Coast peoples needed to be supplied with commodities they desired, and this presented Portugal with a problem, as it was not a major manufacturing nation. The raw iron and copper, metal goods, cloth, and other items that were in demand on the Gold Coast had to be purchased elsewhere. Some of the cloth exported to the Gold Coast was in fact brought from Morocco (and may therefore have been in competition with a trade in cloth that had earlier reached the Akan from the north), and the requirements of their Gold Coast customers were a prime factor in leading the Portuguese to develop relations with the kingdom of Benin and the Niger delta, where further supplies of cloth, and also of beads and slaves that were in demand on the Gold Coast, could be obtained.

*São Jorge da Mina (now called Elmina Castle) was the first fort erected by the Portuguese on the Gold Coast in what would become present-day Ghana. Portuguese forts like this one ensured Portugal's monopoly of the gold trade through the 16th century.* Fox Photos/Hulton Archive/ Getty Images

At first the Portuguese hoped to control the trade of Benin and surrounding areas by converting the kingdom, or at least its court, to Christianity and turning it into a satellite protectorate of their empire. Although this kind of policy was initially successful elsewhere in Africa, notably in the Kongo (Bakongo) kingdom of northern Angola, the Benin monarchy was powerful enough to reject European pressures and infiltration. From about 1520 onward, the Portuguese were virtually excluded from Benin, and their trade with the Niger delta was conducted from São Tomé and from the other islands of the Gulf of Guinea that they had colonized. This trade was principally in slaves, from the Congo region and Angola as well as from the delta, who were employed on plantations to grow tropical produce, sugar in particular, for the European market.

Apart from an abortive attempt to intercept the western trans-Saharan trade from a fort that was erected on the island of Arguin off the coast of Mauritania, the other principal Portuguese activity in western Africa was the trade with the coastlands of Upper Guinea that was conducted by the settlers on the Cape Verde Islands (which, together with Madeira, were also developed as plantation colonies employing African slave labour). The empire of Mali was in decline, but the Portuguese were not strong enough to control trade so far into the interior. What ultimately developed, on the creeks and islands of the coast from The Gambia to Sierra Leone, was a number of informal settlements where traders from the Cape Verde Islands did some trade with Mande merchants and with the local peoples. Gradually they married into the local trading and ruling families and, escaping formal Portuguese control, became agents of the African commercial system who sought to secure the best terms they could from any visiting European trader irrespective of nationality.

It may be doubted whether this first period of European involvement with western Africa, from about 1450 to 1600, had much effect on the course of its history. The only Europeans consistently involved were the Portuguese, who were not strong outside the Gold Coast and who were really only interested in controlling some aspects of trade, and these only in a few selected areas of the coastlands where new opportunities had been opened up for a few members of the ruling and trading classes. Perhaps the main changes were that a few Africans acquired some acquaintance with Christianity and with elements of the Portuguese language—a pidgin variety of which became the lingua franca of coastal commerce for some centuries—and that western African farmers were introduced to some new crops and fruits, usually of tropical American provenance, which they quickly adopted if they were more productive than their established cultigens. For example, corn (maize) was more productive than millet and cassava more productive than yams under certain conditions.

The new era of maritime intercourse with the outside world was probably of marked significance only on the Gold Coast. There new avenues of wealth had been opened up for some of the Akan in trade at the coast. There too a new political problem had emerged of how to ensure regular and profitable commercial dealings with the Europeans, while at the same time preventing the coastal footholds, which the Europeans required as entrepôts, from subverting the sovereignty of the indigenous states. This was a very real problem, because the coastal kingdoms were small and divided among themselves in competition for the trade with the Europeans. Elmina certainly, and to some extent Axim also, did in fact develop independent jurisdictions over the mixed European, African, and mulatto trading communities that developed beneath the walls of the forts. Beyond these, the difficulty of maintaining large and effective forces of European soldiers in the tropics meant that the Portuguese could only exert power through African allies. The coastal people were thus able to maintain the principle that the land on which the forts were built was not ceded, but only leased. If the Portuguese lost their allies' confidence, the latter could refuse to supply or help defend the forts, or even destroy them altogether (as happened for the first time at Accra in the 1570s).

## THE RISE OF THE ATLANTIC SLAVE TRADE

The coastal peoples generally, and those of the Gold Coast in particular, were certainly prepared to welcome the merchants of other European nations so as to decrease their dependence on the Portuguese. The first Europeans effectively to break into the Portuguese monopoly of sea trade with western Africa were the Dutch, who had been some of the principal distributors in northwestern Europe of the Asian, African, and American produce imported into Portugal and Spain. After the northern Netherlands had revolted against Spanish rule, however, and Philip II of Spain (who since 1580 had been king of Portugal also) had sought to punish the Dutch merchants by excluding them from the Iberian ports, they were stimulated to organize oceanic trading ventures of their own and from 1598 established on the Gold Coast the first Dutch trading posts in western Africa.

The principal targets for Dutch aggression, however, were in the East Indies and in the Americas, and the effective assertion of Dutch power against Portugal in western Africa was a by-product of the success of the Dutch West India Company in destroying Spanish naval power in the Caribbean and in embarking on the conquest of the plantation colony that the Portuguese had established in Brazil. As a result, by the end of the 1630s the Dutch had established themselves as principal suppliers and customers of the Spanish plantations in the Caribbean, while in Brazil they were themselves in possession of a plantation colony.

The production on American plantations of tropical produce, of which sugar was the most important, and especially the marketing of this produce in western Europe, were extremely profitable activities. But plantation agriculture in the tropics required large and regular supplies of cheap labour. America did not have these, but, just across the Atlantic, western Africa seemed to have relatively great quantities of productive labour. As early as the 1440s, the Portuguese had begun to transport some African slaves to supplement the meagre labour resources of their own country (especially of the southern provinces they had reconquered from the Moors), and their own plantations in Madeira, the Cape Verde Islands, and, ultimately, on the islands of the Gulf of Guinea that had become dependent on African slave labour. The Spaniards, and subsequently other Europeans in America, thus naturally came to look to Africa to make good their labour shortage, and a slave trade to the Caribbean had commenced on a small scale in the 1520s.

Spain had little in the way of trade in Africa itself, so the authorities gave out contracts for the supply of slaves to other merchants, and the ultimate suppliers were usually Portuguese. From the 1570s onward, Portugal's slave traders had a further American market in their own colony of Brazil. The large slave population on their Gulf of Guinea islands was getting out of control, with the result that many Portuguese planters were abandoning these islands and reestablishing their activities in Brazil.

By the time the Dutch West India Company entered the scene in the mid-1620s, in all probability about 400,000 slaves had been imported into the Americas, and the annual volume of imports had risen to about 10,000 a year. This was a sizable business compared with the earlier trades in African slaves to Europe (which had virtually ceased by the 1550s, when perhaps 50,000 slaves had been imported) or to the Atlantic and Gulf of Guinea islands (which by the 1620s had probably received rather more than 100,000 slaves, but whose imports were then less than 500 a year). The demand for slaves in the Americas was also beginning to increase rapidly. In the wake of the Dutch defeat of Spanish naval power, English and French colonists were beginning to settle the smaller Caribbean islands and were seeking to exploit their soils for tropical agriculture with as many slaves as possible, while Spanish official restrictions on the volume of slave imports in their territories were hardly effective.

The labour needs of the plantations it had conquered in Brazil made it imperative that the Dutch West India Company should begin to secure slaves from Africa, and it very quickly recognized that the supply of slaves to European colonists elsewhere in the Americas was an extremely profitable business. To ensure its sources of supply, the Dutch company embarked on the conquest of all the Portuguese bases on the western African shores. Some of these, for example the island of São Tomé in the Gulf of Guinea, were subsequently lost to it, but by 1642 the Dutch were firmly in possession of

*A ship of the Dutch West India Company, whose primary purpose was the waging of economic warfare against Spanish and Portuguese interests.* Mansell/Time & Life Pictures/ Getty Images

the Portuguese forts on the Gold Coast, and they dominated Europe's trade with western Africa. By the 1660s probably as many as 15,000 African slaves were being landed in the Americas each year. Nearly half of this trade was Portuguese, for this nation had by then recovered its possessions in both Brazil and Angola and had a near monopoly of the trade south of the equator, but the remainder, the growing part, was in northern European hands.

The Dutch West India Company's activities in the Atlantic slave trade aroused interest throughout the ports of northwestern Europe, and soon merchants from France, Britain, Germany, and Scandinavia, as well as private Dutch traders, were competing with the Dutch company. French and British competition soon became of major importance. Both countries were resentful of the growing economic power of the Netherlands that was based on foreign trade, and both possessed colonies in the Americas. Their governments decided that their colonists should not be dependent on Dutch merchants for their supplies of labour (nor, for that matter, for capital or for the marketing of their produce in Europe). Through grants of monopolies of their nations' trade with western Africa or the West Indies, French and English merchants were encouraged to form companies strong enough to challenge the power of the Dutch West India Company, and these challenges were supported by the warships of their respective royal navies.

Between 1652 and 1713 there was a succession of wars involving France,

Britain, and the Netherlands. The main battles were usually fought far away from Africa, but throughout the period the traders of each nation sought to increase the number of their trading posts on the western African coast and to deny trade to their rivals. A large number of new forts was built, and these forts were constantly changing hands.

## ANGLO-FRENCH COMPETITION

By 1713, however, a pattern of European activity had emerged that was to remain more or less constant until the Atlantic slave trade was brought to an end during the first half of the 19th century (and that was considerably to influence the subsequent partition of western Africa between European empires). The hold that the Dutch had established over Europe's oceanic commerce was destroyed, and Britain and France competed with each other for its inheritance. The Anglo-French wars of the 18th century had less direct effect on western Africa than did the earlier wars involving the Dutch, but the development of trade with western Africa to supply slaves for their American colonies continued to be an important aim of both countries.

France emerged as master of the coastal trade north of the Gambia River, where it had taken the strategic naval base on Gorée Island from the Dutch in 1677 and was developing a fort and town at Saint-Louis at the mouth of the Sénégal River as a major commercial

## DUTCH WEST INDIA COMPANY

*The Dutch West India Company is the byname of the West India Company (Dutch: West-Indische Compagnie), a Dutch trading company founded in 1621. Its primary purpose was to carry on economic warfare against Spain and Portugal by striking at their colonies in the West Indies and South America and on the west coast of Africa. While attaining its greatest success against the Portuguese in Brazil in the 1630s and '40s, the company depleted its resources and thereafter declined in power.*

*Governed by a board representing various regions of the Netherlands, the company was granted a monopoly of the trade with the Americas and Africa and the Atlantic regions between them. With military and financial support from the States General (the Dutch national assembly), the company acquired ports on the west African coast to supply slaves for plantations in the West Indies and South America. The company's trade, however, was never sufficient to finance operations against Spain, Portugal, and England in areas where the latter were well equipped to defend themselves.*

*Using booty acquired from the capture by the Dutch seaman Piet Heyn of part of a Spanish treasure fleet off Cuba in 1628, the company challenged the Portuguese hold on Brazil beginning in 1630 and attained its greatest success during the administration of Count John Maurice (1636–44). The effort proved too costly, however, and the Dutch company capitulated to the Portuguese in 1654.*

*The company also established several colonies in the West Indies and Guyana between 1634 and 1648, including Aruba, Curaçao, and Saint Martin, but later lost many of them to the French. The Dutch colony in North America, New Netherland (renamed New York in the mid-1660s), became a province of the company in 1623. A combination of low Dutch immigration, autocratic administration, and under-investment, however, damaged the ability of New Netherland to compete with the neighbouring English colonies, and it was ceded to the English in 1667.*

*The Dutch West India Company was much less successful than the Dutch East India Company, its counterpart in Southeast Asia. The West India Company was taken over by the state in 1791 and was dissolved in the wake of the French invasion of the Dutch Republic in 1794.*

centre. By and large, however, this part of the coast produced relatively few slaves, and the French companies operating from Saint-Louis sought compensation by developing the trade of the Sénégal basin in gum and hides and by penetrating upriver toward the alluvial goldfields of Bambuk. Little of permanence was achieved in the 18th century, however, in part because of the resistance of the local peoples, but mainly because of the growing naval power of Britain. Britain's strategic interests almost invariably led it to occupy Gorée and Saint-Louis in each of the sea wars of the century, and from 1758 to 1779 its government attempted to consolidate its conquests there into a formal colony.

But the Colony of the Senegambia was not a success. Britain's merchants were not willing to follow up its naval and military successes in this region, and French traders were allowed to creep back. The main results of Britain's initiative were to interrupt French imperial ambitions in the Sénégal valley for nearly a century, and, on the British side, to contribute to a growing opinion—associated particularly with the loss of the North American colonies and the views of Adam Smith—that formal empire was less important and valuable than the independent operations of a growing host of individual British traders, operating wherever there was profit to be found under the general cover of British naval supremacy.

British traders competed with the French on the Gambia River, where both nations' companies maintained forts, and also established themselves to some extent on the coast of Sierra Leone, but initially the main centre of British activity in western Africa was the Gold Coast. Because the Gold Coast had been the scene first of the major Portuguese and then of the major Dutch successes in western African trade, its peoples were better organized than most to provide European traders with what they sought, and the fact that they could supply gold as well as slaves remained of major importance.

During the period of intensive competition in the later 18th century, the number of major European forts on this 300-mile- (482-km-) long coastline had risen to approximately 30. The Dutch West India Company still had more Gold Coast forts than anyone else, and these by and large were the strongest and best maintained. But their headquarters at Elmina was now rivaled by the British castle at Cape Coast only a few miles away, and indeed almost every Dutch fort had an adjacent British establishment competing with it. The French never succeeded in getting a permanent foothold on the Gold Coast; Swedish and German ventures eventually came under Dutch or British control, and traders from Denmark retained forts only on the eastern Gold Coast, where there was little gold and slaves were the main articles of trade.

Although the formal position of the Dutch on the Gold Coast remained strong throughout the 18th century, and indeed into the 19th century, they steadily lost trade to the British merchants. One reason for this was simply that Britain had displaced the Netherlands as the major naval and sea-trading power in western Europe and, through the developing Industrial Revolution, was better able to supply overseas traders with cheap goods for the world market. The British were also more successful than their rivals in adapting the nature of their operations to changing conditions of trade.

The Dutch on the Gold Coast and the French in Senegal tended to hold to the view that the African trade should be conducted through large corporations, which had military and administrative as well as commercial responsibilities and which were rewarded for these by their monopoly rights. Such companies had been essential if the original Portuguese monopoly of African maritime trade were to be broken, or if the national interest in it were to be maintained in the subsequent period of militant European rivalry for the trade. The intensity of the competition during about 1650 until about 1713 had made the business of building or capturing and of maintaining and defending coastal forts extremely expensive. On the other hand, the breakthrough into trade with Africans had been made, and the ever-increasing demand for slaves led to a great widening of European commercial activities along the coast. Thus by the beginning of the 18th century there were few parts of the coastlands where African rulers and merchants were not prepared and organized to sell slaves in some numbers.

Hence the future lay not with the cumbersome companies, with large amounts of capital locked up in costly forts, but with a host of small European traders, who were not tied to particular shore installations but were seeking for the best terms of trade they could find along the coast. This type of European trader was naturally welcomed by African rulers, newly embarking on trade with the Europeans, who had no wish to see the latter establish permanent bases on their coasts, which, as the Gold Coast forts had done, might develop political claims to challenge their own traditional jurisdictions. It was the British traders, protected by their country's command of the sea and backed by the abundant supplies of goods and capital produced by its revolutionary economic growth, who were most successful in exploiting the new pattern of trade.

The old monopoly companies had never been strong on the coast between the Gambia River and the Gold Coast. In the north this was largely due to the effects of the breakdown of the early Portuguese attempts at controlling the trade. Farther south, the territories of modern Liberia and Côte d'Ivoire had not excited much interest among early European traders. Their coastline was treacherous for navigation, and their thick forests supported a scanty population that was little organized for commerce. Such trade as had developed, principally in ivory and in agricultural produce, did not warrant much investment in shore establishments. Thus, as the American demand for slaves increased, the Upper Guinea coast became frequented by increasing numbers of small traders who competed bitterly with each other for slaves.

The greatest opportunities for the new class of individual European traders lay not to the west but to the east of the Gold Coast, where populations were denser and much better organized, not only politically but also commercially and specifically in their access to developed trade routes linking them with inland centres of population, production, wealth, and organized government. European sea captains knew this coast well enough, for the best sailing routes to return to Europe from the Gold Coast ran via the Gulf of Guinea and its islands.

European trade had been held back there only because there had been no staple export to compare with the gold of the Gold Coast. Nevertheless, their ships' need of provisioning for the return voyage, the local trade between the Niger delta and the Gold Coast, and the early slave trade to São Tomé and Brazil had led to a demand developing among the African peoples for European manufactures such as metals and metalware, cloth, guns and ammunition, and spirits, and there was a network of traders and trade routes to expand trade with the interior if a staple African export could be found.

The rapidly increasing demand for slaves as West Indian and American plantation production began to boom provided this staple. In the second half of the 17th century, Dutch, French, English, and Portuguese traders became increasingly involved in trade on the coast between the Gold Coast and Benin, which soon in fact received the name of the Slave Coast. Initially the company-fort pattern of trading was applied here, but it never took root to the extent that it had done on the Gold Coast, in part because the local rulers insisted that the forts should be built in their own inland towns. As the slave trade further developed, both on the Slave Coast itself and also further east, in the Niger delta region, it became typically an enterprise of individual European or American traders or small partnerships, who acknowledged the authority of the local rulers and paid the fees and duties these demanded.

As has been seen, in the 1620s, on the eve of the great growth of the Atlantic slave trade that followed the Dutch entry into it, the number of African slaves reaching the Americas was about 10,000 a year. In the last quarter of the 17th century, the average annual American import was some 25,000, and the total number of African slaves imported during the century has been estimated at 1,494,000. In the following century it operated on a vastly greater scale; the best available estimate for the number of Africans imported into the New World in the 18th century is some 5.2 million. After about 1815, and especially after the 1840s, the measures taken to outlaw European and American slave dealing, and also—more significantly—the possession of slaves in the Americas, began to take effect, and in the 1860s the Atlantic trade was finally brought to an end after a further 2,780,000 slaves had been landed in the Americas.

The peak of the Atlantic slave trade seems to have been reached in the 1780s, when on average some 78,000 slaves were brought to the Americas each year. About half these slaves were transported in the ships of British merchants. Their nearest competitors, the French and Portuguese traders, carried each about a fifth of the total. Subsequently the French trade (and also the Dutch and Danish trades) virtually ceased as a result of the British blockade of Europe during the Revolutionary and Napoleonic wars of the turn of the century, and the British predominance was even more marked, possibly 60 percent of the trade being in

British hands, compared with perhaps 25 percent for Portugal and 15 percent for North American merchants.

## THE SLAVE-TRADE ERA

All the estimates for the volume of the Atlantic slave trade that have been given so far are for numbers of slaves landed in the Americas, as such numbers are generally more readily ascertainable than figures for slaves leaving Africa. A fair proportion of these slaves never reached the other side of the Atlantic because of deaths from disease, maltreatment, or maritime disaster. Evidence from the 18th and 19th centuries, when the vast majority of the slaves were transported, suggests that on average the loss may have been about 15 percent; in earlier times losses are likely to have been higher, perhaps averaging 20 percent.

Not all the slaves were taken from western Africa as defined in this chapter. Considerable numbers were always taken from Africa south of the equator, and in the 19th century the measures taken to stop the North Atlantic slave trade were quicker and more effective than those against the trade across the South Atlantic. It seems safe to suggest that, up to and including the 18th century, 60 percent of the slaves were taken from the western African coasts from the Sénégal River to the Cameroons and that in the 19th century the proportion dropped to about one-third. It is thus possible to arrive at the following estimates for the loss of population to western Africa.

It is not easy to assess what effects such a loss of population may have had on western Africa and on the course of its history. In the first place, it must not be forgotten that almost all statistics concerning the slave trade involve some degree of estimation. Those used here are based on the analyses of the available data by the American historian Philip D. Curtin and by the Canadian historian Paul E. Lovejoy; they are unlikely to be more than ±20 percent from the reality.

Second, there is really no means of knowing the size of the population of western Africa at any time during the period of the Atlantic slave trade. Working backward from the population data available in the 20th century (which are not themselves always very reliable) and from the evidence these provide for rates of growth, it is possible to suppose that at the beginning of the 18th century, when the Atlantic slave trade was entering its dominant phase, the total population of western Africa may have been about 25 million and its natural rate of increase may have been some 0.15 percent per annum. Although these estimates can be little more than guesses, they do tend to suggest that the commonly held idea that the export slave trade actually depopulated western Africa is not likely to be right.

When the slave trade was at its height during the 18th century, the export of slaves was averaging 45,000 a year. This loss would have been about equal to the assumed natural increase in population, so that the effect might have been to have checked population growth rather than to have actually diminished the population. In earlier centuries or in the 19th century, it would not even have had this effect: population would have been growing, albeit more slowly than with no export of slaves.

But these are gross calculations that take no account of the uneven selection of slaves for export. Since the American planters, and hence the slave traders, looked in particular for fit slaves in the prime of life, between about 15 and 35 years old, it may be argued that robbing western Africa of people particularly from this group of its population would especially tend to reduce births and thereby reduce the capacity of the population to maintain its numbers. On the other hand, however, the planters preferred their slaves to be male, and only about a third of those exported were women. Thus, since western African men who could afford it were polygynous, the birth rate may have been less affected than might have been expected. There is also evidence to suggest that the fitter or more intelligent slaves were often kept at home, and that less fit individuals were in many ways prepared to deceive the European buyers as to their age or condition.

It can also be argued that, since some parts of the coast saw the export of many more slaves than did others, the regions adjacent to these coasts suffered much more severely than the overall figures for western Africa as a whole might suggest. In the peak period of the 1780s, the distribution of exports along the coast was approximately as follows: from the Senegambia and Sierra Leone, about 7,000 slaves a year (about 15 percent of the total from western Africa as a whole); from the Gold Coast, about 9,400 (20 percent); from the Slave Coast and the Benin region, about 16,000 (35 percent); and from the Niger delta and the Cameroons, about 13,400 (29 percent). The three last zones—Lower Guinea—today have populations as dense as any to be found in tropical Africa, and the available evidence suggests that their population was also relatively great in the 18th century—certainly by and large denser than that of most parts of Upper Guinea.

It is therefore possible to conclude that the largest numbers of slaves came from just those regions that could most afford to export population. It is also unlikely to be a coincidence that it was this same area—from the Gold Coast to the Cameroons—which was the most highly developed coastal region in terms of government, economic production, and trade. It was only in areas of low population and poor indigenous organization that foreign slave traders ever needed to set out to capture slaves for themselves. This naturally made the Africans involved hostile to further dealings with the traders, while it also tended to reduce the power of the population to maintain and feed itself, so that in both cases supplies of slaves were ultimately fewer. For the most part, the European traders bought the slaves they needed from African merchants and rulers who had organized to offer slaves for sale.

*Engraving depicting a slave merchant in Gorée Island in present-day Senegal.* The Bridgeman Art Library/Getty Images

About half these slaves were unfortunates in their own societies: criminals, the mentally or physically handicapped, debtors or those who had been sold for debt or pledged as security for a debt, those who had offended men of power or influence, or simply those who in some way had become outcasts from the family and societal systems. Selling such people was usually simply an alternative to keeping them in some kind of servitude in domestic society or, in more extreme situations, condemning them to execution or to serve as human sacrifices in the festivals of ancestral or land cults.

The remainder of the slaves exported were strangers to the societies that sold them, sometimes unwary travelers or border villagers who were kidnapped, but for the most part prisoners of war. Europeans sometimes argued that African kings went to war often with the prime purpose of securing slaves for the slave trade. In the 19th century, when the Europeans themselves had outlawed the slave trade, this argument was used to justify the advance of European colonial rule. On the other hand, in the 18th century, some European slave traders claimed that the acquisition of slaves was simply a consequence of wars which were natural occurrences. From this they argued that they were actually doing a service to such captives and to humanity by buying them and selling them into hard labour on the American plantations. They claimed that they were rescuing the slaves from the danger of being executed or of becoming human sacrifices and that slavery under civilized Christian masters was preferable to slavery in primitive, pagan African society.

Despite the speciousness of the latter claim, the 18th-century slavers' argument seems nearer the truth than that of the 19th-century abolitionists. African wars, like wars anywhere else, were the consequence of rivalries for wealth and power between states. Whereas elsewhere the wealth and power of a monarchy might be measured in terms of the amount of territory it controlled, or in terms of the monetary value of its resources, the prime measure of both power and wealth in Africa was people. By and large land in Africa had very little economic value. There was almost invariably far more land available than there were people to cultivate it or to develop its mineral and other resources. The key to the strength of a kingdom thus lay in its ability to gain control of human energy, and an obvious way to do this was to take people away from its neighbours and rivals. This, indeed, was how western African kingdoms had come to be built up, by the natural rulers of particular small kinship groups securing for themselves and their units more clients and slaves than their neighbours, and by using them to extend their power over these neighbours and even farther afield.

People then were the important resource. Often, indeed, a person was the unit of value in which other resources were measured: thus the value of horses, or guns, or parcels of trade goods was often expressed in terms of the numbers of slaves (i.e., disposable people) for which they might be exchanged. If more people were available, then more land, or gold or iron or salt, might be exploited or more trade might be done (the environment was hostile to transport animals, so that trade depended heavily on the availability of porters and canoemen). Thus there would be greater surpluses available to support the monarch, his household, his administration, and his army, and to maintain specialized manufactures, crafts, and services.

The purpose of wars was thus to increase the power and wealth of a kingdom by increasing its human power and diminishing that of its rivals. The ruling philosophy cannot therefore have been one favouring the export of slaves. But it was one in which the economic value of a person was very well established. With the growth of trade, and especially of international trade which made available desirable commodities that seemed as valuable or sometimes more valuable than people, it was natural for African kings and their traders to think of selling some men and women in exchange for these commodities, and especially so if the foreign merchants who offered these commodities were themselves interested in acquiring slaves.

## PRE-EUROPEAN SLAVE TRADING

This situation had first arisen, and at a very early stage, in the trans-Saharan trade. Labour was needed to work the Saharan salt deposits, and the civilizations of the Mediterranean and Middle East had long had a demand for slaves. Some North African and Middle Eastern exports, particularly perhaps horses, were so valuable in the Sudan that its kings were quite ready to exchange some of their scarce human power to secure these. However, the problems involved in marching slaves across the Sahara with its scarce and widely separated resources of water were formidable. Although reliable estimates are lacking, it is generally supposed that the trans-Saharan slave trade could rarely if ever have transported more than 6,000 or 7,000 slaves a year. After the middle of the 17th century, however, the demand of the Atlantic trade for slaves was practically insatiable, and, as has been seen, at its peak during the 18th century, each year about seven times as many slaves were leaving the western African coasts.

A high proportion of these slaves, nearly a third, were being exported—as has been seen—from the Niger delta region. The communities of Ijo (Ijaw), Ibibio, and Efik fishermen and salt makers, who controlled the waterways to the interior, developed city-states whose whole fortunes came to be bound up with the slave trade. Most of their slaves were brought from their immediate hinterland. It is probably significant that some of this hinterland, particularly that inhabited by the Igbo and the Tiv, today has the highest population densities to be found anywhere in tropical Africa—some Igbo densities being as much as 1,500 persons to the square mile. Igbo country is not rich in natural resources, however, and its water supplies are poor. In the 20th century one result was the emigration of many Igbo to sell their labour in other parts of Nigeria. Some scholars believe that something of this population pressure may have already been evident during the slave-trade era.

It is noteworthy that, although the American demand for slaves was rising steadily from about 1630 onward, every other part of the coast seems quite soon to have reached a figure for slave exports which thereafter remained more or less constant until the 19th century. Then two things happened: first, there was a breakdown in the system of law and order that had hitherto operated in Yoruba country to the west of the Niger delta, with the result that exports from the Slave Coast began to increase; and second, after the early 1860s, the American demand fell off sharply. There is a strong implication that in the 17th and 18th centuries the other major slave-exporting regions with relatively large populations had developed politico-economic systems which were able more or less consciously to calculate the balance of advantage for themselves of engaging in the export slave trade. By and large their conclusion seems to have been that it was more profitable to exchange some of their labour for European goods than it was to keep it all at home, but that it was dangerous to export more than a certain controlled quantity.

The Atlantic slave trade was not simply a rape of African labour to serve European purposes in the Americas. In any case, slaves were not the sole African exports by sea during the slave-trade era. Gold, gum, hides, timbers, palm oil, and other commodities were also traded, and the European merchants needed to buy large quantities of provisions to feed the slaves during the Atlantic crossing. The slaves and other exports had to be purchased, and in exchange Africans received supplies of other goods—cloth, metals, tools, knives and other hardware, guns and ammunition, beads and small manufactures, tobacco and spirits—that, however much their prices may have been inflated in relation to their cost in Europe or America, were thought by their purchasers to be at least as valuable as the slaves or other goods they had sold.

From the African point of view, the main importance of the slave trade may have been that it led to a great growth of all kinds of trade at the coasts and to a considerable stimulation of economic and political activity and organization for some distance into the interior of Guinea, a region which had hitherto been remote from the main centres of trade in western African history, which had been in the Sudan. It is difficult to quantify this growth of commercial activity, but coastal exports and imports combined, negligible prior to about 1500, may—in contemporary values—have been worth something like $3.5 million a year by 1700 and $8 million or more by 1800. This was a considerable trade by the standards of the time, as can be seen from comparison with an estimate in the 1850s of the value of the trade of Kano, then the most prosperous of the Sudanic kingdoms, at some $500,000 a year.

Some consequences of this rapid increase of trade on the Guinea Coast were fairly general. One was the appearance on the coast itself of a new class of African merchants, who freed themselves from some of the restrictions of traditional society and were able to accumulate personal wealth and power to rival that of the local kings. Sometimes, indeed, as at Komenda on the Gold Coast or at Opobo in the delta, the new men actually set themselves up as kings. This development owed much to the direct influence of the European trade on the coast. Some Europeans settled more or less permanently in Africa, married local women, and created new merchant dynasties, such as the Brews of the Gold Coast. Others of the new men were former slaves who had returned from America, particularly perhaps from Brazil to the Slave Coast. Many were local Africans, but usually men who had started by gaining useful contacts and training in the service of European merchants. All the new men were experienced in European ways and often secured for their sons elements of a European education.

The growth of Guinea's international trade encouraged the spread and acceptance of regular systems of currency. Many, perhaps most, of the Guinea currencies were already extant on the coast when the Europeans arrived, but the growth of trade meant that certain of these became the sole acceptable currency within relatively large and well-defined areas, such as iron bars in Upper Guinea and much of the Niger delta, ounces of gold dust on the Gold Coast, and cowrie shells on the Slave Coast. Another development was the emergence on a considerable scale of production for sale. In Asante (Ashanti), for example, some villages were given over to the production of a particular commodity, such as cloth, and some of the chief men ran plantations with slave labour (as also, in the 19th century, did the kings of Dahomey).

The emergence of the trading city-states of the Niger delta represented a social revolution as well as a political innovation. The kinship system gave way to the "House" system, by which both freemen and the large numbers of slaves needed to operate trading canoes and strategic and trading settlements were bound together by common economic interests into large corporations headed by the leading merchants. On the Gold Coast and Slave Coast, however, political development was more akin to that which had earlier taken place in the Sudan under the influence of trans-Saharan trade.

Behind the Gold Coast the original centres of Akan trade and power had been north of the forest and northward-looking. The growth of trade at the coast led to new developments among the settlements in the forest, which had hitherto served only to produce gold and kola nuts for the northern trade. In the 17th century three major forest kingdoms emerged: Denkyera in the west, Akwamu to the east, and between them, Akyem. These competed with each other in expansion parallel to the coast to control as many as possible of the paths of trade to the European forts. Akyem lost, while Denkyera achieved such an overweening power that some of its northern tributaries secured guns and new techniques of political and military organization from Akwamu and rose in revolt. This was the effective origin of the new monarchy of Asante based on Kumasi, situated in the central forest where the major trade routes from the Gold Coast converged and met with the major routes of the Hausa and the Mande-Dyula traders from the north.

By the beginning of the 18th century the power of Denkyera had been crushed, and in the next 70 years Asante armies went on to build up an empire that in the north engulfed Bono and Gonja (Guang) and levied tribute on Dagomba and in the south incorporated or made tributary virtually all the small states that had been involved in the rise of Denkyera, Akyem, and Akwamu. The only part of modern Ghana that was not under the sway of Kumasi was the central coastlands, where the small Fanti (Fante) states, gaining some measure of protection from their close association with the various European forts, began to come together in a federation to resist Asante influence.

## THE SOUTHWARD EXPANSION OF OYO

As the Atlantic trade began to expand east of the Gold Coast to the Slave Coast, similar political developments began to manifest themselves in its hinterland also. Toward the end of the 17th century the northernmost Yoruba kingdom, Oyo, began to turn away from its traditional rivalry with the adjacent savanna kingdoms of Nupe and Borgu and to use its cavalry to assert control of the trade routes through the open country southwestward to the small Aja states on the coast in which the Europeans had established trading posts. A measure of control was also asserted more directly to the south over other Yoruba peoples and kings in the forest. Here a boundary was established with the kingdom of Benin, which in the late 17th century decided that it was in its interests to open up its ports to European merchants and to sell slaves to them to secure a share of the goods they were offering.

By the early 18th century strains caused by the virulent competition between the European traders and their African associates were leading to the dissolution of traditional social and political controls among the Aja, who had a number of small kingdoms under the nominal leadership of the king of Allada. The resultant disorder was not to the liking of the kings of Dahomey, the youngest of these monarchies, who, in colonizing the northern marches of Aja territory, had evolved much more authoritarian and militant forms of government and society. Between 1724 and 1734, Dahomey enforced its concepts on the other Aja peoples by conquest and began to build up a centralized state to control the entire Slave Coast.

Initially Dahomey, wishing to conserve labour, was reluctant to sell slaves to the Europeans. This was not to the liking of Oyo, whose foreign trade was dependent on its being able to sell slaves to the Europeans on the Slave

Coast. Nor was it really in the long-term interests of the centralized trading system of the Dahoman kings themselves, for these had little but slaves to offer in return for the guns and other goods they needed to buy from the Europeans. From 1726 to 1748 the consequence was continual warfare on the Slave Coast, the ultimate results of which were that Dahomey was led by force of arms to recognize Oyo suzerainty and that the slave trade became firmly established, both under strict royal control in Dahomey's port of Whydah (Ouidah) and, increasingly, in ports beyond its control to the east, such as Badagri and Lagos.

The armies of Denkyera, Akwamu, Asante, and Dahomey all made use of firearms, and Akwamu seems to have been a pioneer in the development of tactics suited to the new weapons. The Portuguese had not imported guns into western Africa on any scale and as a matter of policy had sold them only to their allies. In the highly competitive trading situation that followed the Dutch breaking of the Portuguese monopoly, all the European trading nations vied with each other to sell guns, and they soon became an essential article of trade.

The muskets exported to western Africa were cheap varieties specially made for the African market. They were undoubtedly serviceable for hunting and for the protection of crops from the depredations of birds and wild animals, but it is debatable how significant their acquisition was in the rise of the new Guinea kingdoms of the 17th and 18th

centuries. It is notable, for instance, that Oyo's military victories were attributed to its employment of cavalry and that it was consistently successful against Dahomey, whose soldiers were equipped with muskets.

From the African point of view, guns were expensive—though less perhaps to buy than to keep in working order and supplied with powder. In this respect, guns were not dissimilar to horses and, like horses, they became the particular prerogative of kings and their henchmen, symbols of prestige but also elements in the growth of royal power at the expense both of subjects and of unfortunate neighbouring peoples who did not evolve state systems. It followed that the trade in firearms—and also in those African exports, such as slaves and gold, which were most in demand by the European sellers of firearms—tended to be under strict royal control. Similarly, competition to secure supplies of guns and ammunition—as of horses in the Sudan—and to deny such supplies to rivals was a factor of some significance in the new era of power politics in Guinea.

By the 18th century the kingdoms and empires of Guinea, especially those of Lower Guinea, though commonly less extensive, were as powerful as those that had been established in the western Sudan. As with the latter, control of trade with the outside world had been an important element in the growth of these states. However, the relationships between the growth of trade and the growth of states in the two systems, those of Guinea and of the Sudan, were not entirely identical. The rise of the Guinea states, for instance, was associated with a growth of trade that was particularly dependent on the growth of a demand for one particular African export, slaves. Any cessation of this demand was therefore likely to create strains for the Guinea states; and Asante, Dahomey, and Oyo had hardly established paramountcies in their areas when Europeans began seriously to question both the morality and the economic value of slave labour.

It is also noteworthy that the Guinea peoples did not generally establish networks of itinerant traders extending far beyond their homelands, as the Mande and Hausa had done. The Asante, Dahomey, and Benin trading systems seem essentially to have been state corporations operating under royal control or license only within the boundaries of their political influence. The northern limits of the Guinea trading system hardly extended more than 300 miles (483 km) from the coast. Conversely, Mande–Dyula and Hausa traders had ventured far beyond the political and military limits of their kings' authority (which, in the case of the Hausa, were always very restricted). Even after the rise of the Atlantic trade and of the Guinea kingdoms, traders from the north continued to be of prime importance to the commerce of Guinea and, sometimes, to its political life. The community of Muslim northerners settled in Kumasi, for example, sometimes played a significant role in Asante politics, and the northern trade also led to Islam gaining important ground among the Yoruba. Thus the Guinea states were also likely to be affected by any important changes in the political and economic life of the western Sudan.

# CHAPTER 3

# PRE-COLONIZATION DEVELOPMENTS: ISLAMIC REVOLUTION AND INCREASING EUROPEAN ACTIVITY

In the years prior to the era of colonial administration, western African states were affected by a variety of influences. Of notable impact was the spread of Islam throughout the region and the relationship that developed between the African states and European powers after the slave trade was abolished.

## THE ISLAMIC REVOLUTION IN THE WESTERN SUDAN

One of the major themes of 19th-century western Africa history is the Islamic revolution that swept the region. The spread of Islam was not limited to that particular century, though, as the religion had been gaining adherents in western Africa on a smaller scale for quite some time, and the revolution had its roots in the events of previous centuries.

### DOMINANCE OF THE TUAREG AND AMAZIGH

The Moroccan occupation of the Niger Bend in 1591 meant that the domination of the western Sudan by Mande or

Mande-inspired empires—Ghana, Mali, Songhai—which had persisted for at least five centuries, was at last ended. The Songhai kings were pushed southeast into their original homeland of Dendi, farther down the Niger close to Borgu, and Mande political power was limited to the so-called Bambara—i.e., "pagan"—kingdoms of Segu (Ségou) and, later, of Kaarta, upstream and to the west of Macina. In and around the Niger Bend itself, the long-term effect of the Moroccan conquest was to open up the country to the Tuareg and Arabized Amazigh groups of the Saharan fringes. By the middle of the 18th century the descendants of the Moroccan conquerors, who had settled down in the Niger Bend cities as a ruling caste, the Arma, had become tributary to the desert pastoralists.

The same groups operated, or at least profited from, the trans-Saharan trade, and some of them had acquired leading positions in western African Islam. The Kunta group of Arabized Imazighen had become preeminent in both these respects by the 18th century. It dominated the salt trade to Timbuktu, and in the person of Sīdī Mukhtār (died 1811) it had produced a spiritual leader so respected among the Muslims of the western Sudan that the Kunta were able to exercise on the quarrels between the pastoral groups a mediating influence which was clearly to the general benefit of commerce and urban society.

Mukhtār's position was due to qualities of learning and holiness that were in part personal but also in large measure due to his leading role in the Qādirīyah, one of the Muslim brotherhoods (tariqas) in which particular traditions of both sanctity and learning were passed on from teacher to teacher. These brotherhoods or religious orders had arisen with the growth, from about the 11th century onward, of mystical currents of Muslim thought (especially in eastern Islam, where the Qādirīyah had begun). Mysticism proved to be congenial to Amazigh society in North Africa (where the proselytizing order of Islamic mystics—Tijānīyah—evolved in the 18th century), and from there the tariqa entered the Sahara, arriving in western Africa by the beginning of the 16th century.

Hitherto Islam had been spread in western Africa essentially by merchants who, in order to secure their livelihood, chose to accommodate themselves and their religion within the pagan social and political framework that existed where they settled—which for the most part was only in the towns. But with the coming of the tariqa—of which the Qādirīyah was one of the first and, until the Tijānīyah began to advance in its tracks in the 19th century, certainly the foremost—western Africa began to experience the growth of organized groups of devout Muslims who were both specifically trained and morally compelled to work toward a true Islamic society. Moreover, if the people and their rulers remained irresponsive or hostile, it was the Muslims' duty to preach the doctrine of conversion by force, through the jihad, divinely justified war or rebellion against rulers who were pagans or not true Muslims.

This doctrine was particularly attractive to the Fulani, who, as has been seen, were scattered in stranger communities between the agricultural settlements throughout the western African savannas. As the wealth, organization, and power of agricultural and urban society increased, so there was less scope available for the free movement of the Fulani cattle and less freedom for their herdsmen. The Fulani were subject to increased pressures to pay rents, taxes, and services to the rulers of the settled communities who, from the Fulani point of view, were aliens who had no natural right to these things. Although the bulk of the Fulani were pagans, they were, as pastoralists, naturally open to influence from the Saharan pastoralists who were Muslims and among whom the tariqa had been established. The Fulani also had ethnic links with the long Islamized Tukulor of the far west, and they had a considerable and influential Muslim clerical class of their own. The Fulani clerics were thus particularly receptive to the doctrine of jihad and, throughout the Sudan, could ally themselves with considerable numbers of disgruntled and mobile pastoral kinsmen to make jihad a military reality.

## The First Fulani Jihad

The earliest known Fulani jihad occurred in Bondu, close to the Islamized Sénégal valley, where in the second half of the 17th century Fulani clerics succeeded in taking over political power from local Mande rulers. Early in the following century, considerable numbers of Fulani began to do the same in alliance with the local Muslim Mande traders in the nearby Fouta Djallon. By about 1750 a Muslim theocracy had been erected whose leaders were soon engaged in organizing trade to the Upper Guinea coast on which European traders were active. In the second half of the 18th century the same pattern was repeated in the Fouta-Toro (now Fouta), the homeland of the Tukulor, for there, though the dispossessed rulers were Muslims, as a group they were too self-interested and exploitative to suit the clerics.

News of these developments in the westernmost Sudan naturally spread through the Fulani diaspora to more easterly territories influenced by the teaching of Sīdī Mukhtār and other like-minded tariqa divines. In 1804 the most famous of the western African jihads was launched in Hausaland by Usman dan Fodio.

## The Jihad of Usman Dan Fodio

Usman was the leading Fulani cleric in Gobir, the northernmost and most militant of the Hausa kingdoms. This was in a disturbed state in the 17th and 18th centuries. The growth of Tuareg power in Aïr on its northern frontiers had led the Gobir ruling class to seek compensation to the south and southwest, in the territories of Zamfara and Kebbi. There the breakup of the Songhai empire had led to a power vacuum, which had been an encouragement to Fulani settlement. The kings of Gobir, like other Hausa monarchs, were at least nominally Muslims, and for a time Usman had been employed at their court. He then used the influence he had gained to develop a Muslim community of his own, some miles away from the capital, governed according to the strict principles of law preached by the Qādirīyah. The kings of Gobir gradually came to the conclusion that they could not afford to tolerate this independent jurisdiction within their unsettled kingdom and began to take steps against the Muslim community. By 1804 the situation became such that Usman felt he had no alternative but to declare a jihad and to adopt the role of an independent Muslim ruler (*amīr al-mu'minīn* or, in Hausa, *sarkin musulmi*).

Both sides appealed for wider support. While the Hausa kings proved incapable of concerted action against the movement of Islamic rebellion, discontented Fulani and oppressed Hausa peasantry throughout Hausaland welcomed the opportunity to rid themselves of vexatious overlords and arbitrary taxation. Within three years almost all the Hausa kings had been replaced by Fulani emirs who acknowledged the supreme authority of Usman. The most serious fighting was in and around Gobir itself, where the maintenance of large Fulani forces in the field alienated the local peasantry. Fortresses had to be established for the systematic reduction of the country, and in the process the old kingdom of Gobir was destroyed and two

major military encampments, Sokoto and Gwandu, eventually emerged as the twin capitals of a new Fulani empire.

The core of this empire was composed of the three large former kingdoms of Katsina, Kano, and Zaria (Zegzeg), in which, together with the smaller former kingdom of Daura, a Fulani aristocracy had taken over the Hausa system of government and had brought it into line with the principles of Islam as stated by Usman. But the jihad had not stopped at their boundaries. Hausa clerics and adventurers joined with the Fulani in creating new Muslim emirates farther afield, among the pagan and hitherto largely stateless peoples of the Bauchi highlands, for example, and in the open grasslands of northern Cameroon, where there were large numbers of Fulani. There the vast new emirate of Adamawa was created. In the south Fulani and Hausa clerics intervened in a succession dispute in the old pagan kingdom of Nupe and by 1856 had converted it into a new emirate ruled from Bida. There had also been considerable Fulani and Muslim penetration into northern Yorubaland, and, in about 1817, its governor rashly invoked Fulani and Hausa aid in his rebellion against the king of Oyo. The governor's new allies took over, the new emirate of Ilorin was created, and the disintegration of the Oyo empire was accelerated.

The only serious check to Fulani conquest was in Bornu. By 1808 the forces of Fulani rebellion and invasion had reduced its ancient monarchy to impotence. Bornu and Kanem, however, had their own clerical class and tradition, and in the latter province arose a new leader, Muḥammad al-Kānemī, who asserted that the Fulani clerics did not have a unique right to interpret Muslim law for the government of humanity. Al-Kānemī was able to inspire a spirited national resistance, which by 1811 had turned the tide against the Fulani. By 1826 he was the effective master of a new Islamic state, though the traditional kings were maintained in office until 1846, when the puppet of the time rebelled against al-Kānemī's son and successor, 'Umar, but was defeated and killed.

Usman dan Fodio was a scholar and theologian who had little inclination for the political and military direction of the movement he had inspired. His main role was to maintain the jihad's spiritual and moral force and direction, and he left a remarkable memorial of this in his innumerable writings. The practical commanders of the jihad were his brother, Abdullahi, and his son, Muḥammad Bello, who were men of action as well as considerable scholars. These two eventually became joint viceroys of the new empire, Bello ruling its eastern half from Sokoto and Abdullahi the western half from a seat of government at Gwandu. They oversaw the installations of the provincial emirs, received tribute from them, and endeavoured to ensure that their governments and systems of taxation followed the principles of Muslim law and were not arbitrary and extortionate. Gradually the original scholarly and clerical impulse of the jihad weakened

(though it was never wholly forgotten), and the emirs tended to become more representative of the military Fulani aristocracy, which tended to intermarry into the old Hausa ruling class. Standards of scholarship decayed and Hausa, rather than Arabic, became the language of administration. But for half a century or more after the jihad, some 200,000 square miles (518,000 square km) of territory enjoyed a unified system of relatively impartial law and administration, and this was much to the advantage of its agriculture, industry, and trade.

Both Sokoto and Gwandu were in the extreme northwest of the empire, where the jihad had had its origins and where it continued longest, for Kebbi was never entirely subdued. It is possible also that it was in this direction, looking up the Niger toward the Kunta and to the considerable Fulani population of Macina, that it was thought that there might be further advances. Doubtless it was for these reasons that Abdullahi settled at Gwandu with responsibility for the western empire. The main Fulani successes, however, were to the southeast in Bello's sphere, and it was Bello who in 1817 succeeded to his father's titles of caliph and *sarkin musulmi*.

When, about 1818, a jihad began in Macina, it was an independent movement led by a local Qādirī Fulani, Ahmadu ibn Hammadi. Ahmadu was certainly cognizant of Usman's jihad, and the circumstances in which his own movement was born were very similar to those that had occasioned the jihad in Hausaland.

Ahmadu established an independent Muslim community that brought him into conflict with his local, pagan Fulani chief, who was unwise enough to call for help from his suzerain, the Bambara king of Segu. The result was a general rising under Ahmadu that established a theocratic Muslim Fulani state throughout Macina and extended to both the ancient Muslim centres of Jenne (Djenné) and Timbuktu.

## THE JIHAD OF ʿUMAR TAL

The third major western African jihad of the 19th century was that of al-Ḥājj ʿUmar Tal (c. 1797–1864), a Tukulor cleric from the Fouta-Toro. As a young man, ʿUmar went on the pilgrimage (hajj) to Mecca (hence the honorific al-Ḥājj), and in all spent some 20 years away from his homeland. Twelve of these were spent at Sokoto, where he married a daughter of Bello's. He also spent some time with al-Kānemī in Bornu, and he shared with both men in the great revival of Muslim scholarship in the western Sudan. But ʿUmar had a wider experience of the Muslim world than either Bello or al-Kānemī, and he must have been acquainted with both the modernism of Muḥammad ʿAlī Pasha's regime in Egypt and the new puritanism of the Wahhābīyah in Arabia. Also while in Arabia he seems to have been appointed the western African caliph of the relatively new Tijānīyah brotherhood, which was appreciably more activist in its demand for reform than the Qādirīyah. About 1838 ʿUmar arrived home in the

Fouta-Toro, where he quickly became estranged from the local clerics. In 1848 he moved away with such followers as he had to Dinguiraye, on the borders of the Fouta Djallon. There he built up a community of his own, attracting and training military and commercial adventurers as well as religious reformers. His community traded with the Upper Guinea coast for firearms and was consciously conceived as the nucleus for a new state. In 1852 the Dinguiraye community came into conflict with the adjacent Bambara chiefs. A jihad was launched northward through the gold-bearing valleys across the upper Sénégal, where in 1854 the Bambara kingdom of Kaarta fell. ʿUmar then turned west down the Sénégal toward his own homeland and the French trading posts. But he was repulsed by the French, and after 1859 he sought to join with the Fulani of Macina in the conquest of the more powerful Bambara kingdom of Segu. The Macina Fulani were opposed to the idea of a Tijānī power advancing into their own Qādirī zone in the Niger valley and even gave some aid to Segu. After ʿUmar's forces had conquered Segu in 1861, they continued eastward, and, finding that Ahmadu's somewhat autocratic and intolerant regime had estranged the longer established Muslim communities, they established ʿUmar's hegemony as far as Timbuktu (1863).

In less than 10 years al-Ḥājj ʿUmar's armies had conquered an empire almost as large as that of the Sokoto Fulani. It does not, however, appear to have been as well founded. Outside of the Niger valley and the major trading settlements, the majority of its inhabitants were basically pagans who had only accepted Islam because they had been subjected to the shock of conquest by comparatively small bodies of well-armed and well-led adventurers. This was a different situation from that in which relatively large numbers of Muslim Fulani and Hausa had poured out from the old Hausa states into territories already prepared for them by the infiltration of Islam and the presence of Hausa traders and Fulani settlers. In 'Umar's empire individual captains, exempt from taxation themselves, settled down to exploit their conquests as virtually independent fiefs. Along the Niger axis of empire there were both old, established Muslim towns and Fulani communities whose inhabitants regarded the Tijānī Tukulor as upstarts. In 1864 'Umar was killed attempting to suppress a Fulani rebellion in Macina, and for many years his son and successor, Aḥmadu Seku (died 1898), had to compete for his inheritance with his father's numerous other relations and captains.

The most important result of 'Umar's conquests was that they established the Tijānīyah as the most powerful tariqa in western African Islam, and this, together with the earlier consolidation of Muslim power in the east under Sokoto, ultimately ensured that Islam became the dominant religion throughout the western Sudan, and one capable of peaceful expansion deep into Guinea. Already circumstances had changed, however, since the Fulani cavaliers had built up the Sokoto Muslim

empire. Al-Ḥājj 'Umar's empire builders relied on horses for their mobility, but they were also musketeers who knew the value of trade with the Europeans at the coast. Even more significantly, they had already come into conflict with, and had been worsted by, European military and political power advancing inland from the coast.

## THE GUINEA COASTLANDS AND THE EUROPEANS

In addition to the Islamic revolution in the Sudan, the major themes of western African history in the 19th century are the successful campaign against the export of slaves, the trade that for the previous 200 years had been the mainstay of Guinea commerce; the search by both Africans and Europeans for a stable new relationship in the absence of slave trading; and the failure of the major African kingdoms to adjust to the new economic and social circumstances swiftly enough to withstand growing European pressures.

### THE ABOLITION OF SLAVERY

These three themes are closely interwoven in the course of events in Africa. It should be noted, however, that the major decisions regarding the abolition of the slave trade were taken outside Africa and were responses to economic and political changes and pressures in Europe and America. Many of the Christian churches had never accepted the morality of trading in human beings, and the 18th-century Evangelical movements in Protestant Europe led to open campaigning against the Atlantic slave trade and also against the institution of slavery itself. These things were equally condemned by new secular currents of thought associated with the French Revolution. Because plantation production in tropical America was no longer as profitable a field for investment by northern Europeans as industry, or as trade with other parts of the world, the propaganda against the slave trade began to take effect. Denmark outlawed slave trading by its citizens in 1803, Great Britain in 1807, the United States in 1808, Sweden in 1813, the Netherlands in 1814, and France (for the second time) in 1818.

The most significant of these actions against the slave trade was that of Britain. British ships had been by far the largest carriers of slaves at the end of the 18th century, and only Britain really possessed the naval resources necessary to secure enforcement of anti-slave-trade laws on the high seas. Furthermore, when Portugal, Spain, and some American countries expanded their slave trading to meet the deficiency caused by the British withdrawal, they met with strong opposition from Britain. The underlying reason for this was that Britain, more than any other European nation, had considerable amounts of capital, experience, and goodwill accumulated in trade with Africa. When British merchants tried to develop new lines in African trade to replace their old slave trade, however, they commonly found that, as long as their European or American rivals continued to buy slaves, African kings and merchants were generally not willing to organize alternative exports. Economic interest therefore combined with abstract morality to induce successive British governments to bring pressure on other governments to outlaw their slave trades and to permit the British navy to help enforce their laws on their ships at sea.

But these measures did not stop the export of slaves from Africa. Some nations, notably France and the United States, whose own naval controls were fitful, objected strongly to British warships stopping, searching, and, if need be, arresting their ships at sea. Furthermore, as long as there was a market for slaves in the Americas (i.e., until all the American countries had abolished the institution of slavery), there were lawless individual traders who felt that the profits to be gained from running slaves across the Atlantic more than outweighed the risk of arrest. Except when actually embarking slaves on the African coast or unloading them in American waters, the chances of interception at sea were in fact quite small. Although the British navy maintained in western African waters an anti-slave-trade squadron of up to 20 ships, which between 1825 and 1865 arrested 1,287 slave ships and liberated about 130,000 slaves, during the same period about 1.8 million African slaves are believed to have been landed in the Americas.

The final cessation of the export of slaves from Africa to the Americas took place toward the end of the 1860s. The decisive factor was the abolition of slavery in the United States in 1865. Slavery was then legal only in Cuba and Brazil—and only to the 1880s—and the risks of transporting slaves to these two markets became too high. Before this, British governments had already embarked on a policy of taking or supporting active steps in Africa to stop slaves from being offered for sale on its coasts and to encourage the production of alternative exports. The immediate results of these efforts were often not very great. For example, many African governments and merchants were no more inclined than many European or American governments or merchants to enforce or to observe the anti-slave-trade treaties that British officials wished upon them. They saw no reason why their economic interests, which were bound up with slavery and trade in slaves, should be subordinated to the new economic interests of British traders following what was to them the capricious decision that slavery and the slave trade were wrong.

## THE BRITISH PRESENCE IN SIERRA LEONE

What was significant was that Britain, through its desire to stop the export of slaves from western Africa and to protect the interests of British merchants desiring to trade in other commodities, maintained a substantial naval presence in western Africa and was also acquiring new political, commercial, and missionary presences. These led to increasing interference in the domestic affairs of African societies and their governments.

This interference began with the British naval squadron's need of shore stations to serve as bases for its patrolling ships and as landing places for the appreciable numbers of slaves it was intercepting. The slave ships had to be taken to a European jurisdiction to be condemned, and the slaves they had carried could not simply be returned to the societies that had sold them, but needed to be maintained as wards for whom Britain accepted political and moral responsibilities. British political officers and missionaries therefore became established on African soil, and the area of their activities was continually increasing. Explorers were penetrating the hinterland in search of new avenues for trade. British traders were competing with the slave traders. The liberated Africans were branching out into trade for themselves or simply returning home with new Western and Christian attitudes. All these were apt to ask for political or missionary support, and, behind this, naval action could be called upon if there were difficulties with the local African rulers.

For the greater part of the 19th century the prime centre for British naval, political, and missionary activities on the western African coast was Sierra Leone. Toward the end of the 18th century the Sierra Leone peninsula had been chosen by British philanthropists as a suitable place to which Africans who had been taken to Britain as slaves and freed there, or who had fought on the British side in the American Revolution, might be repatriated. A first group was sent out and settled on the site of the future Freetown in 1787. Although many of the early settlers did not survive, others were brought, and by 1811 Freetown had a liberated African population of about 2,000.

After a first false start, the philanthropists hoped to find funds for the maintenance of their settlement by placing it under the control of a company they had floated to trade with the interior. But the only trade that prospered in the Sierra Leone region was the slave trade, in which the company naturally did not engage, and after 1799, their colony, whose indeterminate constitutional status caused many difficulties, was able to survive only with the help of annual grants-in-aid from the British government. Eventually, in 1808, the British government agreed to take over direct responsibility for the colony from the Sierra Leone Company.

Freetown was not the only British settlement on the western African coast.

*Freetown, Sierra Leone, shown here in the late 19th century, was established by an English abolitionist as a settlement for freed slaves in 1787.* Hulton Archive/Getty Images

Officials of a descendant of the old African Company of slave trading days still occupied a number of forts on the Gold Coast and one in The Gambia, and these were now meant to provide support for British merchants engaged in other trades. In 1817, after the settlements on the Sénégal, which had been in British hands during the Napoleonic Wars, had been handed back to France, a considerable number of British traders and their African associates moved to the mouth of the Gambia River and established there the new settlement of Bathurst (Banjul). Neither The Gambia nor the Gold Coast were exclusive British spheres, however. The French were strong competitors on the former, and both the Dutch and the Danes still held forts on the latter, and where European interests were divided, there was no certainty that the British settlements would prosper in competition with slave traders, nor that they could be developed as effective bases in an active campaign against that trade.

From 1808, however, British policy required that such a base be maintained

*British troops land on the Gold Coast to aid the Fanti in their persistent struggle against the Asante.* Rischgitz/Hulton Archive/Getty Images

in western Africa, and Freetown was the obvious choice. It had one of the best natural harbours on the coast, and it was already experienced in the resettlement of liberated slaves. Christian missions had begun to establish themselves there since 1806, and it became the seat of a British governor and of anti-slave-trade courts and the headquarters of the navy's western African squadron. During the next 60 years this squadron was to swell the population under British rule by landing some 60,000 men and women, from all over western Africa, whom it had taken from arrested slave ships. Freetown's only serious disadvantage was that it was at one end of the slave-exporting coast. In 1827, therefore, the British navy also began to use the island of Fernando Po in the Gulf of Guinea as an alternative base and freed-slave settlement. But this activity aroused the interest of the Spanish government, which had had a legal claim to the island since 1778, and in 1834 the settlement was abandoned.

From 1814 to 1824 the British governor and commander in chief at Freetown was Sir Charles M'Carthy, an active military man who thought that the most effective means of achieving Britain's aims in western Africa was to extend its formal dominion over the most vexatious outlets for the slave trade. The home government for a time countenanced this policy and in 1821 transferred the forts on The Gambia and Gold Coast to M'Carthy's administration. During the 10 years of his government its expenditure quadrupled to nearly $400,000 a year.

There was no corresponding increase in British trade (nor any diminution of the slave trade), however, with the result that the cost had to be met by British taxpayers who were antagonistic to spending money on colonies. In 1824 M'Carthy's forward policy led him to make common cause with the Fanti against Asante claims to overlordship on the Gold Coast. In the war that followed, however, he was defeated and killed, and the British government decided that it should withdraw from all formal commitments in western Africa except at Sierra Leone.

## THE BRITISH IN THE NIGER DELTA

In fact the most prosperous British trade was developing on a part of the coast on which there was no British interference other than naval action to intercept slave ships and to secure anti-slave-trade treaties. That was the Niger delta. British shipping had been paramount there when the British slave trade had been abolished in 1807, and the merchants of the delta city-states had quickly adapted themselves to offering palm oil as an alternative export to slaves.

Britain's Industrial Revolution had occasioned a growing demand for vegetable oils as lubricants and for the manufacture of soap, and the new Lancashire cotton industry was producing in quantity a commodity with which palm oil might readily be purchased. By the 1830s the British purchases of palm oil in western Africa were worth nearly $2 million a year. About nine-tenths of this trade was initially with the Niger delta. The oil palm grows throughout a belt just behind the western African coast, and the oil from its fruit was already widely consumed and traded locally. Africans of the delta were much quicker and more successful in developing an export trade in palm oil than were those of other coastal regions. One reason was simply that the oil was not easy to transport in quantity, and its value was not high in proportion to its bulk. Canoe transport was thus easier and cheaper than headloading or cask rolling, and the delta afforded a ready-made system of waterways. But its hinterland also had an unusually dense population in a relatively poor agricultural environment and therefore had both a greater need to exploit the semiwild palm trees than was usually the case and more labour with which to do this and to manufacture and transport the oil. Moreover, the collection of the fruit and the manufacture of the oil were traditional household activities, and to exploit these for export necessitated a commercial system that was both wide and intensive and, in addition, highly responsive and flexible.

The small, highly competitive city-states of the Niger delta, built up and ruled by merchants, could exploit the overseas demand for palm oil much more quickly and efficiently than was possible elsewhere. In Liberia and western Ivory Coast, for example, the trading network, like the population, was thin and little advanced. Elsewhere export trading (for example, in slaves or gold) had been directed, or at least controlled, by

large-scale organizations that were less flexible, politically motivated, and much less responsive to commercial changes; among these were the traditional political hierarchies of large kingdoms such as Benin, Asante, and Dahomey, or the new politico-religious administrations of the Fouta Djallon or of al-Ḥājj ʿUmar. It may be noted, incidentally, that the successful development of palm-oil exports from Yorubaland followed upon the collapse of the Oyo empire there. It was not until about the 1860s, when the total British purchases of palm oil were worth about $6 million a year, that exports from the rest of western Africa, with Yorubaland in the vanguard, began to equal those of the Niger delta.

British official policy toward western Africa remained one of minimum intervention until the 1870s. Indeed, the view that Britain should withdraw from all commitments other than in Sierra Leone was most forcefully asserted by a Parliamentary Select Committee as late as 1865. In fact, however, both positive and negative results of the active British campaign against the Atlantic slave trade made it impossible for the policy of non-intervention to be maintained in practice.

The growth of the spirit of European scientific inquiry during the 18th and 19th centuries combined with a practical interest in finding out what Africa produced besides slaves that could be of value to world trade and what political, economic, and transport systems existed to permit such products to be brought down to the coast, to lead to a great movement of European exploration of the interior of western Africa between 1788 and 1855. This movement was primarily directed from Britain, and from 1805 the British government sponsored many of the major expeditions.

These explorations suggested a possible strategy of breaking through the barrier of the established slave-trading states at the coast by using the Niger River to trade directly with the interior. This seemed attractive after the rejection of the M'Carthy policy of positive coastal action, and from 1832 onward the British government sponsored or helped to sponsor a number of expeditions designed to develop navigation up the Niger. By 1854 quinine and the steamship had solved the technical problems of navigating the lower river, but a new political problem had been created in the objections of both black and white traders in the delta to their established trading system being bypassed in this way.

## THE FALL OF THE AFRICAN KINGDOMS

By the middle of the century the development of the liberated African community in Sierra Leone under the tutelage of British administration, churches, and education meant that some of its members were providing a considerable reinforcement for the British interest in western Africa. Economic activities in Sierra Leone itself were limited, and Sierra Leoneans were soon finding their way along the coast as independent pioneers of trade and Westernization or as auxiliaries to British traders, officials, and missionaries. Their most significant influence was in Yorubaland. By the 1840s at least half the liberated Africans were of Yoruba extraction, and by this time their homeland afforded considerable scope both for independent traders and for people seeking to introduce Christian and Western ideas and ways into African life. Both these circumstances derived from the failure of the Oyo empire in the 18th century to establish a stable form of central government capable of maintaining a firm control over the provinces it had conquered. There remained a dangerously uncertain balance of power between the king and the traditional chiefs of the capital.

Such a situation was by no means unique in the history of the kingdoms of Guinea (or, for that matter, of western Africa). Dahomey seems to have avoided it only because its kings, initiating their kingdom through the conquest of peoples who were not of their own stock, had been able to build up an unusually authoritarian form of government. But in both Benin and Asante traditional kinship organizations imposed restraints on royal authority, and tensions could develop when it came to sharing the rewards of empire and trade. There was a near disastrous civil war at Benin at the end of the 17th century, though the king emerged from it with his authority strengthened, apparently because he was able to play off the town chiefs against the chiefs of his palace. Asante had come into being as an alliance of petty kingdoms against Denkyera, and its kings, desiring to be more than merely *primus inter pares (Latin*: first aomng equals), began by entrusting the new kingdom's conquests mainly to the chiefs of their capital, Kumasi. But the chiefs then sought to control the monarch, and the latter had to turn for help from the provincial rulers to release him from this situation. Ultimately, however, from the time of Osei Kojo (*c.* 1764–77), the kings secured their preeminence throug hout the kingdom by building up a new hierarchical military and civil administration, which was responsible uniquely to them and which limited the power of both sets of chiefs.

At Oyo the traditional town chiefs, who commanded the army of the capital, converted the kings into puppets during the 1750s and '60s. About 1774 they gave the throne to a king, Abiodun, who escaped from their control and used provincial forces to establish royal authority over the capital. After Abiodun's death (*c.* 1789), the provincial chiefs began to act with increasing independence. When (*c.* 1817) the viceroy of the north invited Fulani aid to help consolidate his rebellion, the result was not simply that the kings of Oyo lost their northern provinces to the Fulani; they also lost control over the northern trade routes on which they depended for their vital supplies of horses and slaves, and eventually (*c.* 1836) they had to evacuate their capital to the south. By this time there was no longer any central authority, and everywhere ambitious men were vying with each other to create personal dominions over as many clients and slaves as possible.

One consequence of this situation was a great increase in the number of slaves available for export from nearby Dahomey, which by 1818 had thrown off the last vestiges of Oyo suzerainty and was soon sending its armies deep into Yorubaland, and from independent traders at ports such as Lagos and Badagri. It was the close attention given by the British navy to these coasts that had led to the build-up of Yoruba former slaves in Sierra Leone. By the 1840s considerable numbers of these people were returning to Lagos and Badagri and, especially, the new inland town of Abeokuta, originally built up as a refuge where Egba (southern Yoruba) peoples could withstand pressures from Ibadan, the most powerful of the new Yoruba political units, and from Dahomey. The advent of the settlers from Sierra Leone soon brought British missionaries, and a new British-aligned influence was added to the tangled web of Yoruba politics.

British officialdom soon followed. In 1848 a British consulate had been established for the Gulf of Guinea to maintain British interests in the complex situation arising from the splintered politics of the Niger delta and the beginnings of navigation on the river itself.

The consuls joined with naval officers in attempts to stop the king of Dahomey from exporting slaves, and, when repulsed, turned to Lagos, where they saw their opportunity in a split in the royal family. In 1851 the British navy restored to his throne a deposed monarch who had promised to stop the Lagos slave trade. He was in fact powerless to do this without continued British support. Lagos became the seat of a second British consulate in 1853, and in 1861 it was annexed. British and Sierra Leonean traders endeavouring to develop palm oil trade with Yorubaland were soon trying to persuade the colonial government at Lagos that only a further advance of its authority into the hinterland would stop its wars and its export of slaves and allow their own affairs to prosper.

The first serious advance of British power in western Africa occurred on the Gold Coast. After the withdrawal of British officials and troops in 1828, the British Gold Coast traders took on a young army officer, George Maclean, to represent their interests there. Maclean negotiated a peace with Asante and established an informal jurisdiction through the coastal states, which brought security for both British and Asante merchants. The consequent fourfold increase in British trade combined with the uncertain legal status of Maclean's jurisdiction to bring British officials back to the forts in 1843. In 1850 they took over the Danish forts also, but the continued Dutch presence on the coast prevented them from raising an effective revenue from customs duties, and they quarreled with the coastal peoples over the issue of direct taxation. They therefore failed to erect an effective coastal administration of their own on the foundation laid by Maclean, and they equally rejected alternatives proffered by educated Africans in cooperation with the coastal chiefs. Trade declined, and Asante's armies began to invade the coastlands to protect its interests there. Eventually the Dutch were led to withdraw altogether (1872) and the British to invade Asante and destroy its capital and to declare the whole coast a colony (1874).

Three-quarters of a century of turmoil following the British decision to campaign against the Atlantic slave trade and to foster the interests of legitimate trade and Christian civilization in western Africa had therefore resulted in the establishment of the new colony of Sierra Leone and direct British intervention in African affairs in much of the most prosperous area of the old trade—the Gold Coast, Lagos, and the delta and lower river of the Niger.

African sovereignty had also been infringed between Sierra Leone and the Ivory Coast where, inspired by the Sierra Leone example, private U.S organizations had settled freed slaves for whom there was no place in their own society prior to 1863. British and French merchants questioned the right of the settlers to control and to tax their trade and, since formal U.S. policy was anticolonial, the result, in 1847, was the proclamation of the Republic of Liberia. The settler government then embarked on a long struggle to assert control over the local Africans. Because, unlike a colonial government, it had no metropolitan resources or finance to help, this was a prolonged business.

*Louis Faidherbe, governor of Senegal from 1854–61 and from 1863–65.* Apic/Hulton Archive/ Getty Images

The growth of British trade, and of British influence and power, in western Africa was by no means to the liking of the government, traders, and navy of France—Britain's principal competitors in the previous century. But France's mercantile interest in western Africa was not as strong as Britain's, and its traders there received less official and naval support than did the British. Not until the 1870s and the opening of the European scramble was any serious effort made to develop the trading footholds that were established on the coast between Senegal and Sierra Leone, on the Ivory Coast, and between the Gold Coast and Lagos.

France's main effort in western Africa was devoted to developing its old interests in Senegal following the British withdrawal in 1817. Initially an attempt was made to replace the former business of exporting labour to the West Indies by developing a local plantation economy. By the 1820s this was foundering, and matters then drifted until the arrival in 1854 of a new governor, Louis Faidherbe, a soldier with experience in the conquest of Algeria and in the government of its peoples. Faidherbe's concept was to secure control of the exports of the westernmost Sudan by extending French military and political control up the Sénégal River and to encourage local African production of the peanut (groundnut) to help meet the growing French and European demand for vegetable oils. By the time of his departure in 1865, Senegal had become the prototype for subsequent European colonization in western Africa and a springboard from which the French could think of conquering the whole Sudan.

# CHAPTER 4

## COLONIAL ERA

The formal colonial era in western Africa is generally recognized as beginning in the late 19th century. France and Britain were the primary colonial powers, although Germany, Portugal, and Spain were also present in the area.

### COLONIZATION

The European scramble to partition and occupy African territory is often treated as a peripheral aspect of the political and economic rivalries that developed between the new industrial nations in Europe itself and that were particularly acute from about 1870 to 1914. Its opening has commonly been taken to be either the French reaction to the British occupation of Egypt in 1882 or the Congo basin rivalry between agents of France and of Leopold II of the Belgians that led to the Berlin West Africa Conference of 1884–85, both of which are seen as being exploited by Otto von Bismarck, prime minister of Prussia, for purposes of his European policy.

### EFFECT OF LOCAL CONDITIONS

In western Africa, however, it seems fair to say that the beginnings of the scramble and partition were evident at least a generation before the 1880s and that they were determined by the local situation as much as or more than they were by European domestic rivalries. Already during 1854–74, the logic of the situation in western Africa had led France and Britain to take the political initiatives of creating formal European colonies in Senegal, in Lagos, and in the Gold Coast. All along the coast, in fact, the traditional African political order was becoming ineffective in the face of European economic and social pressures. For most of the 19th century these pressures had been predominantly British, but in the 1870s French companies began to offer effective competition to the British traders not only in Upper Guinea, where they had always been strong, but also on the Ivory Coast, in the ports immediately to the west of Lagos, and even in the lower river and delta of the Niger. An unstable situation was developing in which the European traders were likely to call for further intervention and support from their governments, and especially so if the terms of trade were to turn against them. Low world prices for primary produce during the depression years from the 1870s to the mid-1890s certainly caused difficulties for Europeans trading to western Africa and led them to think that an increase in European control there would enable them to secure its produce more cheaply.

The changing balance of power in western Africa was not confined to the coastlands. By the 1870s formal French and British armies had already ventured into the interior and had inflicted defeats on such major African powers as those of al-Ḥājj ʿUmar and Asante. In 1879 Faidherbe's heirs on the Sénégal River had launched the thrust that was to take French arms conquering eastward across the Sudan to Lake Chad and beyond.

By the end of the 1870s France and Britain, therefore, were already on the march in western Africa. The principal effect of the new forces stemming from domestic power rivalries in Europe itself—the most dramatic of which was the appearance in 1884 of the German flag on the Togoland coast, between the Gold Coast and Dahomey, and in the Cameroons—was to intensify and to accelerate existing French and British tendencies to exert their political and military authority at the expense of traditional African rulers.

## FRENCH AREAS OF INTEREST

There can be no question but that, by the end of the 1870s, the advance of the British interest in western Africa had been more rewarding than the advance of the French interest. Devoting their attention primarily to the active economies of the Niger delta, the Lagos hinterland, and the Gold Coast, British traders had secured $24 million of business a year, compared with the French merchants' trade of $8 million, three-quarters of which was concentrated on the Sénégal River. Initially, therefore, the French had much more incentive for expansion than the British.

Britain was already in political control of the Gold Coast, and the arrival of the German treaty makers in Togo and in the Cameroons in 1884 hastened it to declare its protectorate over most of the intervening coastline on which

British traders were active. The gap left between Lagos and Togo was swiftly filled by the French, and from 1886 they also established formal authority over all other parts of the coastline that were not already claimed by the governments of Liberia, Portugal, or Britain. In this way the baselines were established from which France subsequently developed the colonies of Dahomey, the Ivory Coast, and French Guinea.

France's advance inland from these southern coasts was subsidiary, however, to the main thrust, which was eastward from the Sénégal region through the Sudan. The glamour of its past had persuaded the French that the Sudan was the most advanced, most populated, and most productive zone of western Africa. Once they had reached the upper Niger from the Sénégal (1879–83), the French forces had a highway permitting them further rapid advances. By 1896 they had linked up with the troops that had conquered Dahomey (1893–94) to threaten the lower Niger territories which British traders had penetrated from the delta.

## BRITISH AREAS OF INTEREST

The rapid French advance across western Africa from the Sénégal River had denied the British any chance of exploiting the commercial hinterland of the Gambia River and had severely restricted their opportunities from Sierra Leone. Government and mercantile interests nonetheless were able to agree on the need for British action to keep the French (and also the Germans from Togo and from the Cameroons) out of the hinterlands of the Gold Coast, Lagos, and the Niger delta. Asante submitted to an ultimatum in 1896 (the real war of conquest was delayed until 1900–01, when the British had to suppress a widespread rebellion against their authority), and a British protectorate was extended northward to the limits of Asante influence.

On the Niger, British interests were first maintained by an amalgamation of trading companies formed in 1879 by Sir George Goldie to combat French commercial competition. In 1897 the British government agreed to support Goldie's Royal Niger Company in the development of military forces. Three years later, however, it recognized the foolishness of allowing the company's servants and soldiers to compete for African territory with French government officials and troops and to enforce its monopolistic policies on all other traders within its sphere. The company was divested of its political role, and the British government itself took over direct responsibility for the conquest of most of the Sokoto empire. Thus, although the French eventually reached Lake Chad, they were kept to the southern edges of the Sahara, and most of the well-populated Hausa agricultural territory became the British protectorate of Northern Nigeria. In 1914 this was merged with the Yoruba territories, which had been entered from Lagos during the 1890s, and with the protectorate over the Niger delta region to constitute a single Colony and Protectorate of Nigeria.

## Royal Niger Company

*The Royal Niger Company was a 19th-century British mercantile company that operated in the lower valley of the Niger River in western Africa. It extended British influence in what later became Nigeria.*

*In 1885 Sir George Goldie's National African Company, an amalgamation of British companies, signed treaties with the Nigerian emirs of Sokoto and Gando by which it hoped to secure access to the Benue River and to Lake Chad—an avenue of expansion that the Germans, operating from the Cameroons, were preparing to close.*

*In 1886 the company received a charter of incorporation as the Royal Niger Company and was authorized to administer the Niger delta and the country on the banks of the Niger and Benue rivers. It engaged in a three-way struggle—with the French to the west and the Germans to the southeast—for the trade of the central Sudan.*

*The company imposed prohibitive dues on the people of Brass, in the Niger delta, who wished to trade at their traditional markets in the company's territory, and it incurred such hostility that in 1895 its establishment at Akassa was attacked. In the north, it did not manage to subdue the Fulani empire, but it did conquer several emirates and compelled them to recognize its suzerainty.*

*The continuation of the company's commercial and territorial disputes with France, together with continuing complaints from the people of Brass, led to the transference of the company's charter to the imperial British government on Dec. 31, 1899.*

## CLAIMS OF TERRITORIAL BOUNDARIES

As early as 1898 Europeans had staked out colonies over all western Africa except for some 40,000 square miles (103,600 square km) of territory left to the Republic of Liberia. Portugal had taken virtually no active part in the scramble, and its once extensive influence was now confined within the 14,000 square miles (36,300 square km) that became the colony of Portuguese Guinea. Germany, the latecomer, had claimed the 33,000 square miles (85,500 square km) of Togo (together with the much larger Cameroon territory on the eastern borders of what is usually accepted as western Africa). France and Britain remained, as before, the main imperial powers.

France claimed by far the larger amount of territory, nearly 1.8 million square miles (4.7 square km) compared with some 450,000 square miles (1.2 square km) in the four enclaves secured by Britain. In other terms, however, France had done less well. Its territory included a large part of the Sahara, and the three inland colonies of French Sudan (modern Mali), Upper Volta (modern Burkina Faso), and Niger were by and large scantily populated and, because of their remoteness from the coast, were contributing little or nothing to the world economy. In 1897 the trade of the four British colonies was worth about $24 million, compared with about $14 million for the seven French territories, and their combined population of more than 20 million was more than twice as great.

The political boundaries established by the Europeans by 1898 (though usually not surveyed or demarcated on the ground until much later) largely determine the political map of western Africa today. The only subsequent change of significance followed the British and French conquests of the German colonies during World War I (1914–18). While the larger parts of both Togo and Cameroon were entrusted by the League of Nations to the French to administer as separate colonies, in each case a smaller western part was entrusted to Britain to be administered together with the Gold Coast and Nigeria respectively. Ultimately British Togo chose to join with the Gold Coast and so became part of the new independent Ghana. The northern part of British Cameroon similarly joined with Nigeria, but the southern part chose instead to federate with the former French Cameroon.

## PROBLEMS OF MILITARY CONTROL

If 20 years had sufficed for the European powers to partition western African lands, at least a further 20 years were needed to establish colonial regimes that were effective throughout all the vast territories claimed by Europe and that were accepted by all the Africans involved. The first problem was a military one.

Small and mobile columns of African soldiers, led and trained by European officers and noncommissioned officers and equipped with precision rifles, machine guns, and artillery, rarely experienced much difficulty in defeating the great empires created by the 19th-century jihadists. These chose to meet the invaders in pitched battles in which their massed feudal levies, with few modern weapons and limited skill in their use, served only as targets for the superior firepower and discipline of their opponents. Once these battles had been lost, the surviving leaders were usually ready to acknowledge the Europeans as new overlords. The main problems were really ones of distance and logistics. Thus it was not until 1900–03 that Sir Frederick Lugard's forces were sufficiently established in northern Nigeria to defeat the Sokoto Fulani, while the French "pacification" of the even more remote territory further north, which eventually became their colony of Niger, was not really completed until the 1920s.

A much more serious military problem was often presented by smaller political units, which were ethnically more homogeneous and often more densely populated than the jihad empires. Their subjugation was often a protracted business in which the Europeans had to fight virtually for each settlement. This was the case with the British campaign against Asante in 1900–01, with the subjugation of the Sierra Leone protectorate

*Mande leader Samory Touré.* Roger Viollet/Getty Images

in 1898–99, and above all, perhaps, with the advance of British power into the densely populated Igbo and Tiv territories, which was hardly complete until as late as 1918. Similarly, the most formidable resistance faced by the French came not from the Tukolor, but from the more southerly empire established from the 1860s onward from the hinterland of Sierra Leone to western Gonja by the Mande leader Samory Touré. Though Samory was a Muslim whose activities did much to consolidate the hold of Islam in his territories, he was not a cleric like Usman dan Fodio or al-Ḥājj 'Umar. He came from a family of Dyula traders and soldiers, and the principles of his government recalled those of ancient Mali rather than of the jihad empires. Samory established his network of military and political control over territories long subject to Mande commercial penetration and settlement, and a number of campaigns had to be fought against him until he was finally captured and exiled by the French in 1898.

Once the superior firepower and organization of the Europeans had secured their military supremacy, they were faced with an even larger problem; namely, how the small forces they commanded were to maintain a permanent occupation and effective control over the vast territories they had overrun. Lugard, for instance, had conquered the Sokoto empire with only about 3,000 soldiers, only 150 of whom were Europeans, and to administer his northern Nigerian colony of some 250,000 square miles (650,000 square km) and 10 million people he had a civil establishment of only 200 Europeans. This kind of situation persisted almost throughout the colonial period. At the end of the 1930s, for example, the European establishment available to the British governor of the Gold Coast to control nearly four million people was only 842. It is obvious, then, that the conquerors were often very slow to extend effective rule throughout their empires, and particularly to those parts of them that were most remote, presented serious political problems, or seemed least profitable.

## INITIAL DIFFICULTY OF EUROPEAN ADMINISTRATION

No European control could be exercised without the cooperation of large numbers of Africans. This was secured in two ways. First, just as the Europeans had relied on Africans for the rank and file of their armies and police, so their administrations and economic enterprises could not function without a host of Africans employed as clerks, messengers, craftsmen of all kinds, and labourers. All of this employment offered new opportunities to Africans, and to ensure an efficient labour force all European administrations began to supplement and develop the schools begun by the missionaries.

As well as recruiting and training large numbers of Africans as auxiliaries in all spheres of European activity, the colonial powers also came to rely on African chiefs as essential intermediaries in the chain of authority between the colonial governments and their subjects at large. Both the French and the British colonial regimes were essentially hierarchical. The administration of each colony was entrusted to a governor who was responsible to a colonial minister in the government in Europe (in the French case, via a governor-general at Dakar). These governors were assisted by senior officials and a secretariat in the colonial capital, and their decisions and orders were transmitted for implementation to provincial and district commissioners. A district officer, however, could not deal directly with each of the tens, or even hundreds, of thousands of Africans in his care. He therefore gave orders either to the traditional chiefs or to Africans who had been recognized as local rulers by his government, and these intermediaries passed them on to the people at large.

In this connection a difference of theory began to be discernible between French and British policy. The French regarded the local African chiefs as the lowest elements in a single administrative machine. This administration was to be conducted on entirely French lines. The British, on the other hand, came to believe more and more in "indirect rule." British authority was not to reach directly down to each individual African subject. While the British retained overall control of a colony's administration, it was to be made effective at the district level by cultivating and by molding the governments of the traditional African rulers.

Indirect rule was neither a new nor a specifically British expedient. George Maclean had been an indirect ruler on the Gold Coast in the 1830s; Goldie had proposed indirect rule for the empire his Royal Niger Company had hoped to conquer; and, in the early days of their expansion, the French had often had no alternative but to seek to control their newly won territories through the agency of the African governments they had conquered. Once they were firmly established, however, the French almost invariably moved away from the practice. The British, on the other hand, evolved a theory of indirect rule that they tried to apply systematically to their colonies during the first half of the 20th century. This was largely due to the influence of Lugard. In 1900–06 he had seen no other way to control the vast population in northern Nigeria, whose rulers he had defeated, and he had subsequently been promoted governor-general (1912–19) of a united Nigeria, which was by far the most important British colony in Africa. After his retirement to Britain, he became a dominating influence on the formation of colonial administrative policy, so that indirect rule became accepted as the ideal philosophy of government for British tropical Africa.

Not all areas of western Africa were as suitable for Lugardian indirect rule as northern Nigeria. Lugard himself experienced considerable problems in trying to apply it to the largely chiefless societies of eastern Nigeria and to the Yoruba of the southwest, where authority and law were not as clear-cut. In the Gold Coast indirect rule proved more acceptable to the Asante than the direct rule imposed after the conquest of 1900–01. Farther south, however, the Western-style economy and modes of thought had made such inroads that there were endless problems in the implementation of indirect rule, and the full constitutional apparatus for it was hardly installed until the 1940s.

The development of indirect rule also implied a contradiction with an earlier tradition of British colonial government, that of the colonial legislative council. The governors of British colonies were allowed more initiative than French governors and were supposed to exercise this in the interests of their individual territories insofar as these did not contradict the overriding British interest. To help them in this, each colony was equipped with a legislative council that included representatives of local opinion, and this council's consent was normally required before laws were enacted or the colonial government's budget was approved.

The institution of the legislative council had evolved from experience with settler colonies outside Africa; when such councils were introduced into tropical Africa from the 1840s onward, most of their members were colonial officials. A minority of "unofficial" members represented trade and the professions rather than the traditional communities, and these were not elected but were nominated by the governor. However, 19th-century colonial officials, traders, and professionals were almost as likely to be black as white, and the early legislative councils were by no means ineffective vehicles for the expression of African

interests and of criticisms of British policy. It was thus possible both for the British and for the educated African elite in their colonies to view the legislative councils as embryo parliaments that would eventually become composed of elected African members who would control the executive governments, which would themselves, through the growth of education in the colonies, become more and more composed of African officials.

Although very little thought was given to the matter, because it was supposed that the development might take centuries, it was supposed that the British colonies in Africa would follow the example of Canada and Australia and ultimately emerge as self-governing members of the empire. The equally remote future for the French colonies, on the other hand, was thought to be the acculturation (*assimilation*) of their people, so that ultimately they would all become full French citizens, the colonies would be integrated with metropolitan France, and the African citizens would share equally with the French-born in its institutions.

Both of these ideals were more appropriate to the colonial situations in western Africa before the great scramble for territory that began in 1879, when the colonies were comparatively small territories in which European influence had been slowly but steadily gaining ground for a considerable period. They were effectively shelved when it came to grappling with the problem of governing the enormously greater numbers of Africans without any real previous contacts with European ways who were quickly brought under colonial rule in the years after 1879. Thus, on the French side, though those born in the four major communes (Saint-Louis, Gorée, Rufisque, and Dakar) of the old colony of Senegal continued to enjoy the French citizenship that they had been granted prior to 1879, other Africans became French subjects (possessing the obligations of citizens but not their rights), who could only qualify for citizenship after stringent tests. By 1937, out of an estimated 15 million people under French rule in western Africa, only some 80,500 were citizens, and only 2,500 of these had acquired their citizenship by means other than the accident of birth in one of the four communes.

In the British colonies, however, where the legislative councils were already a reality, there was a dichotomy between them and the institution of indirect rule. Initially, insofar as this was resolved at all, it was at the expense of the development of the legislative councils. Thus the competence of the council in the Gold Coast was not extended to Asante before 1946, while in Nigeria until 1922 the council's competence was restricted to the small territory of Lagos. It was not until 1922 that any elected members appeared in the councils, and they remained for a generation a small proportion of the total unofficial membership, chosen only by tiny electorates in a few coastal towns. For the rest, the African population remained firmly under British control through the mechanism of indirect rule. The

implication was not only that the norms of African society and political behaviour were far removed from those of western Europe but also that the British had by no means accepted that African society and politics would or should evolve in that direction. Those few Africans who had become educated and acculturated in Western ways were not thought to be representative of the mass. There was a move to exclude local Africans from the colonial administration, which became regarded as a professional service, liable to serve anywhere in Africa, with the role of holding the ring until, in some unexplained fashion, the native administrations under indirect rule had developed sufficiently to make British control superfluous.

## Colonial Rule

In fact, of course, the very existence of colonial rule meant that the fabric of African societies was exposed to alien forces of change of an intensity and on a scale unparalleled in the previous history of western Africa. Hitherto remote territories like Niger and Mauritania, where there had been very little change since the introduction of Islam, were from about 1900 suddenly caught up in the same tide of aggressive material changes that had for some time been affecting the coastal societies in Senegal or in the southern Gold Coast and Nigeria. From the African point of view, there was little to choose between the European colonial powers. Portugal, despite the fact that it was virtually bankrupt at the onset of the colonial period, was as significant a bringer of change as France, Germany, and Britain. In fact, in the long run, a strange combination of its poverty with memories of its older colonial tradition were to make Portugal's sense of a *mission civilisatrice* even more pervasive than that of its stronger rivals.

Liberia's formal status as an independent republic did not mean that the forces of change associated with the colonial period were excluded from its territory. Its African American ruling elite were orphaned members of a very rapidly changing Western society, who felt it essential to impose its ethos on black Africa. While colonial administrators often had a narrow, 19th-century concept of government as an arbiter, rather than as an active protagonist of change, the Liberians felt a need actively to enlist the support of Western capital and enterprise if they were to consolidate their rule over African peoples and to maintain the independence of their republic.

Up to 1912 the inexperience and relative weakness of Liberia's ruling elite meant that it achieved little except to run up a dangerous indebtedness to ingenuous and potentially rapacious European investors. In 1925–26, however, the tide began to turn for them when the American Firestone Tire & Rubber Company, worried lest its supplies of raw material should become a British colonial monopoly, secured a new American loan for Liberia and began to operate a one-million-acre plantation concession in the hinterland of Monrovia. The country was now supplied with a sure access to world trade, and its government with the means to achieve a stable revenue. Within 25 years Liberia's foreign trade grew from less than $3 million a year to some $45 million, and government revenue from a mere $500,000 a year to nearly $10 million. The evident dangers that Liberia might become too dependent on a single export crop, and that it and its administration might become sole fiefs of the American company, began to disappear when during World War II U.S. strategic interests caused its government to begin to give aid to Liberia and to develop its first modern port, and when in the 1950s both American and European interests began to exploit Liberia's large-scale deposits of high-grade iron ore. By the 1960s Liberia was on the way to becoming one of the richer western African countries, and the ruling elite began to feel sufficiently secure to share both some of its political power and some of its prosperity with the native peoples.

A cardinal rule for all colonial administrations in Africa before the 1930s was that colonies ought not to be a financial burden on the metropolitan governments and their taxpayers: the cost of colonial administration and development should be covered by the local revenues they could raise. So long as such a doctrine was maintained, it was impossible for any but the richest colonial administrations to devise coherent plans for the economic development of their territories; indeed, prior to the 1940s, the colonial government of the Gold Coast was virtually unique in putting forward such a plan, and then only in the 1920s, which were by and large exceptionally prosperous years.

The principal sources of revenue were (1) duties on the trade entering and leaving the territory and (2) direct taxation (usually a poll tax or hut tax). But only those coastal colonies that had already entered the world economy prior to about 1880 had much in the way of trade on which customs duties might be levied or a sufficient internal production of commodities and circulation of money to produce any significant income from direct taxation. Other territories—such as British northern Nigeria, or the French colonies of the Sudan (Mali) and Niger—could not really provide enough revenue to support even the most essential administrative services, such as policing or—for that matter—tax gathering. For some time, therefore, these administrations were in receipt of grants-in-aid from some central source, and it was an attempt to shift this burden from metropolitan resources that as much as anything led the French in 1895 to bring together their western African colonies under a government general and that led Lugard to argue for the unification of the Nigerian colonies, which he eventually achieved in 1912–14. In each case it seemed advisable to use some of the comparatively buoyant revenues of the coastal territories to subsidize the administrations of those in the interior.

It was obvious enough that what was needed was to increase the European commercial penetration of western Africa. But only the prospect of the most lucrative prizes could induce private European investors to place substantial amounts of capital in Africa in advance of adequate European administrations that could guarantee the safety and security of their investments and in advance of the economic infrastructures that would ensure their efficient deployment. The only lure that really operated to attract European investment in advance of the provision of such services was the prospect of rich mineral deposits. The greater part of western Africa's mineral wealth lies in ores such as those of iron, aluminum, and manganese, which are extremely bulky in relation to their value and require very large investments in transport and other facilities before they can be economically worked, and for which there was relatively little overseas demand before the 1930s. The possibilities of diamond mining in Sierra Leone and the Gold Coast were not really recognized until the 1930s. In effect then, it was only the gold of the Gold Coast and Asante forests and, to a lesser extent, the tin of the Bauchi plateau in central Nigeria, that attracted the early attention of European investors.

Modern methods of gold mining first began to be employed on the Gold Coast as early as 1878, but the industry could not make much headway before 1902. By that time the colonial government had taken the decisive steps of defeating Asante, beginning to build a railway system, and establishing an effective civil administration in the relevant areas, which could ensure proper land surveys and some means of controlling and adjudicating disputes over the ownership of land and the validity of concessions of it. Bauchi tin mining began much later, in 1903, but similar, if less acute, difficulties prevented much progress before 1914.

Despite their poverty, and despite the risk of saddling the home governments and taxpayers with unwanted expenditure, colonial governments found that there was no alternative to their providing the basic infrastructures needed by the vast territories they claimed to rule. It was impossible to wait for private European enterprise to provide railways, harbours, telegraph lines, roads, medical services, schools, and all the other things that were needed to support an effective government, let alone to provide some possibility of economic growth sufficient to pay for better government.

## FRENCH TERRITORIES

The problems facing the French were much more formidable than those facing the British. The British colonies were essentially based on territories close to the sea, in which European trade had been long established and whose African peoples were already accustomed to producing for the world market. The French had such a colony in Senegal, but from this they had expanded over vast, remote, and thinly populated territories that required very considerable investment before they could be efficiently administered or developed. By and large the French public had appreciably less capital to invest overseas than the British public had. By 1936 it was estimated that, whereas the British colonies in western Africa had attracted about $560 million of capital, the total outside investment in French West Africa amounted only to some $155 million.

French strategy was initially to open up and develop its western African empire from a base in Senegal on the same Sénégal–Niger river axis along which it had been conquered. As early as 1882 work was begun on a railway to link the heads of navigation of the two rivers at Kayes and at Bamako (which became the capital of the French Sudan). But this line was not completed until 1906, by which time it had become evident that Saint-Louis, at the mouth of the Sénégal River, was not capable of development into a modern port, and that the Sénégal was really suitable for navigation for only three months in the year. So first a railway was completed from Saint-Louis to the new harbour of Dakar in the lee of the Cape Verde peninsula (1885), and then during 1907–24 a line was built directly from Dakar (since 1902 the federal capital for French West Africa) to Kayes to bypass the Sénégal River altogether.

The construction of an effective west–east transport system from the coast to the upper Niger thus took some 42 years to complete, and the only part of it that was profitable was that serving the peanut-growing areas of Senegal. There was a lag of some 20 years after 1924 before the thinly populated and impoverished French Sudan could respond to the stimulus of its improved communications with the outside world. Indeed the only major crop developed for the world market that could withstand the high costs of transport to the coast—over some 700 miles (1,127 km) of railway—was cotton, and that only after considerable further investment in irrigation. Ultimately the main economic role of the Sudan was to provide foodstuffs for Senegal, whose peasant farmers found it more profitable to concentrate on growing peanuts for export.

By 1914 French economic strategy had shifted from the concept of opening up the inland territories of the French Sudan, Upper Volta, and Niger, to the encouragement of agricultural production in the coastal colonies. To a limited extent, the way was pioneered by European plantations, more especially perhaps in the Ivory Coast. Generally these colonies were made remunerative by administrative pressures to induce African farmers to produce for export. Ultimately, just as the economy of the Senegal had become largely dependent on the export of peanuts, so that of French Guinea became dependent on bananas (though at the very end of the colonial period, European and American capital began the successful exploitation of considerable deposits of bauxite and iron ore), and the economies of Dahomey and of Togo (after its conquest from Germany) became dependent on palm produce. The most dramatic successes were achieved in the

Ivory Coast, where considerable exports were developed of coffee, cocoa, bananas, and lumber. Railways were built from suitable points on the coast to facilitate the export of these crops.

In the 45 years from 1912–13 to 1956–57, the French had boosted the foreign trade of their western African empire from about $58 million a year to about $600 million a year, with the result that the revenues available to their colonial administrations increased from about $8.5 million a year to as much as $315 million. (These figures exclude the part of Togo that was incorporated in the French empire only after 1914–18, and the trade and revenue of which by the mid-1950s were worth some $24 million and $4 million a year respectively.) In absolute terms in relation to the total population, which in the same period is thought to have doubled to an estimated 19 million, the results were not so spectacular; in 1956–57 foreign trade per capita overall amounted to about $32 and government revenue to about $17. The significance of the figures is also obscured by the federal system to which all the colonies except Togo were subject and which was deliberately used to enable the richer colonies to help the poorer. The trade and revenue figures cannot be easily broken down between the individual colonies. Whereas the estimated gross national products (GNPs) for Senegal and the Ivory Coast were in the order of $180 and $160 per capita respectively (the former considerably inflated by the colony's possession of the federal capital), only

Togo (about $73) and French Guinea and Sudan (about $58 and $53, respectively) were thought to have GNPs per capita higher than $40.

## BRITISH TERRITORIES

Each of the four British colonies must necessarily be treated as an independent unit, as each was so treated in British policy. The Gambia was merely a strip of land, averaging only 7 miles (11.3 km) in width, on either side of 292 miles (470 km) of navigable waterway penetrating into what otherwise was French Senegal. Even in the 1950s its population did not exceed 300,000, and the possibilities for any sort of development were limited. In fact the colony achieved a fair degree of prosperity by concentrating on the production of peanuts, grown in part by farmers who migrated annually from Senegal for the purpose. By 1956–57 foreign trade was some $60 per capita and government revenue $14.

The Sierra Leone situation was one of a relatively dense population exploiting or even overexploiting a poor environment for its subsistence, and initially the most that was achieved was to develop some palm produce for export. During the 1930s the situation began to change when European companies began to exploit extensive diamond-bearing gravels and to mine high-grade iron ore. By the mid-1950s foreign trade, which had been $14 million ($9 per capita) in 1913–14, had risen to $101 million ($44). About half of this was based on the activities of the foreign-owned mining companies.

These provided little local employment; and furthermore, large numbers of people had been led to abandon farming to dig for diamonds on their own account. This gave rise to numerous social, economic, and political problems, because legally the diamond-bearing grounds had been conceded to the European companies. These factors may explain why the increase in government revenue, and hence the capacity of the government to sponsor further development, was low in comparison with other western African territories. It rose from $3.6 million ($2.40 per capita) in 1913–14 to $27 million ($11.70) in 1956–57, a factor of increase of 4.9, which compares unfavourably with a factor of 21.1 for French West Africa as a whole, 11.4 for the Gold Coast, 6.1 for Nigeria, or even 5.9 for The Gambia.

The Gold Coast was a complete contrast, indeed one of the most successful examples of colonial development anywhere in British tropical Africa. The people of its coastlands were long accustomed to world trade, and indeed to British rule, with the result that the Gold Coast entered the colonial period with a very high level of economic activity. In 1912–13 its foreign trade was worth $42.5 million ($28.30 per capita) while government revenue was $6.5 million ($4.30 per capita). Subsequent development was facilitated by the possession, within a manageable area that was adequately but not too densely populated, of a considerable variety of resources.

The first railway was built inland from Sekondi in the southeastern Gold

Coast between 1898 and 1903 with the dual purpose of supporting gold mining and ensuring political control of Asante. This railway subsequently was used for the removal of manganese ore and bauxite. Extensive diamond diggings, worked equally by individual Africans and by European companies, began to be developed from 1919 onward. But the mainstay of the economy became cocoa, which local farmers began to produce on small plots in the forest toward the end of the 19th century. They found a reliable market for their produce. Cocoa became the most valuable export when it outranked gold in 1913, and thereafter went on to contribute more than four-fifths of exports and to constitute something between a third and a half of the world's supply.

The prosperity derived from cocoa in the 1920s enabled the governor, Sir Frederick Gordon Guggisberg, to pledge the country's revenues for loans to finance a coherent program of economic and social development. The Gold Coast's first deep-water port was built at Takoradi, the cocoa-producing forestlands were equipped with a comprehensive railway and road system, and the foundations were laid for educational and medical services as good as any in tropical Africa. Subsequent development was severely checked by the Great Depression of the 1930s and by events of World War II, but by the mid-1950s the postwar demand for tropical produce generated trade for the Gold Coast, estimated to have fewer than five million people, of about $500 million a year, not far short of that

generated by all the 19 million people living in French West Africa. Government revenue reached the high level of $27.50 per person, by far the highest in western Africa, while the GNP of about $200 per person was probably higher than that of any tropical African country.

Nigeria provides yet another contrast. The people of its southern territories, like those of the southern Gold Coast or of Senegal, had long been in touch with the world economy. In 1912–13 the country's trade, at some $65 million a year, was 50 percent higher than the Gold Coast's and greater even than the combined total for the eight French colonies, including Senegal. But Nigeria was a giant territory, three times as large as the other three British colonies put together, and though compared with the French federation it was relatively small and compact (373,000 square miles [966,000 square km]), it had the same problem of extending over a considerable area of the remote western Sudan. This could not be ignored—as the much smaller northern Gold Coast or such northern French colonies as Niger were effectively ignored—because the Nigerian Sudan contained more than half the country's enormous population. By the mid-1950s the Nigerian population was more than 32 million, more than half that of western Africa.

Two things were clearly needed: first, to develop a transport system to make it possible to control and open up the populous north; and, second, to use some of the wealth generated from the growth of foreign trade in the south to stimulate development in the north. No coherent policy was possible, however, before the amalgamation of the separate colonial administrations, which was achieved under Lugard in 1912–14. Initially, even railway building tended to provoke disunion. The first line was built inland from Lagos in 1898–1901 to open up Yorubaland. Before this line was extended to the north across the Niger, the northern government had begun its own railway, from the highest point of navigation on the river, through its new administrative capital of Kaduna, to Kano. In 1912 this was intercepted by an extension of the Lagos line, and subsequently branches were built to areas active in tin mining and the cultivation of peanuts. Finally, another line was built from a new eastern port, Port Harcourt, to the coal mines around Enugu (1916), and this was subsequently extended to Kaduna (1927). By the 1930s Nigeria had 1,900 miles (3,058 km) of railway, nearly as many as those possessed by all the French territories together (2,160 miles [3,476 km]) but built at nearly twice the cost.

While southern Nigerian development, based essentially on cocoa production in the west and processing of palm oil and kernels in the east, followed much the same pattern as that of the southern Gold Coast, and with essentially similar social consequences, the development of peanuts as the prime export crop of the north did not produce comparable results for its appreciably larger population. By the mid-1950s the trade of Nigeria, at some $800 million a year, was still greater than that of all French

West Africa in total, but it was appreciably less per capita, $25.30 compared with $32.20, and the annual revenue available to government, at $173 million, was small in proportion to the total population, only about $5.50 per capita. Inevitably a serious gap had developed between the economic and social progress of the south and that of the north.

## DECOLONIZATION AND THE REGAINING OF INDEPENDENCE

The end of the colonial period and the establishment during 1957–76 of all the former colonies as independent states was attributable both to a change in European attitudes toward Africa and the possession of colonies and to an African reaction to colonial rule born of the economic and social changes it had produced.

Europeans had colonized western Africa in the later 19th and early 20th centuries confident that their civilization was immensely superior to anything Africa had produced or could produce. Yet hardly had their colonies been established than these convictions began to be challenged. World War I, and the immense misery and loss of life it caused, led some Europeans to doubt whether nations who could so brutally mismanage their own affairs had any moral right to dictate to other peoples. Some reflection of this view was seen in the League of Nations and the system of mandates applied to the former German colonies.

Although in western Africa these were entrusted to either French or British administration, the mandated territories did not become the absolute possessions of the conquerors, and the role of the new rulers was declared to be to equip the mandated territories and their peoples for self-government.

A second shock to European self-confidence came with the Great Depression of the 1930s, when trade and production shrank and millions of Europeans had no work. It began to be argued that a remedy lay in more active development of the overseas territories controlled by Europe. If more European capital and skills were directed to the colonies, so that they could produce more raw materials for European industry more efficiently, both Europe and the colonies would gain; as the colonies became wealthier through the exploitation of their resources, the people of the colonies would buy more from Europe.

In 1929 Britain had enacted the first Colonial Development Act, providing that small amounts of British government money could be used for colonial economic development, thus breaking the deadlock by which the only colonial governments that could embark on development programs to increase the wealth of their subjects, and to improve their own revenues, were those that already commanded sufficient revenue to pay for the programs or to service the loans the programs required. The idea that the colonies should be actively developed, in the European as much as in the African interest, was broadened during and after

World War II. Transport and currency problems made it urgent for Britain and France to exploit strategic raw materials in their colonies. Furthermore, during 1940–44, when France itself was in German hands, it was only from the colonies and with their resources that Gen. Charles de Gaulle and his associates could continue the fight.

The British funding policy, initiated in 1929, of providing the funds needed for colonial development was greatly expanded in the 1940s and extended to social as well as economic plans. After the war the governments of both Britain and France required their colonial administrations to draw up comprehensive development plans and in effect offered to provide the funds for those that could not be funded from local resources.

In view of past history, the need for such plans was probably greater in the French colonies than in the British, and the French West African program for 1946–55 envisaged the investment of $1,108,000,000, compared with programs totaling $549 million for the four British colonies. Virtually all of the financing for the French program came from France itself. But some of the British colonies had built up considerable reserves from the high prices commanded by their produce during the war and immediate postwar years, and they themselves were able to provide much of the money needed. This tended to accentuate already existing disparities. In the extreme case the Gold Coast plan envisaged spending $300 million, only 4 percent of which was

British money. This was the same level of expenditure, roughly $60 per capita, as envisaged for French West Africa. Nigeria's program, with a contribution from Britain of 42 percent, proposed to spend $220 million—only about $7 per capita. The figures for Sierra Leone were $21 million, 45 percent from the United Kingdom, and $10 per capita; and for the tiny Gambia $8 million, 35 percent, and $27 per capita.

The accompanying political changes were more cautious and turned out to be inadequate to accommodate African aspirations—which had been derived from social changes occasioned during the classical period of colonial rule and further whetted by the policies of active economic development. On the British side, during 1945–48 the legislative councils were reformed so that African representatives outnumbered the European officials. Many of these African members, however, were still government nominees, and, because of the British attachment to indirect rule, those who were elected were mainly representative of the traditional chiefs.

Political advance for the French colonies was naturally seen in terms of increased African participation in French political life. In 1944 it was proposed that the colonies become overseas territories of France. Delegates from the colonies in fact participated in the making of the new postwar French constitution, but this was subject to referenda in which metropolitan French votes predominated. The constitution eventually adopted in 1946 was less liberal to Africans than they had been led to expect.

## THE EMERGENCE OF AFRICAN LEADERS

By the later 1940s, however, there were appreciable numbers of Africans in both the French and the British colonies who had emerged from traditional society through the new opportunities for economic advancement and education. In coastal areas Christian missionaries and their schools had advanced with the European administrations. The colonial governments, requiring African subordinates for their system, commonly aided and developed the elementary and vocational education initiated by the Christian missions and often themselves provided some sort of higher education for the chiefly classes whose cooperation they required. If rather little of this education had penetrated to the Sudan by the 1940s, in some coastal areas Africans had become eager to invest some of their increasing wealth in education, which was seen as the key to European strength.

Relatively few Africans started up the French educational ladder—school attendance by the mid-1950s was some 340,000, about 1.7 percent of the total population—but those who did found themselves in a system identical with that in France. In British West Africa schools had gotten a footing before there was much administration to control them, and their subsequent development was more independent. The British educational system therefore developed into a pyramid with a much broader base than the French one. By the mid-1950s there were more than two million schoolchildren in Nigeria, about 6 percent of the total population and a much higher proportion of the population of the south, in which the schools were concentrated; in the Gold Coast there were nearly 600,000, some 12 percent of the population. Many more people in the British than in the French territories thus got some education, and appreciably more were able to attend universities. In 1948 universities were established in the Gold Coast and Nigeria; by 1960 the former territory had about 4,500 university graduates and the latter more than 5,000. The first French African university was a federal institution at Dakar opened in 1950; by 1960 the total number of graduates in French West Africa was about 1,800.

By the 1940s there was enough education to make European-style political activity possible in all the coastal colonies. Such activity may be traced back to at least the 1890s, when Gold Coast professionals and some chiefs founded the Aborigines' Rights Protection Society (ARPS) to prevent the wholesale expropriation of African lands by European entrepreneurs or officials. The ARPS went on to campaign against the exclusion of qualified Africans from the colonial administration. Following this, in 1918–20, a National Congress of British West Africa was formed by professionals to press for the development of the legislative councils in all the British colonies into elective assemblies controlling the colonial administrations.

In French West Africa early political activity was concentrated in the four towns of Senegal whose people possessed political rights before 1946. Because the seat of power was very clearly in France, with Senegalese electors sending a deputy to the French National Assembly, the result by the 1930s was the emergence of a Senegalese Socialist party allied to the Socialists in France.

By the late 1940s both the French and the British territories possessed an educated, politicized class, which felt frustrated in its legitimate expectations; it had made no appreciable progress in securing any real participation in the system of political control. In fact, anything approaching effective African participation seemed more remote than ever. Implementation of the development programs led to a noticeable increase in the number of Europeans employed by the colonial regimes and their associated economic enterprises. On the other hand, because many Africans had served with, and received educational and technical training with, the British and French armies, the war had led to a great widening of both African experience and skills. Furthermore, the postwar economic situation was one in which African farmers were receiving high prices for their produce but could find little to spend their money on, and in which the eagerly awaited development plans were slow to mature because European capital goods were in short supply.

## THE FORMATION OF AFRICAN INDEPENDENCE MOVEMENTS

There thus developed a general feeling among the intelligentsia that the colonies were being deliberately exploited by ever more firmly entrenched European political and economic systems and that there had developed a new, wider, and mobilizable public to appeal to for support. In 1946 politicians in French West Africa organized a federation-wide political association, the African Democratic Rally (RDA). The RDA and its members in the French National Assembly aligned themselves with the French Communist Party, the only effective opposition to the governments of the Fourth Republic. The result, during 1948–50, was the virtual suppression of the RDA in Africa by the colonial administrations.

In British West Africa the tensions were greatest in the Gold Coast. In 1947 the established politicians brought in Kwame Nkrumah, who had studied in the United States and Britain and had been active in the Pan-African movement, to organize a nationalist party with mass support. In 1948 European trading houses were boycotted, and some rioting took place in the larger towns. An official inquiry concluded that the underlying problem was political frustration and that African participation in government should be increased until the colony became self-governing. In 1951, therefore, a new constitution was introduced in which the legislative council gave way to an assembly dominated by African elected members, to which African ministers were responsible for the conduct of much government business. By this time Nkrumah had organized his own mass political party, able to win any general election, and during the following years he negotiated with the British a series of concessions that resulted in 1957 in the Gold Coast becoming the independent state of Ghana.

Once the British had accepted the principle of cooperating with nationalist politicians, their other western African colonies began to follow the example set by the Gold Coast. But Nkrumah had been greatly aided by the high price for cocoa in the 1950s (which meant that by 1960 Ghana's trade was worth $630 million a year and that government revenue, at more than $280 million, was broadly adequate to give the people what they wanted in the way of modernizing programs) and by the comparatively high level and generally wide spread of education in a sizable yet compact territory that was without too serious ethnic divisions. The other colonies were not so well placed.

The small size of The Gambia was the principal factor contributing to the delay of its independence until 1965. Sierra Leone was a densely populated country that was appreciably poorer than Ghana (its GNP per capita, at about $70, being approximately one-third of Ghana's) and in which there was a wide disparity in levels of education and wealth between the Creoles—the descendants of liberated slaves who lived in and around Freetown—and the rest of the people. When independence was achieved in 1961, these deeply rooted problems had been papered over rather than solved.

Nigeria presented the greatest challenge to British and African policymakers alike. In the south two nationalist parties emerged, the Action Group (AG), supported primarily by the Yoruba of the west, and the National Convention of Nigerian Citizens (NCNC), whose prime support came from the Igbo of the east. These parties expected the whole country quickly to follow the Ghanaian pattern of constitutional change. But any elective central assembly was bound to be dominated by the north, which had some 57 percent of the population and whose economic and social development had lagged far behind. The north's political leaders—most of whom were conservative Muslim aristocrats closely allied with the British through indirect rule—were not at all eager to see their traditional paramountcy invaded by aggressive and better-educated leaders from the south.

The first political expedient was to convert Nigeria into a federation of three regions. In 1957 this allowed the east and the west to achieve internal self-government without waiting for the north, but it left open the questions of how politics were to be conducted at the centre and how Nigerian independence was to be secured. At this juncture it occurred to the northern leaders that by allying themselves to one of the southern parties they might maintain their local monopoly of power and gain prestige in the country as a whole by asking for its independence. The problem of central politics was thus resolved when the northern leaders entered a coalition federal government with the NCNC, and in 1960 Nigeria became independent.

Meanwhile, in French West Africa the RDA, led by Félix Houphouët-Boigny, broke with the Communist Party. The votes of a small bloc of African deputies in the French National Assembly were of considerable value to the shifting coalitions of non-Communist parties that made up the unstable French governments of the 1950s, and the RDA began to seek to influence these governments to allow greater freedom to the colonies.

By 1956 Houphouët-Boigny's policy had secured a widening of the colonial franchises and the beginnings of a system by which each colony was on the way to becoming a separate unit in which African ministers would be responsible for some of the conduct of government. The implications of this approach, however, did not meet with the approval of some other African leaders, most notable among them Léopold Sédar Senghor in Senegal and Ahmed Sékou Touré in Guinea. Senghor had stood outside the RDA since the days of its alliance with the Communists, which he had thought could only bring disaster. Together with Sékou, who had

*Members of the African Democratic Rally (RDA) meet in December 1958, three months after a referendum offering the French colonies in Africa full internal self-government.* AFP/Getty Images

remained within the RDA, he argued that Houphouët's policy would split up the western African federation into units that would be too small and poor to resist continued French domination.

In 1958 the French Fourth Republic collapsed and de Gaulle was returned to power. On Sept. 28, 1958, in a referendum, the colonies were offered full internal self-government as fellow members with France of a French Community that would deal with supranational affairs.

All of the colonies voted for this scheme except Guinea, where Sékou Touré led the people to vote for complete independence. Senegal and the French Sudan were then emboldened in 1959 to come together in a Federation of Mali and to ask for and to receive complete independence within the community. These two territories separated in the following year, but all the others now asked for independence before negotiating conditions for association with France, and by

1960 all the former French colonies were *de jure* (Medieval Latin: by right) independent states.

By that time only the excessively conservative regimes of Portugal and Spain sought to maintain the colonial principle in western Africa. Encouraged and aided by independent neighbours, Guinean nationalists took up arms in 1962 and after 10 years of fighting expelled the Portuguese from three-quarters of Portuguese Guinea. In 1974 the strain of this war and of wars in Mozambique and Angola caused the Portuguese people and army to overthrow their dictatorship. Independence was quickly recognized for Guinea-Bissau in 1974 and for the Cape Verde Islands and São Tomé and Principe in 1975. Spain concluded in 1968 that the best way to preserve its interests in equatorial Africa was to grant independence to its people without preparing them for it. The result was chaos.

# CHAPTER 5

## BENIN

B enin is located on the Atlantic coast of western Africa, along the Gulf of Guinea. The former French colony gained independence in 1960. The capital is Porto-Novo.

### EARLY HISTORY

As a political unit, Benin was created by the French colonial conquest at the end of the 19th century. In the precolonial period, the territory comprised a multiplicity of independent states, differing in language and culture. The south was occupied mainly by Ewe-speaking peoples, who traced their traditional origins to the town of Tado (in modern Togo). During the 16th and 17th centuries, the most powerful state in this area was the kingdom of Allada (Ardra), but in the 18th and 19th centuries its place was taken by Dahomey. In the north, the largest group was the Bariba, the most important state being the kingdom of Nikki, which formed part of a confederacy including other Bariba states located in what is today Nigeria. The Somba, in the northwest, did not form a kingdom.

### THE SLAVE TRADE

The Portuguese first explored the coast of Benin in 1472 but did not begin trading there until 1553. During the 17th century the Dutch, English, French, and other Europeans also entered the trade. The principal export before the mid-19th century was always slaves. The volume of slave exports was at first small, but it increased rapidly in the second half of the 17th century, when this area became known to Europeans as the "Slave Coast," and remained high until the 1840s. The principal centre for the trade was the coastal kingdom of Ouidah (Whydah), which was originally a tributary of Allada but had become an independent state by the 1680s. The slaves exported were predominantly war captives and were drawn from the entire area of modern Benin, including northern peoples such as the Bariba as well as communities near the coast. The Atlantic slave trade had a substantial and deleterious impact in Benin, causing the depopulation of certain areas as well as a general militarization of society. The prominence of slaves from this area in the transatlantic trade is reflected in the survival of elements of its culture in black communities of the New World, especially in the Vodou (Voodoo) religion of Haiti, which incorporates many spirit cults and deities of the Ewe-speaking peoples.

## THE KINGDOM OF DAHOMEY

Dahomey (also called Abomey, after its capital city) was the state of the Fon people. It was originally a dependency of Allada, but during the 17th century a ruler called Wegbaja declared himself king and made Dahomey an independent state. Under King Agaja (reigned 1708?–40) Dahomey overran the coastal area, conquering Allada in 1724 and the commercial centre of Ouidah in 1727, thus establishing itself as the dominant power in the area. A section of the royal family of Allada, however, founded the new kingdom of Porto-Novo, on the coast to the east, which successfully resisted Dahomean authority and competed with Ouidah for control of the Atlantic trade. Dahomey itself was attacked and defeated by the kingdom of Oyo, to the northeast (in modern Nigeria), to which it was obliged to pay tribute from 1730 onward. Dahomey attained the height of its power under the kings Gezo (1818–58) and Glélé (1858–89). Gezo liberated Dahomey from its subjection to Oyo by defeating the latter in 1823. Dahomean attempts at expansion eastward, however, brought it up against the powerful state of Abeokuta (also in Nigeria). Dahomean attacks upon Abeokuta in 1851 and 1864 were decisively defeated.

Dahomey was a despotic and militaristic kingdom. Its power was based upon a highly trained standing army, which included a female contingent (called the "Amazons" by Europeans) drawn from the king's wives. The king's authority was buttressed by an elaborate cult of the deceased kings of the dynasty, who were honoured by the offering of human sacrifices at yearly public ceremonies (the "annual customs"). Its rulers succeeded in uniting the disparate communities which they absorbed into a new national identity, so that the conquered subjects of Dahomey came to regard themselves as Fon. During the 18th and early 19th centuries, Dahomey was a major supplier of slaves for the transatlantic trade, but by the mid-19th century the volume of the slave trade was in decline. In 1852 King Gezo was forced by a British naval blockade to accept a treaty abolishing the slave trade, although this was evaded in practice. From the 1840s onward Gezo promoted the export of palm oil, produced by slave labour on royal plantations, as a substitute for the declining slave trade.

## THE FRENCH CONQUEST AND COLONIAL RULE

During the 17th century several of the European nations engaged in the Atlantic slave trade maintained trading factories in the Dahomey area, and during the 18th century the English, French, and Portuguese all possessed fortified posts in Ouidah. The French first established a factory in Allada in 1670 but moved from there to Ouidah in 1671. Although this factory was abandoned in the 1690s, the French built a fort (known as Fort Saint Louis) in Ouidah in 1704. The European forts in Ouidah were, however, all abandoned about the end of the 18th century, the French establishment being withdrawn in 1797.

In 1842 the French fort at Ouidah was reoccupied as a base for the new trade in palm oil, and in 1851 the French government negotiated a commercial treaty with King Gezo of Dahomey. Subsequently fears of preemption by British colonial expansion led to the extension of formal French rule in the area. A protectorate was briefly established over the kingdom of Porto-Novo in 1863–65 and was definitively reestablished in 1882. Treaties purporting to secure cession of the port of Cotonou, between Ouidah and Porto-Novo, were also negotiated with the Dahomean authorities in 1868 and 1878, though Cotonou was not actually occupied until 1890. King Behanzin, who had succeeded to the Dahomean throne in 1889, resisted the French claim to Cotonou, provoking the French invasion and conquest of Dahomey in 1892–94. Behanzin was then deposed and exiled, and the kingdom of Dahomey became a French protectorate.

French ambitions to extend their control into the interior, north of Dahomey, were threatened by the rival expansionism of the British, who were established in what was to become their colony of Nigeria to the east, and in 1894 both the British and French negotiated treaties of protection with the kingdom of Nikki. The Anglo-French convention of 1898, however, settled the boundary between the French and British spheres, conceding Nikki to the former. The boundary with the German colony of Togo to the west was settled by the Franco-German conventions of 1885 and 1899. The present frontiers of Benin were established in 1909, when the boundaries with the neighbouring French colonies of Upper Volta and Niger were delimited. The colony was at first called Benin (from the Bight of Benin, not the precolonial kingdom of Benin, which is in Nigeria), but in 1894 it was renamed Dahomey, after the recently incorporated kingdom. From 1904 Dahomey formed part of the federation of French West Africa, under the governor-general in Senegal. Descendants of Portuguese settlers, freed slaves returning from Portuguese colonies in the Americas (called Brésiliens, or Brazilians), and missionaries were instrumental in spreading Christianity and Western education in the south but not in the Muslim north; by the 1950s Dahomey was known as the "Latin Quarter" of French West Africa.

## DECOLONIZATION AND INDEPENDENCE

In 1946 Dahomey became an overseas territory of France. It was created an autonomous republic within the French Community in 1959 and achieved complete independence on Aug. 1, 1960. During the period of decolonization, the nationalist movement in Dahomey became fragmented, with the emergence of three regionally based political parties— led by Sourou-Migan Apithy (president in 1964–65), Justin Ahomadégbé (1972), and Hubert Maga (1960–63 and 1970–72), drawing their principal support respectively from Porto-Novo, Abomey, and the north. After independence in 1960, these political problems were exacerbated by economic difficulties, reflected in student and trade union unrest. The ensuing instability resulted in six successful military coups d'état between 1963 and 1972 and periods of army rule in 1965–68

and 1969–70. In a last military coup, on Oct. 26, 1972, power was seized by Maj. (later Gen.) Mathieu Kérékou. From 1974 Kérékou pursued a Marxist-Leninist policy, based on nationalizations and state planning of the economy. The country was renamed the People's Republic of Benin in 1975.

The late 1980s and early 1990s were a turbulent period for Benin. In 1989 Kérékou proclaimed that Marxism-Leninism would no longer be the state ideology, and there followed a period of transition in the direction of greater democratization, including the promulgation of a new constitution in 1990 and the liberalization of the economy. The first multiparty elections were held in 1991, and Kérékou was defeated by Nicéphore Soglo, a former cabinet member.

Soglo's administration worked hard to improve the country's economy, implementing fiscal policies that garnered international respect, and Benin started to make economic gains. Unfortunately, the feeling among many Beninese was that economic progress came at too great a cost to the country—the disregard for democratization and the social well-being of its citizens—and Soglo's support slipped. In the 1996 presidential election, Soglo was defeated by Kérékou, as he was again in 2001 when the two leaders ran against each other.

During Kérékou's tenure the economy continued to be a concern among the Beninese. Workers went on strike several times in the late 1990s and early 2000s to protest issues—some resulting

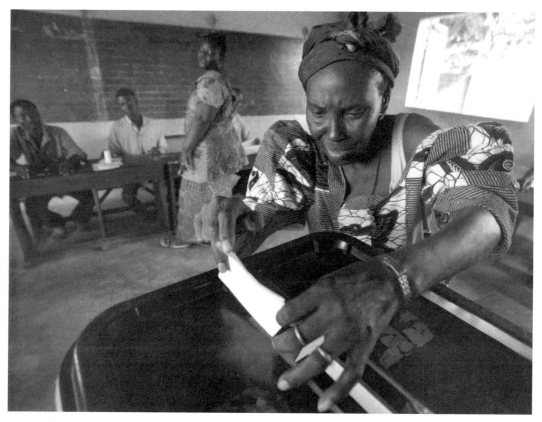

*A voter in Benin casts a ballot at a polling station during the 2006 presidential elections in which Thomas Yayi Boni emerged victorious.* AFP/Getty Images

from economic reform measures—such as low wages and the change to merit-based salary increases and promotions. Corruption was also an issue Kérékou had to address, with two unrelated investigations in 2003 and 2004 implicating many police, judiciary, and finance ministry officials.

Kérékou, barred by the constitution from serving any longer, was set to retire at the end of his term, and there was no clear successor. In presidential elections held in March 2006, Thomas Yayi Boni, former chief executive of the West African Development Bank and relatively new to national politics, emerged victorious after two rounds of voting. The new president focused on economic development as well as the elimination of government corruption. Yayi was the target of an assassination attempt one year later, from which he emerged unscathed.

# CHAPTER 6

## BURKINA FASO

Burkina Faso is a landlocked country in western Africa. The former French colony gained independence in 1960. The capital is Ouagadougou.

### EARLY HISTORY

Axes belonging to a Neolithic culture have been found in the north of Burkina Faso. The Bobo, the Lobi, and the Gurunsi are the earliest known inhabitants of the country. About the 15th century CE, conquering horsemen invaded the region from the south and founded the Gurma and the Mossi kingdoms, in the eastern and central areas, respectively. Several Mossi kingdoms developed, the most powerful of which was that of Ouagadougou, located in the centre of the country. Headed by an emperor, the *morho naba* ("great lord"), the Ouagadougou Mossi state defeated attempted invasions by the Songhai and Fulani empires yet maintained valuable commercial links with major western African trading powers, including the Dyula, the Hausa, and the Asante.

### EUROPEAN EXPLORATION AND COLONIZATION

The German explorer Gottlob Adolf Krause traversed the Mossi country in 1886, and the French army officer Louis-Gustave

## BOBO

*The Bobo are people of Burkina Faso, who speak a language of the Gur branch of the Niger-Congo family. They are a sedentary agricultural people growing such staples as millet and sorghum and a wide variety of other crops. Crop rotation and some irrigation are utilized, and small numbers of cattle and other animals are tended. Hunting, fishing, and the gathering of wild plants provide additional food.*

*The typical household comprises an extended family that dwells in a rectangular house with mud-brick walls, a beaten-earth roof, and, frequently, a defensive outer wall. Local patrilineages constitute clans that dominate a particular locality. There is a high incidence of polygyny, and the levirate (a custom whereby a widow marries a brother of her dead husband) and the sororate (a custom whereby a widower marries a sister of his dead wife) are practiced. Social structure is otherwise relatively egalitarian, although slavery was once present and some castes of smiths and leather workers persist. The Bobo are traditionally animist, although some individuals have converted to Islam and Christianity.*

Binger visited the *morho naba* in 1888. France obtained a protectorate over the Yatenga empire in 1895, and Paul Voulet and Charles-Paul-Louis Chanoine defeated the *morho naba* Boukari-Koutou (Wobogo) of Mossi in 1896 and then proceeded to overrun the Gurunsi lands. The Gurma accepted a French protectorate in 1897, and in that same year the lands of the Bobo and of the Lobi were annexed by the French (though the Lobi, armed with poisoned arrows, were not effectively subdued until 1903). An Anglo-French convention of 1898 fixed the frontier between France's new acquisitions and the northern territories of the Gold Coast.

The French divided the country into administrative *cercles* ("circles") but maintained the chiefs, including the *morho naba*, in their traditional seats. The country at first was attached to Upper Senegal–Niger (as that colony was called from 1904 to 1920; now Mali) but was organized as a separate colony, Upper Volta (Haute-Volta), in 1919. In 1932 it was partitioned between Côte d'Ivoire, Niger, and French Sudan. In 1947, however, Upper Volta was reestablished to become an overseas territory of the French Union, with a territorial assembly of its own. The assembly in 1957 received the right to elect an executive council of government for the territory, which at the end of 1958 was transformed into an autonomous republic within the French Community. When independence was proclaimed on Aug. 5, 1960, the new constitution provided for an executive president elected by universal adult suffrage for a five-year term and an elected Legislative Assembly.

## INDEPENDENCE

Since Burkina Faso became an independent nation, the military has on several

## LOBI

*The Lobi are people residing in the western region of Burkina Faso and in Côte d'Ivoire and speaking a Gur language of the Niger-Congo family. They are farmers and hunters, growing millet and sorghum as staples. Traditionally, the Lobi governed themselves through the clan system, with no formal political organization.*

*Religious beliefs were purely animistic until Islamic influence entered the area around the 14th century. Polygyny is practiced. In 1897, France annexed the Lobi lands, but because of the Lobi's effective use of poisoned arrows the population was not subdued until 1903.*

occasions intervened during times of crisis. In 1966 the military, led by Lieut. Col. (later Gen.) Sangoulé Lamizana, ousted the elected government of Maurice Yaméogo. Lamizana dominated the country's politics until November 1980, when a series of strikes launched by workers, teachers, and civil servants led to another coup, this time headed by Col. Saye Zerbo.

Zerbo's short-lived rule ended in November 1982 when noncommissioned army officers rebelled and installed Maj. Jean-Baptiste Ouedraogo as president. The Ouedraogo government soon split into conservative and radical factions, with the radicals seizing power on Aug. 4, 1983. They set up a National Revolutionary Council (CNR), with Capt. Thomas Sankara as head of state.

A year after taking power, Sankara renamed the country Burkina Faso, meaning "Land of Incorruptible People," and ordered all officials, including himself, to open their bank accounts to public scrutiny. His government was responsible for several concrete achievements: vaccination and housing projects, tree planting to hold back the Sahel, promotion of women's rights, and curbing of waste in government.

During Sankara's rule, tensions with Mali over the mineral-rich Agacher Strip erupted in a brief border war in December 1985. The dispute was settled in the International Court of Justice at The Hague a year later, to the satisfaction of both countries.

Initially a coalition of radical groups that included army officers, trade unionists, and members of small opposition groups, the Sankara regime gradually lost most of its popular support as power became concentrated in the hands of a few military officers—the most important of which were Sankara, Capt. Blaise Compaoré, Maj. Jean-Baptiste Boukari Lingani, and Capt. Henri Zongo. Popular support continued to decline, and on Oct. 15, 1987, a military coup overthrew Sankara, who was killed along with several others.

*Blaise Compaoré, who took power in the late 1980s and was first elected president in 1991, is shown here in 2010.* Fethi Belaid/AFP/Getty Images

Compaoré took power at the head of a triumvirate that included Zongo and Lingani. However, as time went on, Lingani and Zongo disagreed with Compaoré about economic reform issues, and in 1989 they were accused of plotting to overthrow him. The two were arrested and quickly executed, and Compaoré continued to pursue his political agenda. In 1991 a new constitution was promulgated, and Compaoré was elected president in an election that was boycotted by opposition candidates.

Compaoré was reelected in 1998 and 2005. His regime, however, was not without opposition or controversy. Unpopular political and economic developments and the suspicious death in 1989 of Norbert Zongo, a prominent journalist known for speaking out against Compaoré's administration, contributed to periodic episodes of social and political unrest that continued into the 2000s.

In October 2003 several people were arrested and accused of planning a coup to oust Compaoré. Meanwhile, economic troubles were exacerbated by the civil war that had begun in neighbouring Côte d'Ivoire in 2002. The conflict disrupted an important source of trade for Burkina Faso as well as the livelihoods of several hundred thousand Burkinabé who had found work there. Compaoré's administration also faced public discontent over high living costs, which lead to riots in February 2008, weeks of protests, and a general strike in April.

# CHAPTER 7

## CAMEROON

Cameroon is located on the Atlantic coast of western-central Africa, along the Gulf of Guinea. Initially a German colony, administration was divided between the French and British after World War I. The French territory gained independence in 1960 and was joined by the southern portion of the British territory one year later, while the northern portion of the British territory opted to join neighbouring Nigeria. The capital is Yaoundé.

### EARLY HISTORY

From archaeological evidence it is known that humans have inhabited Cameroon for at least 50,000 years, and there is strong evidence of the existence of important kingdoms and states in more recent times. Of these, the most widely known is Sao, which arose in the vicinity of Lake Chad, probably in the 5th century CE. This kingdom reached its height from the 9th to the 15th century, after which it was conquered and destroyed by the Kotoko state, which extended over large portions of northern Cameroon and Nigeria. Kotoko was incorporated into the Bornu empire during the reign of Rābiḥ al-Zubayr (Rabah) in the late 19th century, and its people became Muslims.

Islam became a powerful force in the northern and central portions of the country through conquest, immigration, and the spread of commerce from north and northwestern Africa.

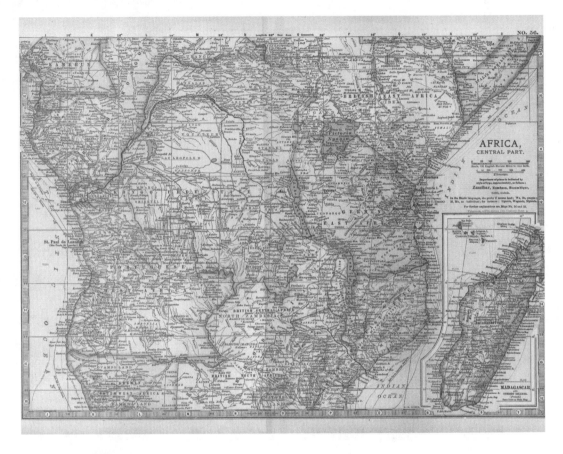

*Map of central Africa, from the 10th edition of* Encyclopædia Britannica, *published in 1902.*

The most significant bearers of this faith, the Fulani, entered northern Cameroon in the 18th century. The first small groups of pastoralists were welcomed by the host populations. Eventually the Fulani, frustrated under non-Muslim rule and encouraged by the teachings of the mystic Usman dan Fodio, revolted. In the early 1800s Modibbo Adama was appointed by Usman to lead a jihad over large areas centred in northern Nigeria, which were subsequently incorporated into Usman's Sokoto empire.

The Fulani expansion reached its southernmost point with the conquest of Bamum, a kingdom founded in the 17th century by Nshare, the son of a Tikar chief. Bamum was one of the largest of numerous kingdoms that emerged in the grassland areas of Cameroon at that time. The Fulani conquest was brief and did not result in Islamization, although this faith was accepted by a later ruler, Sultan Njoya, in the early 20th century.

Islam was a significant influence entering Cameroon from the north.

Other powerful influences entered from the southern coastal region. In 1472 the Portuguese explorer Fernão do Pó was the first European to view the Cameroon coast, although Hanno, a Carthaginian, may have sailed there 2,000 years earlier. Pó was followed by traders, many of whom were involved in the Atlantic slave trade. Cameroon became a significant source of slaves, a number of whom were sold and traded at Bimbia, Douala, and other ports. Routes linked these ports far inland where the Bamileke, Bamum, and other kingdoms provided a greater supply of slaves. In the early 1800s the slave trade declined, and attention turned to trade in rubber, palm oil, and other items. Earlier Portuguese and Dutch influences were largely replaced by the British and the Germans.

Christian missionaries also began to play a role in the region. Under the leadership of Englishman Alfred Saker and West Indians such as Joseph Merrick, a Baptist station was established in 1845 at Akwa Town (now Douala). Saker established a larger post at Victoria (now Limbe) in 1858. The American Presbyterian mission opened a station in 1871. The origin and denomination of the missions changed frequently, but the Presbyterians, Baptists, and Roman Catholics have been the most prominent.

## GERMAN KAMERUN

In spite of the predominant role of the British along the coast, in 1884 the Germans claimed the region as Kamerun.

The explorer Gustav Nachtigal arrived in July 1884 to annex the Douala coast. The Germans moved inland over the years, extending their control and their claims. Initially, their major dealings were with African traders, but direct trade with the interior promised greater profits, and colonial power was used to break the African monopoly. Plantation agriculture was another major German economic activity. Large estates were established in southwestern Kamerun to provide tropical produce for Germany. Traders, plantation owners, and government officials competed for labour, and force was used to obtain it. The system established was harsh, and many workers died serving German interests.

## BRITISH CAMEROONS AND FRENCH CAMEROUN

In World War I British, French, and Belgian troops drove the Germans into exile, beginning a period of British rule in two small portions and French rule in the remainder of the territory. These League of Nations mandates (later United Nations [UN] trusts) were referred to as French Cameroun and British Cameroons.

The British trust territory consisted of a strip of land bisected by the Benue River along the eastern border of Nigeria. British rule was a period of neglect, and this, coupled with the influx of numerous Nigerians, caused great resentment. The old German plantations were eventually united into a single parastatal (government-owned enterprise), the

*German explorer Gustav Nachtigal.* Apic/Hulton Archive/Getty Images

Cameroon Development Corporation, and were the mainstay of the economy. Development also occurred in agriculture, especially in the latter years of British rule. The production of cacao, coffee, and bananas grew rapidly.

The French territory had an administration based on that of the other territories of French Equatorial Africa. Greater agricultural development took place in French Cameroun. Limited industrial and infrastructural growth also occurred, largely after World War II. At independence, French Cameroun had a much higher gross national product per capita, higher education levels, better health care, and better infrastructure than British Cameroons.

Although there were differences in the French and British colonial experiences, there were also strong similarities. Most important, these rulers continued drawing Cameroon into the international economic system. By the time of independence, the trusts produced raw materials for European industries but were dependent on Europe, and especially France, for finished goods. This fragile economy would long continue to plague Cameroon.

## MOVING TOWARD INDEPENDENCE

After World War II, developments in Cameroon and Europe brought about independence. In French Cameroun the major question was the type and intensity of the relationship with France after independence. The first nationalist party, the Cameroon People's Union (Union des Populations Camerounaises; UPC), led by Felix-Roland Moumie and Reuben Um Nyobe, demanded a thorough break with France and the establishment of a socialist economy. French officials suppressed the UPC, leading to a bitter civil war, while encouraging alternative political leaders. On Jan. 1, 1960, independence was granted. In elections held soon after independence, Ahmadou Ahidjo was elected the first president of the Republic of Cameroon. Ahidjo and his party, the Cameroon Union (Union Camerounaise), pledged to build a capitalist economy and to maintain close ties to France.

In British Cameroons the major question was whether to remain with Nigeria or to unite with the newly independent Republic of Cameroon. In a UN-supervised plebiscite in February 1961, the south decided to unite with the former French Cameroun, creating the Federal Republic of Cameroon. The north voted to join the Federation of Nigeria.

## AHIDJO PRESIDENCY

Ahidjo ruled from independence until 1982. He centralized political power in himself and in the capital, Yaoundé. Cameroon became an authoritarian, single-party state (under the Cameroon National Union [Union Nationale Camerounaise; UNC], formed in the mid-1960s by the merger of a number of parties) in which civil rights meant little.

Ahidjo declared nation building to be a major goal, using the fear of ethnic conflict to justify authoritarianism.

Ahidjo's policy of planned liberalism was formulated to encourage private investment, with government to play a strong role in guiding development. Expansion of export crops was to provide the foreign capital needed. The 1973 announcement of the Green Revolution proposed that the country was to become self-sufficient in food and to become the primary food source for its neighbours.

The discovery of exploitable petroleum in the 1970s was of great benefit to the economy, and petroleum swiftly became Cameroon's most valuable export. Petroleum revenues were used to increase prices to farmers, to pay for imports of materials and technology, and to build financial reserves. Unfortunately, petroleum income also paid for a number of costly and poorly planned projects.

Large-scale industrial development projects met with little success, and much capital was lost. Although there was more success in assisting the growth of agribusinesses and small and medium-sized enterprises producing goods for local use, the country still largely depended on imported industrial goods. Exceptions to this were refined petroleum products, cement, textiles and clothing, beverages, and aluminum. Expansion of transportation facilities, the development of hydroelectric capability, and tremendous growth in education took place.

## CAMEROON UNDER BIYA

On Nov. 4, 1982, Ahidjo resigned and was succeeded by Prime Minister Paul Biya under the terms of the constitution. Ahidjo, however, remained head of the UNC, the sole political party.

### TRANSITION

Despite Ahidjo's resignation, he still had expectations of retaining control over the government—intentions that did not sit well with Biya. A confrontation soon followed when Ahidjo tried to assert party domination over the government. The bid was unsuccessful, however, and in August 1983 Ahidjo was forced to resign as head of the party. A minor coup attempt and a subsequent uprising by the Republican Guard on April 6, 1984—perhaps favoured or directed by Ahidjo or his supporters—followed. Biya emerged unscathed, while Ahidjo, who had taken refuge in France, was tried and sentenced in absentia for his role in the plot. What remained of Ahidjo's UNC was soon restyled as Biya's Cameroon People's Democratic Movement (Rassemblement Démocratique du Peuple Camerounaise; RDPC).

### CONSOLIDATION AND CHALLENGE

At first Biya had sought the development of a more democratic society. Competitive elections for party offices and the National Assembly were permitted, even though the country was still a single-party state. The conflict with Ahidjo and the 1984 coup attempt, however, brought back some of the restrictions of the Ahidjo era. As the sole candidate for the country's only legal political party, Biya won uncontested presidential elections in both 1984 and 1988. In the 1990s Biya resisted both domestic and international pressure to democratize. Although he supported legislation in late 1990 that provided for a change to a multiparty political system, he employed a variety of tactics to ensure the status of the RDPC as the dominant party.

At the same time, calls for democracy were also increasing in the English-speaking part of the country. There, many citizens claiming oppression by the French-speaking majority made demands for a return to a federal system, while extremists called for Anglophone independence and threatened violence if their demands were not met. Tensions between the Anglophone community and the Biya administration continued into the 2000s.

In addition to political strife, Biya also had to deal with growing economic troubles. He had inherited a country poised on the brink of severe economic crisis; although the crisis had taken root during Ahidjo's tenure, it did not surface until after his resignation. Cameroon's economy, extremely dependent on such exports as cocoa, coffee, and oil, was adversely affected by decreases in the prices of these commodities during the

1980s. In addition, poor economic management had long plagued the country. Cameroonians placed the blame on Biya, and by the late 1980s opposition to the government had grown. In 1987 Biya admitted that the country faced an economic crisis, and the necessity of an International Monetary Fund structural adjustment program and budget cuts was recognized. The realization that Cameroon had not been able to change the dependent nature of its economy, regardless of the economic progress made since independence, was the cause of much frustration.

Despite the subsequent efforts made toward economic reform, conditions in Cameroon were less than ideal, and corruption was rampant. By the 1990s the country was in severe recession. Numerous jobs had been lost, many workers had received salary cuts, and education and health care funding had been reduced. Discontent with the government—manifested in part by periodic demonstrations and strikes to protest the country's economic policies—was extremely high. Cameroon did benefit from debt relief by international creditors, particularly in 2006, when the majority of the country's sizable debt to the Paris Club, a group of creditor countries, was cancelled.

Despite the array of challenges facing him, Biya's rule was extended with his victories in multiparty elections held in 1992, 1997, and 2004 (the presidential term had been extended, first to five and then to seven years)—all marred by irregularities, although the 2004 election experienced fewer problems than the others and was generally viewed as free and fair. In April 2008 the National Assembly passed a controversial constitutional amendment abolishing presidential term limits, thereby providing Biya with the option to run again in the future.

## FOREIGN RELATIONS

Meanwhile, tensions from a long-standing border dispute with Nigeria over the oil-rich Bakassi Peninsula came to a head in late 1993 and early 1994 when Nigerian troops advanced into the region. New skirmishes occurred in early 1996, and, although a truce was signed, sporadic fighting continued for the next few years. After eight years of investigation and deliberation, the International Court of Justice (ICJ) awarded the peninsula to Cameroon in October 2002. Nigeria and Cameroon entered into two years of mediation and discussion to facilitate the implementation of the

ICJ ruling, reaching an agreement to transfer sovereignty of the peninsula in September 2004. Despite these measures, Nigeria did not meet the deadline, citing technical problems with preparing for the transfer. In August 2006 the handover of the Bakassi Peninsula from Nigeria to Cameroon was largely completed. Although the transfer was not without its problems—including the dissatisfaction of many peninsula residents who would have preferred to retain their Nigerian identity—the region enjoyed relative peace until November 2007, when Cameroonian troops stationed in the peninsula were killed by assailants who were reportedly wearing Nigerian military uniforms. Nigeria quickly declared that its military was not involved and cited recent criminal activity in the Niger delta region, where military supplies—including uniforms— were stolen. A ceremony held on Aug. 14, 2008, marked the completion of the peninsula's transfer from Nigeria to Cameroon.

# CHAPTER 8

## CAPE VERDE

Cape Verde comprises a group of islands in the Atlantic Ocean, located 385 miles (620 km) off the coast of western Africa. The former Portuguese colony gained independence in 1975. The capital is Praia.

### EARLY HISTORY

Although there is no conclusive evidence that the islands were inhabited before the arrival of the Portuguese, cases may be made for visits by Phoenicians, Moors, and Africans in previous centuries. It was Portuguese navigators such as Diogo Gomes and Diogo Afonso, Venetian explorer Alvise Ca' da Mosto, and Genoese navigators such as António and Bartólomeu da Noli, however, who began to report on the islands in the mid-15th century, shortly before a plan of active colonization and settlement was launched.

In 1462 the first settlers from Portugal landed on São Tiago, subsequently founding there the oldest European city in the tropics—Ribeira Grande (now Cidade Velha). Sugar was planted in an attempt to emulate the success of the earlier settlement of Madeira. Cape Verde's dry climate was less favourable, but, with the development of transatlantic slave trade, the importance and the wealth of the islands increased.

Cape Verde served an increasingly important role as an offshore entrepôt with the development of the triangular trade, by which manufactured goods from Europe were traded

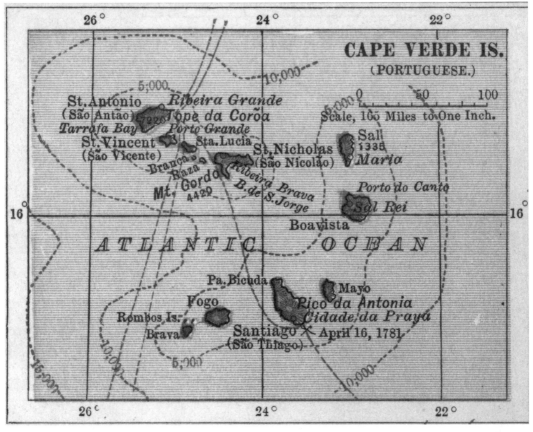

*Map of the Cape Verde Islands, from the 10th edition of* Encyclopædia Britannica, *published in 1902.*

for slaves, who were sold in turn to plantations in the New World in exchange for the raw materials produced there; with these, the ships returned home. Cape Verde was thus a centre for the trade of cheap manufactured items, firearms, rum, cloth, and the like in exchange for slaves, ivory, and gold. Cape Verde was especially known for its *pano* cloths, usually constructed of six strips of fabric made from cotton that was grown, dyed dark indigo, and woven on narrow looms by slaves in Cape Verde; the cloths were a valuable form of currency for the slave trade on the mainland. Tens of thousands of slaves were exported from the coast to the islands and then on to the New World, especially to northern Brazil.

Portuguese efforts to monopolize exploration and trade along the western African coast were disrupted by those who saw the potential of the wealth of Africa for their own interests, and smuggling was rife. Although the slave trade was controlled through the crown-issued monopoly contracts, in the late 16th century the English and Spanish began to wear away the Portuguese monopoly. In addition, the prosperity of Ribeira Grande attracted pirates, who attacked the city in 1541. The English later attacked it twice—in 1585 and 1592—the first time under the command of Sir Francis Drake. After a French attack in 1712, it was decided to move the capital to Praia. With the transfer officially complete in 1770, Ribeira Grande began its long slow decline.

The waning of the slave trade—the Portuguese rulers and merchants reluctantly abandoned the industry in 1876—coupled with increasing drought slowly sapped the islands' prosperity. In the early 1800s Cape Verde experienced not only recurrent drought and famine but government corruption and maladministration as well. In the mid-1850s, the islands enjoyed a period of economic optimism as the age of steam replaced the age of sail, and large long-distance oceanic vessels needed strategic coaling stations such as Mindelo could provide. As a result, Cape Verde was briefly the site of great port activity, before the opening of the Suez Canal in 1869 cut severely into this business. For the wider population there was little relief or improvement, and emigration from the islands became the norm: faced with the prospect of drought and starvation at home, the poorest Cape Verdeans commonly traveled south to work as agricultural labourers picking bananas and cocoa beans on the islands of São Tomé and Príncipe; others found maritime work on whaling ships.

# STRUGGLE FOR INDEPENDENCE

The long-standing joint colonial administration of Cape Verde and Guinea-Bissau was terminated in 1879, when both became separate Portuguese territories. Amid the contemporary African decolonization movement, their status was modified in 1951 to "overseas provinces," and their inhabitants were officially granted full Portuguese citizenship in 1961. Not perceiving these changes as meaningful, however, some members of the colonial population began to agitate for complete independence from Portugal for both Guinea-Bissau and Cape Verde. One such group, the African Party for the Independence of Guinea and Cape Verde (Partido Africano da Independência da Guiné e Cabo Verde; PAIGC) was founded in Bissau in 1956 and headed by Amílcar Cabral, a gifted revolutionary leader and theoretician. Its goal was to achieve independence by using peaceful means of protest; in 1959, however, the Portuguese responded with violence and arrests, which convinced the PAIGC that only a path of armed struggle would be sufficient to end the colonial and fascist regime. After a period of military training and political preparation, the PAIGC launched its armed campaign in January 1963 and showed steady military progress thereafter. On Jan. 20, 1973, Cabral was assassinated; later that year, on September 24, Guinea-Bissau declared independence. This event—compounded by the other lengthy wars in Portuguese colonies—precipitated a crisis in Portugal that resulted in a successful coup there on April 25, 1974. Portugal's new government soon began negotiating with African nationalist movements.

## INDEPENDENCE

Full independence was achieved in Cape Verde on July 5, 1975. Aristides Pereira, the PAIGC secretary-general, and Pedro Pires, a military commander, became the first president and prime minister, respectively. A military coup in Guinea-Bissau in 1980, deeply resented in Cape Verde, broke the political unity between the two countries. The PAIGC subsequently split, with the Cape Verdean branch thereafter known as the African Party for the Independence of Cape Verde (Partido Africano para a Independência de Cabo Verde; PAICV). Pereira and Pires remained in power in the one-party state until PAICV dissidents were permitted to form a second party, the Movement for Democracy (Movimento para a Democracia; MpD), which was organized from as early as March 1990 and emerged victorious in the two-party elections of January 1991. In the presidential election held the following month, Antonio Mascarenhas Monteiro, backed by the MpD, won a decisive victory; he was reelected in February 1996 in an election marked by a low turnout and in which he was the only candidate.

During Monteiro's tenure, the country continued to experience economic struggles, and both the MpD and the PAICV held the troubled economy to be their primary concern. During the legislative and presidential elections of 2001, the PAICV was returned to power, with Pires winning the second round of balloting to secure the presidency despite allegations of irregularities by his opponent, former prime minister Carlos Alberto Wahnon Carvalho Veiga. That same year, food shortages—a common predicament for the country—worsened considerably, and the government relied heavily on foreign aid and food imports to feed the country. Veiga and Pires faced each other once again in the presidential election of 2006, in which Pires—with diasporic support—very narrowly secured reelection.

The poverty and high rates of unemployment that plagued Cape Verde in the 1990s continued into the 2000s, even as the government made strides in reaching economic goals. In the 21st century, the country continued to successfully pursue political and economic relationships around the globe, courting foreign investors and creating and maintaining diplomatic ties in the international community.

# CHAPTER 9

## CHAD

C had is a landlocked country in north-central Africa. The former French colony gained independence in 1960. The capital is N'Djamena.

### EARLY HISTORY

The region of the eastern Sahara and Sudan from Fezzan, Bilma, and Chad in the west to the Nile valley in the east was well peopled in Neolithic times, as discovered sites attest. Probably typical of the earliest populations were the dark-skinned cave dwellers described by Herodotus as inhabiting the country south of Fezzan. The ethnographic history of the region is that of gradual modification of this basic stock by the continual infiltration of nomadic and increasingly Arabicized white African elements, entering from the north via Fezzan and Tibesti and, especially after the 14th century, from the Nile valley via Darfur. According to legend, the country around Lake Chad was originally occupied by the Sao. This vanished people is probably represented today by the Kotoko, in whose country, along the banks of the Logone and Chari, was unearthed in the 1950s a medieval culture notable for work in terra-cotta and bronze.

The relatively large and politically sophisticated king-doms of the central Sudan were the creation of Saharan Imazighen, drawn southward by their continuous search for pasturage and easily able to impose their hegemony on the fragmentary indigenous societies of agriculturalists. This process was intensified by the expansion of Islam. There are indications of a large immigration of pagan Imazighen into the central Sudan early in the 8th century.

## FROM THE 16TH TO THE 19TH CENTURY

The most important of these states, Kanem-Bornu, which was at the height of its power in the later 16th century, owed its preeminence to its command of the southern terminus of the trans-Saharan trade route to Tripoli.

Products of the Islamized Sudanic culture diffused from Kanem were the kingdoms of Bagirmi and Ouaddaï, which emerged in the early years of the 17th century out of the process of conversion to Islam. In the 18th century the Arab dynasty of Ouaddaï was able to throw off the suzerainty of Darfur and extend its territories by the conquest of eastern Kanem. Slave raiding at the expense of animist populations to the south constituted an important element in the prosperity of all these Muslim states. In the 19th century, however, they were in full decline, torn by wars and internecine feuds. In the years 1883–93 they all fell to the Sudanese adventurer Rābiḥ az-Zubayr.

## FRENCH ADMINISTRATION

By this time the partition of Africa among the European powers was entering its final phase. Rābiḥ was overthrown in 1900, and the traditional Kanembu dynasty was reestablished under French protection. Chad became part of the federation of French Equatorial Africa in 1910. The pacification of the whole area of the present republic was barely completed by 1914, and between the wars French rule was unprogressive. A pact between Italy and France that would have ceded the Aozou Strip to Italian-ruled Libya was never ratified by the French National Assembly, but it provided a pretext for Libya to seize the territory in 1973. During World War II Chad gave unhesitating support to the Free French cause. After 1945 the territory shared in the constitutional advance of French Equatorial Africa. In 1946 it became an overseas territory of the French Republic.

## INDEPENDENCE

A large measure of autonomy was conceded under the constitutional law of 1957, when the first territorial government was formed by Gabriel Lisette, a West Indian who had become the leader of the Chad Progressive Party (PPT). An autonomous republic within the French Community was proclaimed in November 1958, and complete independence in the restructured community was attained on Aug. 11, 1960. The country's stability was endangered by tensions between the black and often Christian populations of the more economically progressive southwest and the conservative, Muslim, nonblack leadership of the old feudal states of the north, and its problems were further complicated by Libyan involvement.

Lisette was removed by an associate more acceptable to some of the opposition, N'Garta (François) Tombalbaye, a southern trade union leader, who became the first president of the republic. In March 1961 Tombalbaye achieved a fusion of the PPT with the principal opposition party, the National African Party (PNA), to form a new Union for the Progress of Chad. An alleged conspiracy by Muslim elements, however, led in 1963 to the dissolution of the National Assembly, a brief state of emergency, and the arrest of the leading ministers formerly associated with the PNA. Only government candidates ran in the new elections in December 1963, ushering in the one-party state.

## CIVIL WAR

In the mid-1960s two guerrilla movements emerged. The Front for the National Liberation of Chad (Frolinat) was established in 1966 and operated primarily in the north from its headquarters at the southern Libyan oasis of Al-Kufrah, while the smaller Chad National Front (FNT) operated in the east-central region. Both groups aimed at the overthrow of the existing government, the reduction of French influence in Chad, and closer association with the Arab states of North Africa. Heavy fighting occurred in 1969 and 1970, and French military forces were brought in to suppress the revolts.

By the end of the 1970s, civil war had become not so much a conflict between Chad's Muslim northern region and the black southern region as a struggle between northern political factions. Libyan troops were brought in at Pres. Goukouni Oueddei's request in December 1980 and were withdrawn, again at his request, in November 1981. In a reverse movement the Armed Forces of the North (FAN) of Hissène Habré, which had retreated into the neighbouring country of Sudan in December 1980, reoccupied all the important towns in eastern Chad in November 1981. Peacekeeping forces of the Organization of African Unity (now the African Union) withdrew in 1982, and Habré formed a new government in October of the same year. Simultaneously, an opposition government under the leadership of Goukouni was established, with Libyan military support, at Bardaï in the north. After heavy fighting in 1983–84 Habré's FAN prevailed, aided by French troops. France withdrew its troops in 1984 but Libya refused to do so. Libya launched incursions deeper into Chad in 1986, and they were turned back by government forces with help from France and the United States.

In early 1987 Habré's forces recovered the territory in northern Chad that had been under Libyan control and for a few weeks reoccupied Aozou. When this oasis was retaken by Muammar al-Qaddafi's Libyan forces, Habré retaliated by raiding Maaten es Sarra, which is well inside Libya. A truce was called in September 1987.

## CONTINUING CONFLICT

Habré continued to face threats to his regime. In April 1989 an unsuccessful coup attempt was led by the interior minister, Brahim Mahamot Itno, and two key military advisers, Hassan Djamouss and Idriss Déby. Itno was arrested and Djamouss was killed, but Déby escaped and began new attacks a year later. By late 1990 his Movement for Chadian National Salvation forces had captured Abéché, and Habré fled the country. Déby suspended the constitution and formed a new government with himself as president. Although it was reported that he had received arms from Libya, he denied Libyan involvement and promised to establish a multiparty democracy in Chad.

Déby's takeover of the government was not without resistance. In 1991 and 1992 there were several attacks and coup attempts by opposition forces, many of whom were still aligned with Habré, but Déby maintained his grip on the government and the country. A national conference was held in 1993 to establish a transitional government, and Déby was officially designated interim president. In 1996 a new constitution was approved and Déby was elected president in the first multiparty presidential elections held in Chad's history. Peace was still fragile, however, and periodic skirmishes with opposition groups developed into a full rebellion in late 1998 when the Mouvement pour la Démocratie et la Justice au Tchad (MDJT) began an offensive in the northern part of the country. Other opposition groups later joined forces with the MDJT, and the rebellion continued into the 21st century.

In 2001 Déby was reelected amid allegations of fraud by his opponents; however, international observers found the electoral proceedings largely to be valid. Meanwhile, Déby's government was still coping with major rebel offensives, until peace accords in 2002 and 2003 essentially ended most of the fighting for a few years. Also in 2003, years of planning and construction came to fruition when Chad became an oil-producing country; the revenues generated from this undertaking had the potential to transform the country's economic situation.

Despite the progress Déby's government made with promoting peace and creating an opportunity for economic prosperity, there were additional coup attempts, including those in 2004 and 2006. Rebel offensives also resumed, most notably in 2006, prior to Déby's reelection to a third term as president, and in 2008, when rebels reached N'Djamena before retreating; many Chadians were displaced by the fighting. Several rebel leaders involved in the 2008 offensive were tried in absentia in August of that year, as was former president Habré, who was suspected of directing rebel activity in Chad while living in exile in Senegal. Habré and the rebel leaders were found guilty of attempting to overthrow Déby's government and were sentenced to death. Habré also faced charges in Senegal regarding politically motivated killings

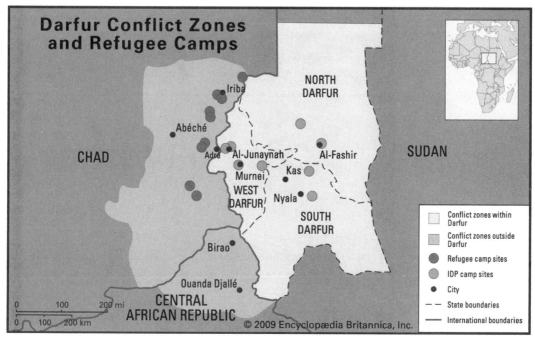

*Map showing Darfur-related conflict zones and camp sites for refugees and internally displaced peoples (IDPs) in The Sudan, Central African Republic, and Chad, 2008.*

and acts of torture allegedly committed during his rule in Chad; Senegal pursued these charges at the request of the African Union.

In addition to internal conflicts, at the beginning of the 21st century Chad had problems along its border with neighbouring countries Niger, the Central African Republic, and most notably Sudan, its neighbour to the west. In early 2003, fighting in the Darfur region of Sudan sent thousands of Sudanese fleeing to Chad; by early 2005 it was estimated that there were some 200,000 refugees in Chad. Chadian troops were drawn into the conflict periodically, as Sudanese militias crossed over the border into Chad while chasing Sudanese rebels or attacking refugee camps; Chadian rebels were also suspected of operating from bases in Sudan. Both Chad and Sudan accused each other of supporting rebel activity in the other's country. In January 2008 a European Union peacekeeping force was deployed to protect refugees of Chad, Sudan, and the Central African Republic in conflict zones along the borders; this was replaced by a larger contingent of United Nations peacekeeping forces in March 2009.

# CHAPTER 10

# CÔTE D'IVOIRE

Côte d'Ivoire is located on the Atlantic coast of western Africa, along the Gulf of Guinea. The former French colony gained independence in 1960. The de facto capital is Abidjan; the administrative capital designate (since 1983) is Yamoussoukro. For many years the name of the colony, and then the country, was more commonly known to the English-speaking world as "Ivory Coast," the English translation of Côte d'Ivoire.

## EARLY HISTORY

Abundant archaeological evidence confirms the presence of early humans in what is now Côte d'Ivoire. Groups in the north were drawn into the trans-Saharan trade networks of the Ghana and Mali empires. Islam arrived with Malinke merchants as trade expanded. Mali's collapse in the 16th century resulted in a great upheaval that sent waves of migrants southward, where they founded new kingdoms in the hinterlands of the forest zone. The original inhabitants were either displaced or assimilated by these new groups.

## PRECOLONIAL KINGDOMS

Important kingdoms flourished in the precolonial period. In the savanna country, towns developed around communities of Dyula traders. Kong existed for several centuries before Sekou Ouattara and his sons established a new dynasty there in the early 18th century. Kong lasted until 1897, when it was destroyed by Samory Touré, who was in the process of creating a new Muslim empire that included what is now northern Côte d'Ivoire. The Bouna kingdom was created in the late 17th century by Bounkani, an immigrant from Dagomba (now Ghana). It, along with Kong, became a major centre of Islamic learning.

The wars associated with the rise of the Asante empire in the late 17th century led to the migration of numerous Akan peoples into the forest region of Côte d'Ivoire. The most powerful of the states established was the Abron kingdom of Gyaman founded by Tan Daté. It was conquered by the Asante in the 1730s, and, despite numerous revolts, remained subject to it until 1875. In much the same circumstances the Anyi kingdoms of Indénié (Ndenye) and Sanwi were founded. Following the death in 1750 of the ruler of the Asante, Asantehene Opoku Ware, a succession struggle in Kumasi (the capital of the Asante empire) forced one contender, Queen Abla Poku (Awura Poku), and her supporters to enter the north-central part of Côte d'Ivoire. They founded the Baule kingdom, remarkable for its blending of Akan and local traditions.

## ARRIVAL OF EUROPEANS

Until the 19th century, European contact was confined to the coast, where French and Portuguese traders sought slaves and ivory. Louis-Édouard Bouet-Willaumez began signing treaties with coastal chiefs in the 1830s that allowed France to build forts and trading posts. France withdrew

in 1870, but private merchants remained. Arthur Verdier sent explorers north and imported the first coffee plants. By the 1890s, inland penetration by traders such as Marcel Triech-Laplène and military missions such as those of Capt. Louis-Gustave Binger in 1887–89 resulted in more treaties and French "protectorate" relationships with many groups.

As the European rush to divide Africa accelerated, France claimed Côte d'Ivoire as a colony in 1893. Borders were determined in 1898, following the capture of Samory Touré. Gov. Gabriel Angoulvant began the military occupation in 1908. Imposition of forced labour and head taxes led to fierce resistance, especially among the Baule, Anyi, and Abe (Abbey). New revolts broke out when France conscripted thousands of Ivoirians to serve with other western African soldiers in World War I. France's superior weaponry eventually triumphed, although the colony was not considered under control until 1918.

## MARCH TOWARD INDEPENDENCE

Following World War I, concerted efforts toward economic development were taken. The railway was extended to Bobo Dioulasso, which, along with most of Upper Volta (now Burkina Faso), was attached to Côte d'Ivoire in 1933. Schools and Western-style health facilities were introduced, exploitation of the forests was intensified, and Africans were encouraged to plant cash crops for export. By 1939, Africans grew 90 percent

*Félix Houphouët-Boigny, first president of Côte d'Ivoire, is shown here in 1960, when the country gained its independence from the French. AFP/Getty Images*

of the cocoa and 80 percent of the coffee produced in the colony.

Forty thousand Ivoirians fought for the French army during World War II. Between 1940 and 1942 the colony, along with the rest of French West Africa, chose to remain under the Vichy government. Racist legislation, economic discrimination against African planters, increased forced labour, and a depression caused by Britain's naval blockade created enormous discontent. Educated Africans thus welcomed the subsequent Free French regime. In 1944 Félix Houphouët-Boigny and Auguste Denise formed the African Farmers Union (SAA), which, with the support of the colony's governor, André Latrille, secured equal treatment for African planters. Houphouët-Boigny's all-African slate swept local elections in 1945. The following year, with Côte d'Ivoire part of the French Union, he was elected to the French Assembly, where he spearheaded the law to abolish forced labour throughout the empire. The present borders were set in 1947, when the north reverted to the country of Upper Volta.

In 1946 Houphouët-Boigny helped found the African Democratic Rally (RDA), a western Africa–based umbrella organization that sought equality for Africans; the Ivoirian branch was the Democratic Party of Côte d'Ivoire (PDCI). Though at first harshly repressed, the RDA achieved many of its goals, including independence in 1960. Houphouët-Boigny, who had been a cabinet minister in two French governments, was elected president of the newly independent Côte d'Ivoire.

# CÔTE D'IVOIRE SINCE INDEPENDENCE

Houphouët-Boigny led Côte d'Ivoire during the country's first three decades of independence and established the country as one of the most prosperous in sub-Saharan Africa. He ruled until his death, in 1993 during his seventh term in office.

## HOUPHOUËT-BOIGNY'S RULE

From the start Houphouët-Boigny pursued liberal free-enterprise policies and developed Côte d'Ivoire's cash-crop agriculture at a time when many other African nations were pursuing costly and abortive attempts at state-run industrialization. Under his leadership the country became a major exporter of cocoa, coffee, pineapples, and palm oil. Houphouët-Boigny welcomed foreign investment and cooperated closely with France in economic matters, even going so far as to employ thousands of French technical and managerial personnel to ensure his country's development. By the early 1980s Côte d'Ivoire had one of the highest per capita incomes of any sub-Saharan African nation without petroleum exports.

Despite reported coup attempts in 1963 and 1973, Houphouët-Boigny had a remarkable ability to reconcile opponents, which sustained the country's peaceful and prosperous relations with France and with its neighbours throughout most of his rule. However, political unrest and strained foreign relations were increasingly evident

# FÉLIX HOUPHOUËT-BOIGNY

(b. Oct. 18, 1905?, Yamoussoukro, Côte d'Ivoire, French West Africa—d. Dec. 7, 1993, Yamoussoukro, Côte d'Ivoire)

*Félix Houphouët-Boigny was a politician and physician who was the first president of Côte d'Ivoire. He served in that role from independence in 1960 until his death in 1993. Under his rule it became one of the most prosperous nations in sub-Saharan Africa.*

*The son of a wealthy Baule chief, Houphouët-Boigny worked as a rural doctor and pursued a second career as a wealthy planter. He began his political career as a cofounder of the African Agricultural Syndicate, formed by disgruntled African planters (1944) to protect their interests against European settlers. In the first Côte d'Ivoire elections (1945) he was elected a deputy to the French National Assembly and was easily reelected in 1946. That year he also founded the Democratic Party of Côte d'Ivoire (PDCI); this party was affiliated with the French Communist Party and was an important component of the interterritorial French West African Federation party, the African Democratic Rally, of which he was also president.*

*In the late 1940s the French administration became increasingly hostile to the PDCI, especially after the Communist Party went into opposition in France, and in October 1950 Houphouët-Boigny decided to break his party's ties with the Communists and to cooperate with the French, all the time building up his party's strength and organization through successive elections. In the period from 1956 to 1960 he divided his time between France, where he was a member of the National Assembly and a cabinet minister, and Côte d'Ivoire, where he was president of the territorial assembly and mayor of Abidjan as well as overall party leader. Meanwhile, he strongly rejected the idea of a West African federation of independent states because he was unwilling to have the wealthy Côte d'Ivoire subsidizing its poorer neighbours. When Pres. Charles de Gaulle in 1958 offered French territories a referendum on whether to join a new federal community or to become independent, Houphouët-Boigny campaigned successfully for self-government within the French Community.*

*Houphouët-Boigny became prime minister of the Côte d'Ivoire government in 1959 and was elected the first president of the independent country in 1960. He was reelected to the presidency unopposed in 1965, 1970, 1975, 1980, and 1985. A skillful and pragmatic politician, he won over opponents to his one-party rule through cooperation, consensus, and compromise. In 1990 Houphouët-Boigny was reelected in Côte d'Ivoire's first contested presidential elections.*

from the late 1980s. Côte d'Ivoire's first multiparty elections were held in 1990, and Houphouët-Boigny managed to defeat challenger Laurent Gbagbo of the Ivorian Popular Front (FPI) in a presidential election that was unsuccessfully appealed to the Supreme Court. Upon his death in 1993, Houphouët-Boigny was succeeded by the president of the National Assembly, Henri Konan Bédié, who was, like his predecessor, a member of the Baule ethnic group and the PDCI.

## POLITICAL UNREST

The PDCI and Bédié were victorious again in the 1995 elections that were boycotted by most of the opposition. Long-standing ethnic and religious tensions continued to exist, exemplified by the government's attempt to rewrite the constitution to prevent certain challengers from running for president. With tensions escalating, soldiers mutinied on Dec. 23, 1999, and Brig. Gen. Robert Guei, a former member of Houphouët-Boigny's government, took control of the country the next day. Although he pledged that he would allow legislative and presidential elections by October 2000 and that he would not be a candidate, he changed his mind and ran for president. After a controversial election in which Guei tried to manipulate the outcome, Gbagbo of the FPI was eventually installed as president.

## CIVIL WAR AND ITS AFTERMATH

Gbagbo's rule was not without discord, culminating in a failed coup on Sept. 19, 2002. Guei, who the government claimed was behind the coup, was killed during the fighting. The failed coup fueled unrest and ignited civil war, leaving the country divided into the rebel-held north and the government-controlled south. Peacekeeping troops from France, the Economic Community of West African States (ECOWAS), and later the United Nations (UN) created a buffer zone between the rebels and the Ivoirian government troops.

Although the government and rebel forces reached a peace agreement in January 2003, months of stalemate followed, and the cultural and nationalistic issues that had ignited the civil war—including land ownership, the basis for nationality, and qualifications for holding office—were never completely settled. Despite an initiative by UN and African leaders to restart the implementation of the peace agreement, simmering tensions exploded in November 2004 when the government violated the cease-fire agreement by bombing rebel-held areas in the north. The already volatile situation worsened when French peacekeeping troops were accidentally killed in one of the Ivoirian bombing raids, prompting retaliatory bombing by France that in turn resulted in anti-French demonstrations and the looting and burning of French businesses, schools, and residences. In response to the escalating situation, the UN Security Council imposed a 13-month arms embargo on Côte d'Ivoire in an attempt to stem the influx of weapons into the region. In April 2005, peace talks held in South Africa led to a new cease-fire agreement between the Ivoirian government and the rebels, with all parties declaring an end to the war. However, the terms of the agreement were not immediately implemented, and fighting resumed. In 2007, talks in Burkina Faso resulted in a power-sharing agreement signed by both sides, and a new transitional government was inaugurated that year.

# CHAPTER 11

# EQUATORIAL GUINEA

Equatorial Guinea is located on the Atlantic Coast in west-central Africa, along the Gulf of Guinea. The former Spanish colony gained independence in 1968. The capital is Malabo.

## EARLY HISTORY

The island of Bioko (formerly Fernando Po) was sighted by the Portuguese explorer Fernão do Pó, probably in 1472. At first it was called Formosa ("Beautiful"). The island of Annobón was probably sighted by Ruy de Sequeira on a New Year's Day (hence the name, which means "good year") between 1472 and 1475, most likely that of 1474.

By the Treaty of Tordesillas (June 7, 1494), the Portuguese had exclusive trade rights in Africa, and it was not until 1778 that they agreed to cede to Spain the islands of Annobón and Fernando Po as well as rights on the mainland coast between the Ogooué and Niger rivers. These cessions were designed to give Spain its own source of slaves in Africa for transport to Spanish America, where, in exchange, the Spanish confirmed the rights of the Portuguese west of the 50° W meridian in what is now Brazil. The Spanish were soon decimated by yellow fever on Fernando Po, and they withdrew in 1781. No European occupation was made on the mainland.

*This black sand beach on the southern coast of Bioko (formerly Fernando Po) shows the island's volcanic origin.* Tim Laman/National Geographic Image Collection/Getty Images

## BRITISH ADMINISTRATION

After the British abolition of the slave trade in 1807, bases were required by the Royal Navy for the effective suppression of the trade. Fernando Po was unoccupied and lay in a strategic situation from which the Niger mouths and the portion of western Africa known as the Slave Coast could be watched for slavers. In 1827 the Spanish leased bases for this purpose to the British at Port Clarence (later Santa Isabel, now Malabo), a fine deepwater harbour on the north coast, and in San Carlos Bay (now Luba Bay) on the west coast.

In the absence of the Spanish, the British also became responsible for administering the island. Thereafter the British resettled many freed slaves there, in default of knowing their origin or of being able to repatriate them. Freed slaves also came to the island from Sierra Leone

## FERNANDO PO

The island of Fernando Po (now known as Bioko) is part of Equatorial Guinea. The island is located in the Bight of Biafra (Gulf of Guinea), lying about 60 miles (100 km) off the coast of southern Nigeria and 100 miles (160 km) northwest of continental Equatorial Guinea.

Volcanic in origin, the island is parallelogram-shaped with a north–south axis, embracing 779 square miles (2,017 square km), and rises sharply from the sea with its highest point being Santa Isabel Peak (9,869 feet [3,008 m]). Equatorial Guinea's capital and chief port, Malabo, stands near a crater breached by the sea.

The island was first sighted by the Portuguese explorer Fernão do Pó, probably in 1472, and was originally named Formosa ("Beautiful"). It was claimed by Spain after 1778, although the first attempt at firm Spanish control came only in 1858. For a short time (1827–34) Britain used the island as an antislavery base.

The original inhabitants, the Bubi, are descendants of Bantu-speaking migrants from the mainland. The so-called Fernandinos are of a later origin, being descendants of liberated slaves, mixed with settlers from former British West Africa. Both these groups have declined in status, as the Fang, who have flocked to the island from continental Equatorial Guinea, came to occupy most of the civil service posts. There was formerly a large transient population of contract plantation workers from Nigeria; most of these returned to Nigeria, however, following repressive acts by the government of Equatorial Guinea in the mid-1970s. The island was named after the first president of the country, Macías Nguema Biyogo, in 1973, but Bioko became the name after he was deposed in 1979.

Bioko was one of the first African territories to grow cocoa. Timber and coffee are other important products. The discovery and development of the country's oil reserves in the 1980s and '90s led to an increase in business and development on the island.

and Jamaica, and in the 20th century the descendants of these several groups continued to speak a form of English. Because of the existence of these freed slaves and the lack of any Spanish administration in the area, the United Kingdom made several unsuccessful offers to Spain for the purchase of Fernando Po, particularly from 1839 to 1841. In 1843 the Royal Navy concentrated its antislavery patrol at Freetown in Sierra Leone, and its buildings on Fernando Po were sold to a Baptist mission.

## SPANISH GUINEA

In 1844 the Spanish made a second effort at effective occupation of Fernando Po, and their first exploration of the mainland was carried out in the two decades ending in 1877. Meanwhile, the Spanish had expelled the British Baptists from Fernando Po in 1858, and in 1879 they began to use it as a penal settlement for Cubans. Following the Spanish-American War (1898), Spanish Guinea remained as Spain's last significant tropical colony. Profiting from the weakness of Spain, France was able to confine mainland Spanish Guinea to its present limited extent. Economic development started only at that time and was concentrated on the richer and healthier Fernando Po. The mainland received significant attention from Spain only after the Spanish Civil War (1936–39).

In 1959 the status of Spanish Guinea was changed, and the region was reorganized into two provinces of overseas Spain, each of which was placed under a civil governor. The citizens, including the Africans, were granted the same rights as those enjoyed by the citizens of Spain. In 1963 a measure of economic and administrative autonomy for the two provinces—which were henceforth known as Equatorial Guinea—was agreed on by plebiscite.

## INDEPENDENCE

The movement toward independence began to take shape at the end of 1967. Early the following year the Spanish government suspended autonomous political control and, with the subsequent approval of the Organization of African Unity (OAU), proposed that a national referendum be held to approve the new constitution. The constitution was overwhelmingly approved on August 11 and was followed by parliamentary elections in September and by the proclamation of independence on Oct. 12, 1968.

The first president was Francisco Macías Nguema (also known as Macías Nguema Biyogo Masie). After his election in 1971, he assumed wide powers and pushed through a constitution that named him president for life in July 1972. He assumed absolute personal powers in 1973, and the island of Fernando Po was renamed Macias Nguema Biyogo Island in his honour. He controlled the radio and press, and foreign travel was stopped. In 1975–77 there were many arrests and summary executions, which brought protests from world leaders and the human rights organization Amnesty International. During this period there was a mass exodus by citizens of Equatorial Guinea, and the Nigerian government repatriated its nationals, who had been working as migrant labourers on Equatorial Guinea's plantations, by 1976.

Macías was overthrown in 1979 by his nephew, Lieut. Col. Teodoro Obiang Nguema Mbasogo, and executed. Obiang led a Supreme Military Council, to which he added some civilians in 1981. A less authoritarian constitution was instituted in 1982, followed by the election of 41 unopposed candidates to the legislature in 1983. Although another new constitution in 1991 provided for a multiparty state—leading to the first multiparty elections, held in 1993—there was no indication that Obiang would willingly give up power, and his regime was the subject of much international criticism for its oppressive nature. In the 1990s and early 2000s, the president and the members of his party repeatedly won reelection by lopsided margins in ballots that were fraught with charges of fraud, most recently in November 2009. Further, accusations abounded that a clique surrounding the president had systematically pocketed the bulk of the country's considerable oil revenue, which grew dramatically beginning in the late 20th century. As it had done since the 1980s, Obiang's regime continued to claim that it was the subject of several attempted coups, but most of the allegations could not be confirmed. A notable exception was a plot to replace Obiang with exiled opposition leader Severo Moto; uncovered in 2004, the plan involved foreign mercenaries. In July 2008 a Malabo court sentenced a British mercenary, Simon Mann, to 34 years in prison for his role in the affair, but Obiang pardoned him in November 2009.

# CHAPTER 12

## THE GAMBIA

The Gambia is located in western Africa, on the Atlantic coast. The former British colony gained independence in 1965. The capital is Banjul.

### EARLY HISTORY

Gambian history before the arrival of Europeans has been preserved to some degree in oral traditions. Its history is closely tied to that of neighbouring Senegal, since it was only in the late 19th century that a distinction was made between Senegal and The Gambia; until that time the region is often referred to as Senegambia.

The Malinke and Wolof kingdoms, fully established by the 19th century, were still in the formative stages when the Venetian explorer Alvise Ca' da Mosto (Cadamosto)—in the service of Portugal's Prince Henry the Navigator—arrived in 1455. The Malinke were the westernmost peoples of the old Mali empire. The Wolof probably migrated from the Songhai regions, and the Fulani pastoralists were part of a migration from the Futa Toro. Although locally powerful, none of the small Gambian kingdoms were ever strong enough to dominate Senegambia. Continuing internecine warfare made it easy for the French and British to dominate the territory.

## EUROPEAN COLONIZATION

The first Europeans in the Gambia River regions, the Portuguese, established trading stations in the late 1400s but abandoned them within a century. Trade possibilities in the next two centuries drew English, French, Dutch, Swedish, and Courlander trading companies to western Africa.

A struggle ensued throughout the 18th century for prestige in Senegambia between France and England, although trade was minimal, and no chartered company made a profit. This changed in 1816 when Capt. Alexander Grant was sent to the region to reestablish a base from which the British navy could control the slave trade. He purchased Banjul Island (St. Mary's) from the king of Kombo, built barracks, laid out a town, and set up an artillery battery to control access to the river. The town, Bathurst (now Banjul), grew rapidly with the arrival of traders and workers from Gorée and upriver. The Gambia was administered as a part of British West Africa from 1821 to 1843. It was a separate colony with its own governor until 1866, when control was returned to the governor-general at Freetown, Sierra Leone, as it would remain until 1889.

British domination of the riverine areas seemed assured after 1857, but the increasing importance of peanut cultivation in Senegal prompted a new imperialism. By 1880 France controlled Senegal; in the 1870s the British attempted twice to trade The Gambia to France, but opposition at home and in The Gambia foiled these plans. Complicating matters was the series of religious conflicts, called the Soninke-Marabout Wars, lasting a half century. Only one Muslim leader, Maba, emerged who could have unified the various kingdoms, but he was killed in 1864. By 1880 the religious aspect had all but disappeared, and the conflicts were carried on by war chiefs such as Musa Mollah, Fodi Silla, and Fodi Kabba.

## BRITISH PROTECTORATE

As a result of a conference in Paris in 1889, France ceded control of the Gambia River to Britain, and the present-day boundaries of The Gambia were drawn. In 1900 Britain imposed indirect rule on the interior, or protectorate (established in 1894), dividing it into 35 chiefdoms, each with its own chief. The real power was concentrated in the British governor and his staff at Bathurst.

Except for some trouble with slave-raiding chiefs, The Gambia enjoyed peace after its separation from Sierra Leone. Slavery was abolished throughout the protectorate in 1906. During World War II The Gambia contributed soldiers for the Burmese campaign and was used as an air-staging post.

## INDEPENDENCE

Political parties were late in developing, but by 1960 there were several demanding independence. Britain, believing that eventually The Gambia would merge with Senegal, gave the territory revised constitutions in 1954, 1960, and 1962 and finally granted it independence within the Commonwealth in February 1965. The Gambia became a republic on April 24, 1970. The first president, Sir Dawda Jawara, head of the People's Progressive Party (PPP), was returned in all elections after 1972. In 1981 an attempt to overthrow the government was put down with the aid of Senegalese troops after heavy fighting in Banjul. In the aftermath, leaders of both countries created the confederation of Senegambia. This plan called for each state to retain independence of action in most areas, but military and economic resources were to be integrated. A Senegambian executive and legislature were also established, but the confederation was dissolved in 1989.

The Gambia faced serious economic problems during the early 1980s. Foreign donors began to refuse aid requests, and food and fuel shortages, common in the rural areas, started affecting Banjul. In 1985 the government initiated a series of austerity measures and reforms that moved the government toward a more disciplined fiscal and monetary policy. The reform program improved The Gambia's overall economic outlook, and foreign assistance once again returned. For the vast majority of peasant farmers, however, there was virtually no change in their harsh economic plight, with bad harvests and falling peanut prices continuing throughout the 1980s. Yet Jawara and the PPP easily won reelection in 1987 and 1992, although opposition parties gained some support in each election.

## POLITICAL CHANGE

In July 1994 a group of young army officers, led by Capt. (later Col.) Yahya Jammeh, staged a bloodless coup, justifying it by citing the corruption and mismanagement of Jawara and the PPP. The Senegalese government did not intervene as it had done in 1981, and Jawara went into exile. The military leaders promised a return to civilian rule once corruption had been eliminated but meanwhile ruled by proclamation. Dissent was brutally repressed, and political activity was banned until August 1996. Presidential elections were held late that year, with elections for the National Assembly following in early 1997. Jammeh, now retired from the military, was elected president, and his political party, the Alliance for Patriotic Reorientation and Construction, dominated the National Assembly. A new constitution, approved by voters in 1996, came into effect after the legislative elections.

The return to civilian rule improved The Gambia's international reputation; aid organizations that had left after the coup began assisting the country once again. The Gambia sent peacekeeping forces into war-ravaged Liberia and worked on improving relations

*Yahya Jammeh was first elected Gambian president in 1997.* Seyllou/AFP/Getty Images

with Senegal, though areas along the border on the upper river remain in dispute. Eventually, though, signs of domestic discord appeared. Jammeh's rule became increasingly authoritative, and by 1998 the corruption he had pledged to eliminate was evident in his own administration. Media freedom was restricted, and an increasing number of human rights abuses were cited by international observers. Jammeh's administration was the subject of coup attempts in 2000 and 2006, which, although unsuccessful, seemed to underline growing discontent in the country. Still, Jammeh was reelected in 2001 and 2006 in elections generally deemed free and fair.

# CHAPTER 13

# GHANA

Ghana is located on the Atlantic coast in western Africa, along the Gulf of Guinea. The former British colony gained independence in 1957. The capital is Accra.

## EARLY HISTORY

The modern state of Ghana is named for the African empire that flourished until the 13th century and was situated close to the Sahara in the western Sudan. The centre of the empire of Ghana lay about 500 miles (800 km) to the northwest of the nearest part of the modern state, and it is reasonably certain that no part of the latter lay within its borders. The claim that an appreciable proportion of modern Ghana's people derived from emigrants from the empire cannot be substantiated with the evidence available at present. Written sources relate only to Muslim contacts with the empire of Ghana from about the 8th to the 13th century or to the period since European contact with the Gold Coast—i.e., modern Ghana—which began in the 15th century. Many modern Ghanaian peoples possess well-preserved oral traditions, but, even though some of these may reach as far back as the 14th century, this is after the final disappearance of the empire of Ghana and such very early traditions often present considerable problems of interpretation. Little progress has so far been made in linking the surviving traditions with the available archaeological evidence.

## TRADE ROUTES OF ISLAM

More archaeological research, especially into the Iron Age, will undoubtedly do much toward resolving present uncertainties about the early history of modern Ghana, but, for the moment, little more can be said than that the traditions of many of the states into which the country was divided before it came under British rule refer to their people having immigrated within the last 600 years either from the north or northwest or from the east or northeast. Such traditions link up with other evidence to suggest that the area which is now Ghana was for many centuries a meeting place for two great streams of western African history. Ultimately, these streams stemmed from the existence of two major trans-Saharan routes, a western one linking the headwaters of the Niger and Sénégal rivers to Morocco and a more central one linking the region between the Niger Bend and Lake Chad with Tunisia and Tripoli. At the end of the western route arose the great Mande states, notably the empires of Ghana and Mali, while around the more easterly termini developed Songhai, the Hausa states, and Bornu. There is evidence that parts of modern Ghana north of the forest were being reached by Mande traders (seeking gold dust) by the 14th century and by Hausa merchants (desiring kola nuts) by the 16th century. In this way the inhabitants of what is now Ghana were influenced by the new wealth and cross-fertilization of ideas that arose in the great empires of the western Sudan following the development of Islamic civilization in northern Africa.

## MIGRATIONS

It is against this background that the traditions of origin of the Ghanaian states must be viewed. It would seem that the first states of the Akan-speaking peoples who now inhabit most of the forest and coastlands were founded about the 13th century by the settlement, just north of the forest, of migrants coming from the direction of Mande; that the dominant states of northern Ghana, Dagomba, Mamprusi, and their satellites were established by the 15th century by invaders from the Hausa region; that a little later the founders of the Ga and Ewe states of the southeast began to arrive from what is now Nigeria by a more southerly route; and that Gonja, in the centre, was created by Mande conquerors about the beginning of the 17th century.

Tradition tends to present these migrations as movements of whole peoples. In certain instances—for example, Dagomba, Mamprusi, and Gonja—it can be shown that the traditions relate in fact to comparatively small bands of invaders who used military and political techniques acquired farther north to impose their rule on already established populations whose own organization was based more on community of kin than on allegiance to political sovereigns. It is probable that the first Akan states—e.g., such influential states as Bono and Banda north of the forest or the smaller states founded on the coast by migration down the Volta

River—were also established in this way. The later Akan infiltration into the forest, which then was probably sparsely inhabited, and the Ga and Ewe settlement of the southeast may have been more of mass movements, though in the latter case it is known that the immigrants met and absorbed earlier inhabitants.

## CONTACT WITH EUROPE AND ITS EFFECTS

A revolution in Ghanaian history was initiated by the establishment of direct sea trade with Europe following the arrival on the coast of Portuguese mariners in 1471. Initially Europe's main interest in the country was as a source of gold, a commodity that was readily available at the coast in exchange for such European exports as cloth, hardware, beads, metals, spirits, arms, and ammunition. This gave rise to the name Gold Coast, by which the country was known until 1957. In an attempt to preserve a monopoly of the trade, the Portuguese initiated the practice of erecting stone fortresses (Elmina Castle, dating from 1482, was the first) on

*The British fort at Cape Coast, located only a few miles from Elmina Castle, was one of many rival forts that threatened Dutch supremacy along the Gold Coast.* Chris Caldicott/Axiom Photographic Agency/Getty Images

the coast on sites leased from the native states. In the 17th century the Portuguese monopoly, already considerably eroded, gave way completely when traders from the Netherlands, England, Denmark, Sweden, and Prussia—Protestant sea powers antagonistic to Iberian imperial pretensions—discovered that the commercial relations developed with the Gold Coast states could be adapted to the export of slaves, then in rapidly increasing demand for the American plantations, as well as to gold trading. By the mid-18th century the coastal scene was dominated by the presence of about 40 forts controlled by Dutch, British, or Danish merchants.

The presence of these permanent European bases on the coast had far-reaching consequences. The new centres of trade thus established were much more accessible than were the Sudanese emporia, and this, coupled with the greater capacity and efficiency of the sea-borne trade compared with the ancient overland routes, gradually brought about the reversal of the direction of the trade flow. The new wealth, tools and arms, and techniques and ideas introduced through close contact with Europeans initiated political and social as well as economic changes. The states north of the forest, hitherto the wealthiest and most powerful, declined in the face of new combinations farther south. At the end of the 17th century, the Akan state of Akwamu created an empire that, stretching from the central Gold Coast eastward to Dahomey, sought to control the trade roads to the coast of the whole eastern Gold Coast. The Akwamu empire was short-lived, but its example soon stimulated a union of the Asante (Ashanti) states of the central forest, under the leadership of the founding *Asantehene* (king) Osei Tutu. The Asante union, after establishing its dominance over other neighbouring Akan states, expanded north of the forest to conquer Bono, Banda, Gonja, and Dagomba.

Having thus engrossed almost the whole of the area that served as a market and source of supply for the coastal trade, the Asante turned toward the coastlands. There traditional ways of life were being increasingly modified by contact with Europeans and their trade, and when, beginning in the latter part of the 18th century, Asante armies began to invade the coastal states, their peoples tended to look for leadership and protection to the European traders in the forts. But between 1803 and 1814 the Danes, English, and Dutch had each in turn outlawed their slave trades, and the gold trade was declining. The political uncertainty following the Asante invasions led by *Asantehene* Osei Bonsu impeded the development of new trades meant to replace the slave trade. In these circumstances the mutually suspicious European interests were reluctant to embark on new political responsibilities. However, during 1830–44, under the outstanding leadership of George Maclean, the British merchants began to assume an informal protectorate over the Fante states, much to the commercial benefit of both parties. As a result, the British

Colonial Office finally agreed to take over the British forts, and in 1850 it was able to buy out the Danes. However, trade declined under the new regime, which was averse to assuming formal control over the territory influenced from the forts, and in the 1860s, as a result of this British reticence and of the growth, from the 1820s onward, of Christian missionary education, the Fante states attempted to organize a European-style confederacy independent of British and Asante control. The Mankesim constitution (1871), written by Fante leaders, was immediately rejected by the British, who, finally prompted to action, now sought more direct control. Further Asante incursions into Fante and the final evacuation of the coast by the Dutch (1872) combined to impel a British military expedition into Asante in 1874, though it was unable to carry out a complete conquest and merely sacked the capital, Kumasi. The Gold Coast was declared a British colony in that same year, with the Asante still outside the colonial borders.

## COLONIAL PERIOD

French and German activity in adjacent territories and the demand for better protection of British mining and commercial interests led to a further active period of British policy from 1896–1901, during which Asante was conquered and its northern hinterland formed into a British protectorate. The 56 years of British rule that followed did not immediately weld into one state the three elements of the territory—the colonies of the Gold Coast and Asante and the protectorate of the Northern Territories—to which after World War I was added a fourth, under mandate from the League of Nations, the western part of former German Togoland. But this was hardly the result of deliberate policy. The ever-increasing assimilation of European ways by the people on the Gold Coast had already made possible there the introduction of such organs of government as a legislative council (1850) and a supreme court (1853), but for many years Asante and the Northern Territories remained the sole responsibility of the governor, whose officials were from the 1920s onward encouraged to work with and through the authorities of the indigenous states. Attempts to introduce similar elements of indirect rule in the Gold Coast served mainly to stimulate a nationalist opposition among the educated professional classes, especially in the growing towns, which aimed at converting the legislative council into a fully responsible parliament.

What really brought the country together was the great development of its economy following the rapid expansion of cocoa growing by farmers in the forest. The cacao tree and its seeds—cocoa beans—were introduced in the 1870s. By the 1920s the Gold Coast, while continuing to export some gold, was producing more than half of the world's supply of cocoa; timber and manganese later became additional exports of note. With the wealth created by this great increase of trade, it was possible to provide modern transport

*Ghanian workers processing cocoa pods. By the early 20th century, cocoa farming had spurred the expansion of Ghana's economy and produced one its primary exports.* Simon Rawles/The Image Bank/Getty Images

facilities—harbours, railways, roads—and social services, especially education (to the university level), all of which tended toward the conversion of the traditional social order, of groups bound together by kinship, into one in which individuals were linked principally by economic ties.

## INDEPENDENCE

Political advancement tended to lag behind economic and social development, especially in the south (for the role of the Northern Territories was principally the supply of cheap labour for the Gold Coast and Asante). World War II, to which the Gold Coast contributed many men and materials, accentuated this lag, and in 1948 there were riots of workers and veterans in the larger towns. The Watson Commission of Inquiry reported that the Burns constitution of 1946, which had granted Africans a majority in the legislative council, was "outmoded at birth." An all-African committee under Justice (later Sir James Henley)

## KWAME NKRUMAH

(b. Sept. 1909, Nkroful, Gold Coast [now Ghana]—d. April 27, 1972, Bucharest, Rom.)

*Kwame Nkrumah was a Ghanaian nationalist leader as well as a Pan-Africanist leader. He led Ghana from its creation in 1957 until he was overthrown by a coup in 1966.*

*Baptized a Roman Catholic, Nkrumah attended Roman Catholic elementary school. After graduation from Achimota College in 1930, he started his career as a teacher. Increasingly drawn to politics, Nkrumah decided to pursue further studies in the United States. He entered Lincoln University in Pennsylvania in 1935 and, after graduating in 1939, obtained master's degrees from Lincoln and from the University of Pennsylvania. He studied the literature of socialism, notably Karl Marx and Vladimir I. Lenin, and of nationalism, especially Marcus Garvey, the black American leader of the 1920s. He also immersed himself in political work, reorganizing and becoming president of the African Students' Organization of the United States and Canada. He left the United States in May 1945 and went to England, where he organized the 5th Pan-African Congress in Manchester.*

*Nkrumah returned home in late 1947 after being invited to serve as the general secretary of the United Gold Coast Convention (UGCC), a group that was formed to work for self-government by constitutional means in the British colony. He spoke throughout the Gold Coast and began to create a mass base for the new movement. When extensive riots occurred in February 1948, the British briefly arrested Nkrumah and other leaders of the UGCC.*

*When a split developed between the middle-class leaders of the UGCC and the more radical supporters of Nkrumah, he formed in June 1949 the new Convention Peoples' Party (CPP), a mass-based party that was committed to a program of immediate self-government. In January 1950, Nkrumah initiated a campaign of "positive action," involving nonviolent protests, strikes, and noncooperation with the British colonial authorities. In the ensuing crisis, services throughout the country were disrupted, and Nkrumah was again arrested and sentenced to one year's imprisonment. The Gold Coast's first general election (Feb. 8, 1951), however, demonstrated the support the CPP had already won. Elected to Parliament, Nkrumah was released from prison to serve in the government and, in 1952, became prime minister of the Gold Coast.*

*When the Gold Coast and the British Togoland trust territory became an independent state within the British Commonwealth—as Ghana—in March 1957, Nkrumah became the new country's first prime minister. It soon became apparent that Nkrumah's style of government was to be authoritarian. His popularity in the country rose, however, as new roads, schools, and health facilities were built and as the policy of Africanization created better career opportunities for Ghanaians.*

*In 1960 Ghana became a republic and Nkrumah became its president, with wide legislative and executive powers under a new constitution. Nkrumah then concentrated his attention on campaigning for the political unity of black Africa, and he began to lose touch with realities in Ghana. His administration became involved in magnificent but often ruinous development projects, so that a once-prosperous country became crippled with foreign debt.*

*The attempted assassination of Nkrumah at Kulugungu in August 1962—the first of several—led to his increasing seclusion from public life and to the growth of a personality cult, as well as to a massive buildup of the country's internal security forces. Early in 1964 Ghana was officially designated a one-party state, with Nkrumah as life president of both country and party. While the administration of the country passed increasingly into the hands of self-serving and corrupt party officials, Nkrumah busied himself with the ideological education of a new generation of black African political activists. Meanwhile, the economic crisis in Ghana worsened. On Feb. 24, 1966, while Nkrumah was visiting Beijing, the army and police in Ghana seized power. Returning to western Africa, Nkrumah found asylum in Guinea. He later died of cancer in Bucharest.*

Coussey was appointed to work out a new constitution in which some executive power would be transferred to African ministers responsible to an African assembly. Meanwhile, a radical politician, Kwame Nkrumah, had established the Convention People's Party (CPP), which, with wide popular support, campaigned with strikes and other actions under the slogan "Self-government now." In 1951 the CPP won almost all the elective seats in the post-Coussey legislative assembly, whereupon Gov. Sir Charles Arden-Clarke invited Nkrumah to lead the new administration. A partnership developed between the two so that power was rapidly transferred to an all-African cabinet responsible to a popularly elected national assembly.

In 1956 the trust territory of British Togoland chose by United Nations plebiscite to integrate with the Gold Coast. Having secured some 70 percent of the assembly seats in general elections in 1954 and 1956, Nkrumah and the CPP government were able in 1957 to obtain the recognition of their country, renamed Ghana, as an independent self-governing member of the Commonwealth and a member of the United Nations.

Nkrumah saw independent Ghana as a spearhead for the liberation of the rest of Africa from colonial rule and the establishment of a socialist African unity under his leadership. Ghana became a republic in 1960, and later became identified with a single political party (the CPP), with Nkrumah, as life president of both, taking ever more power for himself. On the Pan-African front Nkrumah's messianism was increasingly challenged by other leaders of an ever-growing number of independent states. By 1966 his dream of African socialism was foundering under haphazard and corrupt administration, massive foreign debts, and declining living standards. In February, while Nkrumah was in Beijing, army and police leaders rose against him, and his regime was replaced by a National Liberation Council chaired by Lieut. Gen. Joseph A. Ankrah. The machinery of government was overhauled and conservative financial policies introduced. But Ankrah failed to redeem a promise to restore parliamentary democracy, and in 1969 he gave way to the dynamic young brigadier Akwasi Amankwaa Afrifa, a principal leader of the coup. A constituent assembly produced a constitution for a second republic, and a general election was held in August 1969. This resulted in a substantial victory for the Progress Party, led by Kofi Busia, a university professor who had consistently opposed Nkrumah. Busia became prime minister, and a year later a former chief justice, Edward Akufo-Addo, was chosen president.

But the civilian regime, handicapped by the great burden of foreign debt it had inherited and the low prices then obtained by cocoa on the world market, was slow to produce the results expected of it. In January 1972 impatient army officers intervened again, and the government was taken over by a National Redemption Council (NRC) of military men chaired by Col. Ignatius Kutu Acheampong. The national assembly was dissolved, public meetings prohibited, political parties proscribed, and leading politicians imprisoned. In July 1972 a retroactive Subversion Decree was enacted under which military courts were empowered to impose the death penalty for offenses such as subversive political activity, robbery, theft, and damaging public property, and, from 1973, for the spreading of rumours and profiteering. The military regime was clearly failing to maintain good order or anything approaching a prosperous or stable economy. Ghana's gross domestic product, export earnings, and living standards began a precipitous decline.

In 1975 the NRC was reorganized to include some civilians, but ultimate power was given to a Supreme Military Council (SMC). In 1977 the SMC proposed a "Union Government to which everybody will belong," with no political parties and the military sharing in government with civilians. But a national referendum held to approve this served mainly to show the unpopularity of the SMC. Acheampong was replaced as SMC chairman by Lieut. Gen. Frederick W.K. Akuffo, who was less effective in governing than his predecessor. Eventually, in 1979, as the economy floundered, the government of the generals was overthrown by young officers and noncommissioned officers, led by an air force flight lieutenant, Jerry Rawlings. Acheampong and Akuffo were executed, and a quick return to parliamentary government was organized. But under Pres. Hilla Limann this failed to produce the radical improvements in the political and economic life of Ghana sought by Rawlings and his colleagues. At the end of 1981, Rawlings decided that he and those who thought like him must take the lead in all walks of life, and he again overthrew the government. His second military coup established a Provisional National Defense Council as the supreme national government; at local levels, people's defense committees were to take the campaign for national renewal down to the grass roots.

Initially, older Ghanaians doubted that Rawlings and his colleagues could provide more effective and less self-interested government than the old politicians or generals, while other young soldiers thought that they could themselves engineer coups to secure the fruits of power. But Rawlings easily snuffed out two countercoups in 1982 and 1983, and it was apparent that there was wide and genuine approval of his purpose of reforming Ghana's political and economic life. This continued even when he decided that there was no alternative but to follow conservative economic policies—such as dropping subsidies and price controls in order to reduce inflation, privatizing many state-owned companies, and devaluing currency in order to stimulate exports—that would secure International Monetary Fund support and other foreign aid. These free-market measures revived Ghana's economy, which by the early 1990s had one of the highest growth rates in Africa.

In 1992, in the first presidential balloting held in Ghana since 1979, Rawlings—representing a new party, the National Democratic Congress (NDC)—was elected president. He was reelected to a second term in 1996 with almost three-fifths of the votes. Despite the economic progress that had been made during Rawlings's rule, much of the Ghana press and many Ghanaian professionals remained highly critical of his economic policies and authoritarian political style. Rawlings stepped down from the presidency in early 2001, succeeded by John Agyekum Kufuor of the New Patriotic Party (NPP), in the first peaceful transfer of power between democratically elected governments since Ghanaian independence in 1957; Kufuor was reelected in 2004. In the December 2008 presidential elections the NPP's candidate, Nana Addo Dankwa Akufo-Addo, won the first round of voting but did not secure a majority of the vote. In the runoff election John Evans Atta Mills of the NDC narrowly defeated Akufo-Addo.

# CHAPTER 14

# GUINEA

G uinea is located in western Africa, on the Atlantic coast. The former French colony gained independence in 1958. The capital is Conakry.

## EARLY HISTORY

Hunting and gathering populations occupied the area of what is now Guinea about 30,000 years ago, and farming has been practiced there for about 3,000 years. About 900 CE the Susu and Malinke (Maninka) began to encroach on the Baga, Koniagi (Coniagui), and Nalu (Nalou) populations who had been living in the area. The towns and villages of Upper Guinea were incorporated into the Mali empire from the mid-13th century, and by the 16th century the Fulani (Fulbe) had established domination over the Fouta Djallon, the mountainous region of what is now west-central Guinea.

The Portuguese presence on the coast dates from the 15th century, when they developed a slave trade that would continue to affect Guinea until the mid-19th century. British and French trading interests on the coast played minor roles in the historical evolution of the Guinean interior until the *almamy* (ruler) of Fouta Djallon placed his country under French protection in 1881. The independent Malinke state, ruled by Samory Touré, resisted the French military until 1898, and isolated small groups of Africans continued to resist the French until the end of World War I (1914–18).

## COLONIAL ERA

The French protectorate of Rivières du Sud was detached from Senegal as a separate colony in 1890. As French Guinea, it became part of the Federation of French West Africa in 1895. Treaties with Liberia and Great Britain largely established the present boundaries by World War I.

Under the 1946 constitution of the French Fourth Republic, a small number of French-educated Africans in Guinea were allowed to vote for deputies to the French National Assembly. In the 1958 referendum on the constitution for the French Fifth Republic, only Guinea—under the influence of Sékou Touré, who later became the country's first president—voted against membership in the French Community. Guinea thus became independent.

## INDEPENDENCE

Guinea came to occupy a special position among African states for its unqualified rejection of neocolonial control. Touré's rule (1958–84) grew increasingly more repressive, however. Denied French assistance, Guinea contracted loans and economic and trade agreements with the Soviet Union and the People's Republic of China. When it failed to become a full economic partner in the Soviet bloc, Guinea turned to France and other Western countries for capital and technical assistance in the waning years of Touré's regime. Under Touré's uncertain economic leadership,

however, the potentially wealthy country did not prosper.

Throughout Touré's rule, difficulties of economic adjustment and political reorganization caused him to become increasingly obsessed with what he perceived as opposition. Probably the event that had the most negative effect was the Portuguese-backed invasion of Conakry by Guinean dissidents. Such real conspiracies, together with a myriad of imaginary ones, led to show trials, imprisonments, and executions of dissidents and other suspects. Gradually power was concentrated in the hands of Touré and his predominantly Malinke associates. Members of his own family occupied leading government posts, from which illicit earnings were drawn on a large scale. Though the Democratic Party of Guinea, which Touré had led since 1953, retained control, it ceased to enjoy the mass support it had had in the late 1950s and early '60s. Touré's death in 1984 left party leaders with little grassroots support. The ensuing military coup began with fairly strong support from the general public.

The Military Committee for National Recovery (Comité Militaire de Redressement National; CMRN), under Col. Lansana Conté, Guinea's second president (1984–2008), endorsed the concept of a pluralist society. Private ownership and international investment were actively supported, while the role of the state in the economy was reduced. In the late 1980s Guinea sought reintegration into French-speaking western Africa and the Franc Zone (a group of African countries whose currencies were linked to the French franc at a fixed rate of exchange), to which it never achieved entry.

Although a new constitution was adopted in 1991 and the first multiparty elections were held in 1993, the Conté government's move toward political and economic liberalization was slow, and civil unrest and protest continued during the 1990s. In 1996 the government survived an attempted military coup. Meanwhile, Guinea became embroiled in the ongoing civil wars in neighbouring Sierra Leone and Liberia. Guinea and Liberia accused each other of supporting opposition dissidents, and in 2000 Guinean dissidents and Sierra Leone's rebel army, the Revolutionary United Front, led large-scale incursions into Guinea. At least 1,000 Guineans were killed during the incursions, and thousands more were displaced. As the civil wars raged, several hundred thousand refugees from Liberia and Sierra Leone poured into Guinea—adding to the tension between Guinea and its neighbours.

A national referendum in 2001 amended the constitution to allow for unlimited presidential terms and to extend each term from five to seven years. In January 2007 a number of unions, political groups, and civilian societies formed an alliance to contest the high cost of living and government corruption in the country, and they demanded Conté's resignation. During demonstrations led by the alliance, several protesters were killed by Guinean security forces. A state of emergency was declared in February; nevertheless, violent protests, this time led by soldiers who demanded better pay, broke out again in May.

Despite ongoing turbulence (and an assassination attempt against him in 2005), Conté maintained power until his death on Dec. 22, 2008. Soon after the news of his death was made public, a faction of the military launched a coup and announced that it had dissolved the government. The National Council for Democracy and Development (Conseil National pour la Démocratie et le Développement; CNDD), with Capt. Moussa Dadis Camara as president, was created to serve as a transitional government. The CNDD promised to hold elections within one year and vowed to fight rampant corruption. Various African and Western governments denounced the coup, and Guinea was temporarily suspended from several international organizations.

In August 2009 Camara announced that presidential and parliamentary elections would be held in January and March 2010, respectively. Despite earlier promises that he and other members of the junta would not stand in the elections, there were rumours that Camara planned to run for president, which he did not deny. On September 28 tens of thousands of people flocked to an opposition rally protesting Camara's potential candidacy; the military's brutal response to the gathering resulted in the deaths of at least 150 people (although the government claimed only 57 people

*Burkinabé Pres. Blaise Compaoré (left) meets with Guinean Pres. Moussa Dadis Camara in October 2009. The two met as part of Compaoré's sustained effort to mediate the conflict between Guinea's military junta and the opposition.* AFP/Getty Images

died) and injuries to more than a thousand. In the days that followed, Camara banned all further opposition gatherings. He also attempted to distance himself from the actions of the military at the rally and called for the opposition to join him in the formation of a unity government; the opposition rejected his call as being insincere and unrealistic. Two weeks after the rally, opposition groups called for a two-day general strike, which effectively disrupted the country's important bauxite mining industry as well as daily life in Guinean cities, where many businesses were closed and most people stayed in their homes in observance of the strike. On October 15 the International Criminal Court announced it was conducting a preliminary investigation into the military's September 28 actions.

On Dec. 3, 2009, the CNDD announced that Camara had been the target of an assassination attempt led by Lieut. Aboubacar Diakite, a former aide who was widely considered to have been a leading figure in the army's brutal reaction to the September 28 rally. Reportedly grazed in the head by a bullet, Camara was flown to Morocco for surgery the next day; CNDD vice president and defense minister Gen. Sekouba Konate served as interim president in Camara's absence.

Camara left Morocco on Jan. 12, 2010, and flew to Burkina Faso. He met with Burkinabé Pres. Blaise Compaoré, who had been working for several months to mediate an agreement between Guinea's military junta and the opposition. A pact was signed on Jan. 15, 2010, in which Camara agreed to continue his recuperation outside of Guinea, allowing Konate to remain as interim head of the junta. Konate was to work with a new prime minister, selected by the opposition, who would lead a new transitional administration that would hold national elections within six months.

# CHAPTER 15

## GUINEA-BISSAU

Guinea-Bissau is located in western Africa, on the Atlantic coast. The former Portuguese colony gained independence in 1974. The capital is Bissau.

### EARLY HISTORY

The precolonial history of Guinea-Bissau has not been fully documented in the archaeological record. The area has been occupied for at least a millennium, first by hunters and gatherers and later by decentralized animist agriculturalists who used iron implements for their rice farming. Ethnogenesis and interethnic dynamics in the 13th century began to push some of these agriculturists closer to the coast, while others intermixed with the intrusive Mande as the Mali empire expanded into the area. Gold, slaves, and marine salt were exported from Guinea toward the interior of the empire. As Mali strengthened, it maintained local, centralized control through its secondary kingdoms and their *farims* (local kings), whose task was to maintain local law and order and the flow of tributary goods and soldiers as needed. In the case of what is now Guinea-Bissau, this state was known as Kaabu, and the agriculturists often suffered in their subordinate relationship to its economic and military needs. The Fulani entered the region as semi-nomadic herders as early as the 12th century, although it was not until the 15th century that they began to arrive in large numbers. Initially they were also subordinate to the kingdom of Kaabu, although there was something of a symbiotic relationship between the Mande farmers and traders and the Fulani herdsmen, both of whom followed a version of Africanized Islam.

Contacts with the European world began with the Portuguese explorers and traders who arrived in the first half of the 15th century. Notable among these was Nuño Tristão, a Portuguese navigator who set out in the early 1440s in search of slaves and was killed in 1446 or 1447 by coastal inhabitants who were opposed to his intrusion. The Portuguese monopolized the exploration and trade along the Upper Guinea coast from the later 15th and early 16th centuries until the French, Spanish, and English began to compete for the wealth of Africa.

Tens of thousands of Guineans were taken as slaves to the Cape Verde island group to develop its plantation economy of cotton, indigo, *orchil* and *urzella* dyes, rum, hides, and livestock. Weaving and dyeing slave-grown cotton made it

*Slaves taken from Guinea-Bissau were often sent to work on cotton plantations, where they would harvest cotton pods, like the one shown above, to produce textiles useful in trade.* Eco Images/ Universal Images Group/Getty Images

possible to make *panos*, unique textiles woven on a narrow loom and usually constructed of six strips stitched together, which became standard currency for regional trade in the 16th century. *Lançados* (freelance Cape Verdean traders) participated in the trade of goods and slaves and were economic rivals of the Portuguese. At times the *lançados* were so far beyond Portuguese control that severe penalties were imposed to restrict them. Often these measures either dried up the trade to the crown or caused even more brash smuggling.

In Guinea-Bissau and neighbouring territories, slaves were captured among the coastal peoples or among interior groups at war. While Kaabu was ascendant, the Fulani were common victims. In 1867 the kingdom of Kaabu was overthrown by the Fulani, after which the numbers of Mande increased on the slave ships' rosters. Groups of slaves were bound together in coffles and driven to the coastal barracoons (temporary enclosures) at Cacheu, Bissau, and Bolama by *grumetes* (mercenaries). There the prices were negotiated by *tangomãos* (who functioned as both translators and mediators), and slaves were sold to the *lançados* and *senhoras* (slave-trading women of mixed parentage).

The Cape Verde Islands were used as a secure offshore post for the trade of goods from Africa, which included slaves, ivory, dyewoods, kola nuts, beeswax, hides, and gold, as well as goods destined for Africa, such as cheap manufactured items, firearms, cloth, and rum. From the islands of Cape Verde, the Portuguese maintained their coastal presence in Guinea-Bissau. Tens of thousands of slaves were exported from the coast to the islands and on to the New World, destined for major markets such as the plantations in Cuba and northeastern Brazil.

European rivalries on the Guinea coast long threatened the Portuguese position in the islands, where irregular commerce, corruption, and smuggling became routine. In the late 18th and early 19th centuries there was an English initiative to abolish or slow the slave trade, and the United States mounted a halfhearted parallel effort. From 1843 to 1859 the U.S. Navy stationed the Africa Squadron, a fleet of largely ineffective sailing vessels meant to intercept American slavers, in the Cape Verde Islands and along the Guinea coast. However, political indifference, legal loopholes, and flags of convenience undermined this program. After four centuries of slaving, the Portuguese gradually abandoned the practice by the late 1870s, although it was replaced by oppressive forced labour and meagre wages to pay colonial taxes.

## COLONIAL PERIOD

Despite the five centuries of contact between Guineans and the Portuguese, one cannot truly speak of a deeply rooted colonial presence until the close of the 19th century. The long-lasting joint administration of the Cape Verde island group and Guinea-Bissau was terminated in 1879 and both became separate colonial territories: Cape Verde and Portuguese Guinea. However, the European rivalries for control of the larger Guinea region only intensified. Long-term Anglo-Portuguese bickering over the ownership of Bolama was finally resolved when U.S. Pres. Ulysses S. Grant adjudicated the dispute in Portugal's favour in 1870. The Franco-Portuguese conflict over the Casamance region, however, was resolved in France's favour in May 1886.

The struggle for dominance around Guinea-Bissau fell within the context of the greater scramble for Africa that characterized the 1884–85 Berlin Congress, which saw English demands for Guinean territories to the south and French demands along the north and east. The Guinean people were certainly not consulted about such matters, and they resisted, revolted, and mutinied by any available means whenever possible. The Berlin Congress had called for the demonstration of "effective occupation," though, and, in an attempt to satisfy this condition, the brutal "pacification" campaign of Capt. João Teixeira Pinto—with the employed support of an African mercenary force—was conducted from 1913 to 1915. The killings and severe punitive measures exacted by the Portuguese and their mercenaries brought a widespread outcry. Nevertheless, the Portuguese continued their pacification efforts against the Guinean population, especially the coastal peoples, and launched three more major campaigns of pacification,

the latest of which was undertaken in January 1936.

During World War II many Africans gained military and political experience while fighting with and for the colonial powers. In the wake of that war came the emergence of African nationalist movements, and, by the early 1960s, most western African countries had achieved independence through protest, petition, demonstration, and other largely peaceful means. To avoid criticism of its colonial policies in Africa, in 1951 the Portuguese had redefined their colonies' status to that of overseas provinces. The African population of Guinea-Bissau did not perceive these changes as meaningful, however, and some members of the colonial population began agitation for complete independence from Portugal for both Guinea-Bissau and Cape Verde.

## LIBERATION STRUGGLE

In 1956 a group of Cape Verdeans founded the national liberation party for Guinea and Cape Verde—the African Party for the Independence of Guinea and Cape Verde (Partido Africano da Independência da Guiné e Cabo Verde; PAIGC). Most notable of its leaders was Amílcar Cabral, a brilliant revolutionary theoretician. At first the PAIGC's goal was to achieve independence through peaceful means of protest; however, in August 1959 the Portuguese responded to a dockworkers' strike with violence, killing and wounding numerous demonstrators, which convinced the PAIGC that only a rurally based armed struggle would be sufficient to end the colonial and fascist regime. After a period of military training and political preparation, the PAIGC launched its armed campaign in January 1963 and showed steady military progress thereafter. The creation of the People's Revolutionary Armed Force (Forças Armadas Revolucionarias do Povo) and the Local Armed Forces (Forças Armadas Locais) provided for both offensive and defensive military action.

Despite being confronted by large numbers of Portuguese soldiers and their accompanying military technology, the PAIGC gained control of some two-thirds of the country, with the Portuguese colonial army under Gen. António de Spínola surviving only in the major towns and heavily fortified bases. On Jan. 20, 1973, Cabral was assassinated; nevertheless, on Sept. 24, 1973, independence was declared. This event, compounded by the drawn-out wars in Portugal's other overseas provinces, precipitated a crisis that led to a successful coup in Lisbon on April 25, 1974. Portugal's new government soon began negotiating with African nationalist movements.

## INDEPENDENCE

Full independence was achieved by Guinea-Bissau on Sept. 10, 1974; Cape Verde achieved independence the following year. The Cape Verdean revolutionary comrades Luís de Almeida Cabral (half brother of Amílcar Cabral) and Aristides Pereira became the first presidents of Guinea-Bissau and the Republic of Cape Verde, respectively. João ("Nino") Vieira became the commander in chief of the armed forces of Guinea-Bissau.

In August 1978 Vieira assumed the position of prime minister in Guinea-Bissau following the accidental death of his predecessor, Francisco Mendes, in July. On Nov. 14, 1980, Vieira led a military coup against Cabral, who was charged with abuse of power and sentenced to death; after negotiations, Cabral was released from that sentence and went into exile. The coup was deeply resented in Cape Verde and severed the military and political unity that had existed between the two countries. The Cape Verdean branch of the PAIGC was replaced by the African Party for the Independence of Cape Verde (Partido Africano para a Independência de Cabo Verde; PAICV), which eliminated reference to Guinea-Bissau.

With his ascent to power, Vieira faced difficult political and economic problems. Guinea-Bissau's poverty required development aid from Portugal, which was in turn seeking to restore its economic relations with Guinea-Bissau. In addition, the poorly performing state-planned economic policy that had been adopted with independence was increasingly liberalized in subsequent years as attempts were made to improve the economy, but the shift toward a free-market economy was not universally embraced and became a source of political unrest.

Guinea-Bissau made the transition to a democratic, multiparty system in the early 1990s, and the country's first free legislative and presidential elections were held in 1994. The PAIGC won a majority of legislative seats, while Vieira narrowly won his race.

In 1997 Guinea-Bissau joined the West African Economic Monetary Union and the Franc Zone. However, fiscal volatility caused in part by these actions contributed to political unrest that came to a head in 1998 when Vieira dismissed military chief of staff Brig. (later Gen.) Ansumane Mané. Almost immediately Mané initiated a revolt that was fueled by widespread frustration and opposition to Vieira. Most observers first thought that the mutineers would tire and Vieira would reemerge as the victor; instead, the conflict broadened. Various cease-fires were called and broken, and troops from Guinea, Nigeria, Senegal, and France intervened. After each round of fighting, Vieira became increasingly isolated in Bissau. In May 1999 he was forced to surrender and later went into exile in Portugal. Subsequent elections, deemed free and fair by international observers, brought to power the country's first non-PAIGC government, led by Pres. Kumba Ialá.

Despite a democratic beginning, Ialá's rule became increasingly repressive. Widespread discontent with the deteriorating economic and political climate led to his removal in a bloodless coup in September 2003. Soon after, Henrique Rosa, a businessman and virtual political newcomer, was sworn in as interim president. Under

Rosa's transitional government, legislative elections were held in 2004, moving Guinea-Bissau on course toward a stable, constitutional government. While forging political peace, Rosa was faced with the task of rebuilding the country's infrastructure and improving the economy, both severely damaged from the civil war and years of political strife.

In March 2005 Ialá announced his intention to contest the elections scheduled for June of that year, although both he and Vieira—who had returned from exile in April—had been barred from politics in 2003. Both candidates were subsequently cleared to run for office in April. The following month, Ialá announced that he was in fact still president and staged a brief occupation of the presidential building. Defeated in the first round of polling, however, he eventually backed Vieira, who won a second round of elections held in July. Although supporters of the opposition raised allegations of fraud, the elections were declared by international observers to have been free and fair.

Ongoing political strife and economic challenges were compounded by drug smuggling, an increasing problem for Guinea-Bissau and other western African countries in the mid-2000s. With a geography favourable to smuggling and the inability to adequately protect its coastline and airspace, Guinea-Bissau was a particularly desirable target, and individuals in the upper echelons of the government, military, and other sectors were allegedly involved in drug trafficking.

Mounting conflict between the military elite and Vieira's administration—fueled in part by ethnic tensions—generated increasing domestic instability, and in November 2008 Vieira survived an attack by mutinous soldiers that was described as an attempted coup. On March 2, 2009, Vieira was assassinated by soldiers who believed he was responsible for the death of the chief of the armed forces, Gen. Batista Tagme Na Waie, who had been killed in an explosion hours earlier. The military denied any intent to seize power, and, under the terms of the constitution, parliamentary leader Raimundo Pereira was sworn in to serve as interim president until elections could be held; they were eventually scheduled for June 28. On June 5, military authorities killed presidential candidate Baciro Dabo, former defense minister Helder Proenca, former prime minister Faustino Embali, and others, alleging that they were part of a group planning to overthrow the current government. Many senior PAIGC members were also detained as part of the operation to foil the alleged coup.

The tension and uncertainty surrounding the alleged coup and the military's response to it did not interfere with the scheduled presidential election, which proceeded as planned on June 28. None of the 11 candidates were able to obtain a majority of votes, so election officials announced that the two front-runners—the PAIGC's Malam Bacai Sanhá, who once briefly served as interim president, and former president Kumba Ialá—would face each other in a runoff election. In the second round of voting, held on July 26, 2009, Sanhá was victorious, receiving more than three-fifths of the vote.

# CHAPTER 16

# LIBERIA

Liberia is located along the Atlantic coast in western Africa. Liberia is notable in that it is the only black state in Africa that was never subjected to European colonial rule. It was declared an independent republic in 1847, making it the oldest republic in Africa. The capital is Monrovia.

## EARLY HISTORY

Outsiders' knowledge of the west of Africa began with a Portuguese sailor, Pedro de Sintra, who reached the Liberian coast in 1461. Subsequent Portuguese explorers named Grand Cape Mount, Cape Mesurado (Montserrado), and Cape Palmas, all prominent coastal features. The area became known as the Grain Coast because grains of Melegueta pepper, then as valuable as gold, were the principal item of trade.

In the beginning of the 19th century the tide started to rise in favour of the abolition of slavery, and the Grain Coast was suggested as a suitable home for freed American slaves. In 1818 two U.S. government agents and two officers of the American Colonization Society (founded 1816) visited the Grain Coast. After abortive attempts to establish settlements there, an agreement was signed in 1821 between the officers of the society and local African chiefs granting the society possession of Cape Mesurado. The first American freed slaves, led by members of the society, landed in 1822 on Providence

Island at the mouth of the Mesurado River. They were followed shortly by Jehudi Ashmun, a white American, who became the real founder of Liberia. By the time Ashmun left in 1828 the territory had a government, a digest of laws for the settlers, and the beginnings of profitable foreign commerce. Other settlements were started along the St. John River, at Greenville, and at Harper. In 1839 Thomas Buchanan was appointed the first governor. On his death in 1841 he was succeeded by Joseph Jenkins Roberts, the colony's first black governor, who was born free in Virginia in 1809; Roberts enlarged the boundaries of the territory and improved economic conditions.

## THE EARLY REPUBLIC

When the American Colonization Society intimated that Liberia should cease its dependency on it, Roberts proclaimed it an independent republic in 1847. Independence was recognized in 1848–56 by most countries, though formal recognition by the United States did not come until 1862.

*The Liberian cabinet in the 1880s.* Library of Congress, Washington, D.C.

At the time independence was declared, a constitution based on that of the United States was drawn up. Roberts, who had been elected the first president of the republic, retained that office until 1856. During that period the slave trade, theretofore illicitly carried on from various nominally Liberian ports, was ended by the activity of the British and U.S. navies.

In 1871 the first foreign loan was raised, being negotiated in London nominally for £100,000. The loan was unpopular, and still more unpopular was the new president, Edward J. Roye, who was deposed and imprisoned at Monrovia. Roberts was called back to office. He served until 1876.

The early days of Liberia were marked by constant frontier troubles with the French on the Ivory Coast and the British at Sierra Leone. The Liberians tried to extend their authority inland, although they were still unable to control all the coastal area they claimed. Efforts to end the frontier disputes resulted in treaties with Great Britain in 1885 and with France in 1892. In 1904 Pres. Arthur Barclay, who was born in Barbados, initiated a policy of direct cooperation with the groups. Having obtained a loan from London in 1907, he made real efforts at reform. The foreign debt, however, was a burden, and the government was unable to exert effective authority over the interior for more than 20 miles (32 km) inland. In 1919 an agreement was signed transferring to France some 2,000 square miles (5,200 square km) of hinterland that Liberia had claimed but could not control.

## OUTSIDE INTERVENTION

In 1909 a commission appointed by U.S. Pres. Theodore Roosevelt investigated political and economic conditions in Liberia and recommended financial reorganization. A loan of $1.7 million (U.S.), secured by customs revenue, was raised by an international consortium of bankers in 1912, and a receivership of customs was set up, administered by appointees of the British, French, and German governments and a U.S. receiver-general. A frontier police force was organized by officers of the U.S. Army, with the result that Liberian authority was better maintained. However, this promising new regime was upset by World War I. Revenues dropped to one-fourth of their previous level, and the financial situation steadily deteriorated.

The Firestone Tire and Rubber Company obtained a concession of one million acres (400,000 hectares) for a rubber plantation in 1926. At the same time, a loan was arranged through the Finance Corporation of America, a Firestone subsidiary. Using this private loan, the Liberian government consolidated and bonded all its external and internal debts and placed the country's finances on a relatively stable basis. Administration of the customs and internal revenue was placed in the hands of a U.S. financial adviser. In 1952 the government was able to liquidate its foreign debt for the first time since accepting the English loan of 1871.

An investigation by the League of Nations of forced labour and slavery in Liberia, involving the shipment of Africans to the Spanish plantations in Fernando Po, brought about the resignations of Pres. Charles King and Vice Pres. Allen Yancy and the election of Edwin Barclay to the presidency in 1931. Liberia appealed to the Council of the League of Nations for financial aid, and a commission of inquiry was established. The next three years were marked by unsuccessful attempts to work out a plan of assistance involving appointing foreign administrators, declaring a moratorium on the Firestone loan, and suspending diplomatic relations with Great Britain and the United States. After the League Council had finally withdrawn its plan of assistance, the Liberian government reached an agreement with Firestone along lines similar to the league's recommendations.

## WORLD WAR II AND AFTER

The new significance of Liberia became apparent after the outbreak of World War II. During the war Liberia's rubber plantation was the only source of natural latex rubber available to the Allies, apart from plantations in Ceylon (now Sri Lanka). In 1942 Liberia signed a defense agreement with the United States. This resulted in a program of strategic road building and the construction of an international airport and a deepwater harbour at Monrovia. U.S. money was declared legal tender in Liberia in 1943, replacing British West African currency. In 1943 William

V.S. Tubman was elected to his first term as president. Liberia declared war against Germany and Japan in January 1944 and in April signed the Declaration of the United Nations. In December 1960 Liberia became a member of the UN Security Council, and from that time it took an active part in African and international affairs. In 1963 the country became a member of the Organization of African Unity (since 2002 the African Union) at its inception.

In 1963 Tubman was elected to his fifth term as president, and the following year the United States and Liberia signed an agreement to transfer the free port of Monrovia to the government of Liberia. Tubman was again elected president in 1967, the only candidate for the office; he died in London on July 23, 1971, shortly after his election to a seventh term as president. He was immediately succeeded by Vice Pres. William R. Tolbert.

A decline in world prices for Liberia's chief exports, iron ore and natural rubber, brought financial hardship to the country during the 1960s and early '70s. Foreign loans helped sustain the economy during that period.

## DECADES OF STRIFE

In April 1980 Tolbert was killed in a coup led by Master Sgt. (later Gen.) Samuel K. Doe, who became head of state and chairman of the People's Redemption Council (PRC). The PRC promised a new constitution—which became effective in 1986—and a return to civilian rule.

*Charles Taylor, former president of Liberia, sits in a courtroom during his trial for crimes against humanity and war crimes.* AFP/Getty Images

Elections were held in 1985 with several parties participating but were widely criticized as fraudulent. Doe was inaugurated as the first president of the Second Republic in January 1986. His rule ended in 1990 after civil war—primarily between the Krahn and the Gio and Mano peoples—erupted. A multinational West African force, the Economic Community of West African States (ECOWAS) Monitoring Group, attempted to restore order, but the leaders of two rebel groups, Charles Ghankay Taylor and Prince Johnson, contended for power after Doe's

## CHARLES TAYLOR

### (b. Jan. 27, 1948, Liberia)

*Charles Ghankay Taylor is a Liberian politician and guerrilla leader. He served as Liberia's president from 1997 until he was forced into exile in 2003. He was widely held responsible for the country's devastating civil war during the 1990s.*

*Taylor was the son of a judge, a member of the elite in Liberia descended from the freed American slaves who colonized the region in the early 19th century. He attended college in the United States, where in 1977 he received a degree in economics from Bentley College in Waltham, Mass. He then became the director of Liberia's General Services Administration under Pres. Samuel K. Doe, the military leader who had gained power in a bloody coup in 1980. In 1983 Doe accused Taylor of having embezzled nearly $1 million, and the following year Taylor fled to the United States, where he was jailed. Before he could be extradited, he escaped and subsequently appeared in Libya, where he formed the National Patriotic Front of Liberia (NPFL), a militia group that invaded the country in late 1989.*

*Taylor's forces advanced on the capital of Monrovia in 1990, but his bid for power was checked by rival groups. Doe was killed in the fighting, and for the next seven years the armed factions fought a brutal civil war in which more than 150,000 people were killed and more than half of the population became refugees. Although the NPFL never took the capital, it controlled the countryside and its rich natural resources. The fighting also spilled over into neighbouring Sierra Leone, and at one point the Economic Community of West African States attempted to intervene with peacekeeping troops. A 1996 peace pact led to elections on July 19, 1997. Critics accused Taylor of unfair tactics, including giving handouts to the largely impoverished and illiterate electorate, but he won the election with 75 percent of the votes.*

*Taylor's presidency was hindered by his alleged involvement in neighbouring Sierra Leone's civil war as well as Liberia's own descent into civil war. He went into exile in 2003 and a few years later was charged with crimes against humanity and war crimes in a special court that was established jointly by Sierra Leone and the United Nations.*

downfall and execution. The war dragged on for seven years as new factions arose and neighbouring countries became enmeshed in the strife. The toll on the civilian population and the economy was devastating. After a series of abortive attempts, a truce was achieved in 1996. In elections held the following year, the National Patriotic Front of Liberia Party, led by Taylor, achieved a clear majority.

At first, Taylor's government was able to maintain a shaky peace, buoyed by the presence of ECOWAS peacekeeping forces. However, those troops left in early 1999, and by the end of the year rebels were on the attack in northern Liberia. The country's economy, already in shambles, was made worse in 2001 when the UN Security Council imposed sanctions for Liberia's support of rebel forces in

Sierra Leone; Taylor's alleged role in Sierra Leone's civil war also resulted in his June 2003 indictment by a UN-sponsored war crimes tribunal. Meanwhile, the rebel insurgency in Liberia had slowly spread southward, killing thousands and displacing tens of thousands in the fighting. Government troops could not stop the rebel advance, and in August 2003 Taylor fled the country and went into exile in Nigeria. In March 2006 the Liberian government requested Taylor's extradition, and Nigeria announced it would comply with the order. Taylor subsequently attempted to flee Nigeria but was quickly captured. Charged with crimes against humanity and war crimes, he was later sent to The Hague; his trial before the Special Court for Sierra Leone began in June 2007.

## RETURN TO PEACE

After Taylor fled Liberia in 2003, the National Transitional Government (NTG), headed by Liberian businessman Gyude Bryant and supported by United Nations peacekeeping troops, was established and ruled until a new administration was democratically elected and installed. Presidential elections were held in late 2005, and Ellen Johnson Sirleaf defeated former football star George Weah in the second round of polling. She became the first woman to be elected head of state in Africa. Sirleaf focused on rebuilding the country's economy and infrastructure, both of which were devastated from decades of conflict and instability, and worked to promote unity and reconciliation within the country. To that end, a Truth and Reconciliation Commission was established in 2006. Sirleaf also addressed the culture of corruption that had been rampant for some time: she fired the entire staff of the Ministry of Finance and promised to investigate and prosecute anyone responsible for graft. In December 2007 Bryant, the former NTG head, was arrested for failing to appear in court to face corruption charges stemming from his time as leader of the transitional government; he was accused of embezzling more than $1 million, a charge that he vehemently denied. Bryant was found not guilty in 2009. In October 2008 Taylor's son, Charles (Chuckie) Taylor, Jr., was convicted in a U.S court on charges of torture and related war crimes; he was sentenced to 97 years in prison in January 2009.

# CHAPTER 17

# MALI

M ali is a landlocked country in western Africa. The former French colony gained independence in 1960. The capital is Bamako.

## EARLY HISTORY

Rock paintings and inscriptions as well as Paleolithic and Neolithic remains have been found throughout Mali. Neolithic human skeletal remains dating to 5000 BCE were found in 1927 in the Sahara at Asselar.

Rich gold deposits in the west and southwest constituted the principal resource in the economic life of early urban entrepôts and a succession of political states. An important trading centre, Djenné-Jeno, arose about 250 BCE in the inland delta of the Niger River and flourished until the 11th century CE; it then declined and eventually was eclipsed by Djenné, a trading centre founded by Muslim Soninke about the 13th century CE. Terra-cotta statues dating to as early as 800 CE have been found at Djenné-Jeno and other sites in Mali.

The export trade in gold and in slaves, ivory, civet, and gum arabic moved over trans-Saharan caravan routes from the Niger River valley to North Africa for almost a thousand years. This trade was controlled by the Soninke kingdom of Ghana (4th–11th century), which was established between the headwaters of the Niger and Sénégal rivers. Ghana was effectively destroyed by the Almoravid invasion of 1076, and its

*Rock paintings depicting symbols and patterns of ritual signficance, like these found in the Bandiagara escarpment, are evidence of the ancient cultures that once inhabited Mali.* Travel Ink/Gallo Images/Getty Images

hegemony was ultimately assumed by the Mandinka empire of Mali (13th–15th century), founded around the upper Niger. Under Mali the caravan routes moved east through Djenné and Timbuktu (founded about the 11th century CE). Mali's decline in the 15th century enabled the Songhai kingdom in the east to assert its independence. Under Songhai, Djenné and Timbuktu flourished as centres of both trade and Islamic scholarship. In 1591 a Moroccan army of 4,000 men armed with muskets succeeded in crossing the Sahara

and easily defeated the Songhai, who did not have firearms. With the destruction of Songhai hegemony, political chaos ensued, resulting in a disruption of trade.

Eventually new trade routes in gold and slaves were established, but these were directed toward the coast, where Europeans were establishing trading posts. The Moroccans exiled or executed the Timbuktu scholars (because they represented a political threat) and dispersed most of their libraries of books and manuscripts. Moroccan military and political influence never extended beyond a short stretch of the Niger in the areas of Gao and Timbuktu, and eventually political ties between Morocco and the descendants of the Moroccan invaders lapsed. In 1737 the Moroccans were defeated by the Tuareg, who seized control of the Niger Bend, and to the west the Fulani kingdom of Macina defeated the Moroccans at Diré in 1833. West of Macina, the Bambara established a powerful kingdom at Ségou beginning in the early 17th century.

## TIMBUKTU

*Timbuktu (French:Tombouctu) is a city in the western African nation of Mali. It has much historical importance as a trading post on the trans-Saharan caravan route and as a centre of Islamic culture (c. 1400–1600). Located on the southern edge of the Sahara, about 8 miles (13 km) north of the Niger River, the city was designated a UNESCO World Heritage site in 1988.*

*Timbuktu was founded about the 11th century CE as a seasonal camp by Tuareg nomads. There are several stories concerning the derivation of the city's name. According to one tradition, Timbuktu was named for an old woman left to oversee the camp while the Tuareg roamed the Sahara. Her name (variously given as Tomboutou, Timbuktu, or Buctoo) meant "mother with a large navel," possibly describing an umbilical hernia or other such physical malady. Timbuktu's location at the meeting point of desert and water made it an ideal trading centre. In the late 13th or early 14th century it was incorporated into the Mali empire.*

*By the 14th century it was a flourishing centre for the trans-Saharan gold-salt trade, and it grew as a centre of Islamic culture. Three of West Africa's oldest mosques—Djinguereber (Djingareyber), Sankore, and Sidi Yahia—were built there during the 14th and early 15th centuries. After an extravagant pilgrimage to Mecca in 1324, the Mali emperor Mansa Mūsā built the Great Mosque (Djinguereber) and a royal residence, the Madugu (the former has since been rebuilt many times, and of the latter no trace remains). The Granada architect Abū Isḥāq as-Sāḥili was then commissioned to design the Sankore mosque, around which Sankore University was established. The mosque still stands today, probably because of as-Sāḥili's directive to incorporate a wooden framework into the mud walls of the building, thus facilitating annual repairs after the rainy season. The Tuareg regained control of the city in 1433, but they ruled from the desert. Although the Tuareg exacted sizable tributes and plundered periodically, trade and learning continued to flourish in Timbuktu. By 1450, its population increased to about 100,000. The city's scholars, many of whom had studied in Mecca or in Egypt, numbered some 25,000.*

*In 1468 the city was conquered by the Songhai ruler Sonni 'Alī. He was generally ill-disposed to the city's Muslim scholars, but his successor—the first ruler of the new Askia dynasty, Muḥammad I Askia of Songhai (reigned 1493–1528)—used the scholarly elite as legal and moral counselors. During the Askia period (1493–1591) Timbuktu was at the height of its commercial and intellectual development. Merchants from Ghudāmis (Ghadames; now in Libya), Augila (now Awjidah, Libya), and numerous other cities of North Africa gathered there to buy gold and slaves in exchange for the Saharan salt of Taghaza and for North African cloth and horses.*

The Djinguereber mosque in Timbuktu is one of Africa's oldest mosques and signifies the important place the city once held as a centre for Islamic scholarship. Jenny Pate/Robert Harding World Imagery/Getty Images

After it was captured by Morocco in 1591, the city declined. Its scholars were ordered arrested in 1593 on suspicion of disaffection; some were killed during a resulting struggle, while others were exiled to Morocco. Perhaps worse still, the small Moroccan garrisons placed in command of the city offered inadequate protection, and Timbuktu was repeatedly attacked and conquered by the Bambara, Fulani, and Tuareg.

European explorers reached Timbuktu in the early 19th century. The ill-fated Scottish explorer Gordon Laing was the first to arrive (1826), followed by the French explorer René-Auguste Caillié in 1828. Caillié, who had studied Islam and learned Arabic, reached Timbuktu disguised as an Arab. After two weeks he departed, becoming the first explorer to return to Europe with firsthand knowledge of the city (rumours of Timbuktu's wealth had reached Europe centuries before, owing to tales of Mūsā's 11th-century caravan to Mecca). In 1853 the German geographer Heinrich Barth reached the city during a five-year trek across Africa. He, too, survived the journey, later publishing a chronicle of his travels.

Timbuktu was captured by the French in 1894. They partly restored the city from the desolate condition in which they found it. In 1960 it became part of the newly independent Republic of Mali. Timbuktu is now an administrative centre of Mali. Small salt caravans from Taoudenni still arrive, but large-scale trans-Saharan commerce no longer exists there. Islamic learning survives among a handful of aging scholars.

## THE 19TH CENTURY

Most of the 19th century was characterized by French colonial expansion from Senegal in the west and by Islamic jihads (religious wars) that led to the establishment of theocratic states. Shehu Ahmadu Lobbo (Cheikou Amadou), a Fulani Muslim cleric, successfully overturned the ruling Fulani dynasty in Macina in 1810 and established a theocratic state with its capital at Hamdallahi. In the west, political events were dominated by al-Ḥājj 'Umar Tal, a Tukulor Muslim cleric who led a series of jihads. 'Umar conquered the Bambara kingdom of Ségou in 1861 and the Fulani empire of Macina in 1864. After 'Umar was killed in a skirmish with the Fulani in 1864, his vast domains were divided among his sons and commanders. His eldest son, Amadou Tal, who had been installed at Ségou, unsuccessfully attempted to exert control over the whole Tukulor empire in a series of civil wars. He became head of the Ségou Tukulor empire, whose predominantly Bambara inhabitants mounted constant revolts against his rule.

The French, who established a fort at Médine in western Mali in 1855, viewed the Ségou Tukulor empire as the principal obstacle to their acquisition of the Niger River valley. Fearful of British designs on the same region, they engaged in a series of diplomatic overtures and military operations to push the limits of their control eastward. Between 1880 and 1881 the French succeeded in expanding their control from

Médine 200 miles (320 km) east to Kita, primarily through the diplomatic efforts of Capt. Joseph-Simon Gallieni, who signed protectorate treaties with chiefs at Bafoulabé and Kita.

In 1883 Gustave Borgnis-Desbordes launched a series of military campaigns against the Tukulor and the forces of Samory Touré, a Dyula Muslim leader who had founded a state to the south in the late 1860s. Borgnis-Desbordes captured Bamako during that year, giving the French a presence on the Niger. Between 1890 and 1893, Col. Louis Archinard launched a series of successful military operations that led to the final conquest of Ségou in 1893. Samory was driven into the Côte d'Ivoire colony and captured in 1898, the same year that the small Dyula kingdom of Kenedougou around Sikasso was conquered by French forces under Col. H.M. Audeod. Timbuktu was conquered in 1894 by the French officers Gaston Boiteaux, Eugène Bonnier, and Joseph-Jacques-Césaire Joffre, and the southern Sahara was finally brought under French control by *méharistes* (camel corps) by 1899.

## FRENCH WEST AFRICA

What is present-day Mali became a part of French West Africa, although its borders were modified repeatedly and its name was changed as well. For most of its existence, the territory was known as the French Sudan and headed by either a governor or a lieutenant governor. The northern border in the Sahara Desert was gradually extended as the colonialists were able to pacify some, but not all, nomadic groups in the northern region. In 1904 the Kayes-Bamako portion of the Ocean-Niger railroad, linking coastal Dakar with the Niger River, was completed. Bamako became the colony's capital, doubling in size from 1902 to 1912 and continuing to rapidly grow thereafter.

During both World War I and World War II the French recruited and drafted heavily in the French Sudan, as Bambara soldiers were reputed to be reliable and brave; many of the *tirailleurs sénégalaise* (Senegalese riflemen) were actually Bambara from French Sudan. After both wars, but particularly after World War II, veterans achieved considerable standing within the colonial administration and garnered respect from the local population.

Throughout the colonial period, the French viewed the colony as markedly less important economically and politically than its neighbours, Senegal and Côte d'Ivoire. Peasant production was emphasized. Forced labour, conscription, and taxation elicited several local revolts, but none was widespread or notably disrupted production and trade. The Tijani (Tijānīyah) brotherhood dominated among Muslims and generally cooperated with the colonial administration, which sent several key religious figures on the hajj to Mecca.

## INDEPENDENT MALI

Political parties were first formed in 1946, when a territorial assembly was established. The Sudanese Union–African Democratic Party (Union Soudanaise-Rassemblement Démocratique Africain; US–RDA) eventually became the dominant party, under its charismatic Marxist leader, Modibo Keita. In October 1958 the territory became known as the Sudanese Republic; on Nov. 24, 1958, it became an autonomous state within the French Community. In January 1959 Senegal and the Sudanese Republic joined to form the Mali Federation under the presidency of Keita. Hopes that other Francophone states would join the union were never fulfilled, and in August 1960 the federation broke up over major policy differences between the two countries. On September 22, a congress of the US–RDA proclaimed the independent country of the Republic of Mali.

### POLITICAL UNREST AND MILITARY INTERVENTION

Keita, the new country's first president, rapidly replaced French civil servants with Africans, distanced the country from France, established close diplomatic relations and economic ties with communist-bloc countries, and built a state-run economy. In 1962 Mali issued its own nonconvertible currency, although Keita entered into monetary negotiations with the French in 1967 to prop up a sagging economy. Keita, while claiming to be nonaligned, regularly supported the communist bloc in international affairs. His radical socialist political and economic policies and a cultural revolution launched in 1967 led to widespread popular discontent, which created a favourable environment for a group of army officers to seize power. On Nov. 19, 1968, they launched a coup that overthrew Keita and his government. Led by Lieut. Moussa Traoré, the officers formed a 14-member Military Committee of National Liberation that ruled Mali from 1969 to 1979, when a civilian government was elected. Disagreements led to the removal of two officers in 1971, and in 1978 four others, who opposed a return to civilian rule, were accused of planning a coup and were arrested; two of them later died in prison.

### TRAORÉ'S RULE

In 1974, Malians overwhelmingly approved a new constitution. Under it the country returned to civilian rule in 1979, with a military-sponsored political party, the Malian People's Democratic Union (Union Démocratique du Peuple Malien; UDPM), in control of the government and Traoré serving as head of state. When elections were held in 1979, Traoré was elected president, and he was reelected in 1985, while the UDPM—the only legal party—occupied all the seats in the National Assembly. During the

1980s Traoré gave civilians access to the government through regular local and national elections, and he also dealt effectively with protests and with a number of coup attempts.

Traoré consistently followed a pragmatic foreign policy, maintaining close relations with both France and the communist bloc. During the 1980s he made concerted efforts to improve relations with other Western countries, including the United States, which were linked to his attempts to attract foreign investments, diversify the economy, and promote a private sector. Mali had two armed conflicts with Upper Volta (renamed Burkina Faso in 1984) over a border area, in 1974–75 and again in 1985. The latter conflict took place in December 1985 and lasted five days; the territory in question was the Agacher Strip, a border region of about 1,150 square miles (3,000 square km). The matter was referred to the International Court of Justice, which in 1986 divided the territory to the satisfaction of both parties.

By 1991 movements for greater democracy had gained a foothold in Mali but were rejected by Traoré's regime, which claimed that the country was not ready for such change. Demonstrations and riots broke out in major urban centres, leading to a military takeover in March 1991 and the imprisonment of Traoré. The new military government, led by Amadou Toumani Touré, promised a quick return to civilian rule and held a national conference attended by major associations and unions. Elections

were held in 1992, and Alpha Konaré, a prominent civilian intellectual, won the presidency.

## TOWARD A MORE DEMOCRATIC FUTURE

A new constitution and a multiparty government raised hopes of a more democratic future. President Konaré's efforts to rebuild Mali were hampered, however, by a weak economy, drought, desertification, inefficient parastatals (agencies serving the state but not officially under government control), a bloated civil service, decreasing foreign aid, and the French government's devaluation in 1994 of the CFA franc. In 1994–95, confrontations between security forces and students protesting these economic hardships often turned violent. The government also faced a continuing crisis caused by Tuareg rebels, who began returning to their homes in the northern part of the country from Libya and Algeria, where they had migrated in times of drought in the 1970s and '80s. Nevertheless, Konaré was reelected in May 1997 amid charges of electoral fraud and human rights abuses. The political situation subsequently became more stable, and a fragile peace was established with the Tuareg rebels.

In 2002 Touré, the former military leader who had handed the government over to civilians in 1992, was elected president of the country on a nonpartisan platform; he was reelected in 2007.

His administration was faced with continuing economic problems, some of which were partially alleviated by debt relief—particularly the significant relief granted in 2003 and 2005. Touré's administration was also occupied with various conflicts: renewed troubles with Tuareg rebels in 2006 were tenuously resolved by peace agreement that same year, and in 2007 skirmishes between Guinean and Malian villagers over land rights resulted in injury, death, and loss of property. The governments of both countries intervened, resuming a long-dormant mixed patrol along the Mali-Guinea border and encouraging the use of peaceful negotiations to reconcile the disputes.

# CHAPTER 18

## MAURITANIA

Mauritania is located on the Atlantic coast of western Africa. The former French colony gained independence in 1960. The capital is Nouakchott.

### EARLY HISTORY

Mauritania's contributions to the prehistory of western Africa are still being researched, but the discovery of numerous Lower Paleolithic (Acheulean) and Neolithic remains in the north points to a rich potential for archaeological discoveries.

In historical times Mauritania was settled by sub-Saharan peoples and by the Ṣanhājah Imazighen. The region was the cradle of the Amazigh Almoravids, a puritanical, 11th-century Islamic reform movement that spread an austere form of Islam from the Sahara through to North Africa. The main commercial routes that connected subsequent empires in Morocco with the south passed through Mauritania, carrying Saharan salt and Mediterranean luxury products such as fine cloth, brocades, and paper in exchange for gold. In the central desert, Chingueṭṭi, the fabled seventh great city of Islam, was one of the major caravansaries along these routes; another was Oualâta, situated to the south and east of Chingueṭṭi and renowned for the elaborately painted walls of the homes there. It was along these routes that the Ḥassānī Arab groups entered the western Sahara, and gradually an amalgamation of Arab-Amazigh, or Moorish, culture emerged. The Ḥassānī and Arabized Amazigh nomadic groups formed several powerful regional confederations that claimed their origin in Amazigh or Arab ancestry and characterized themselves as pacific, religiously minded *zawāyā* (such as the Idaw 'Aish, said to be the original descendants of the Lamtunah group, and the Reguibat, who claim descent from the Prophet Muhammad) or the raiding, warrior Ḥassānī groups (such as the Trarza and Brakna), respectively. The outcome of a famous conflict (or possibly a series of conflicts) between them in the mid-17th century, known today as Shurr Bubba ("the War of Bubba") became a reference point for deciding political and social status in the southern Sahara.

## EUROPEAN INTERVENTION

In 1442 Portuguese mariners rounded Cape Blanco (Cape Nouâdhibou) and six years later founded the fort of Arguin, whence they derived gold, gum arabic, and slaves. These same commodities later drew Spanish, then Dutch trade to the coast in the 17th century when gum arabic was found to be useful in textile manufacture. The French competed for access to this trade, first with the Dutch and, in the 18th century, with the English, and it was to the French that much of the Saharan coast was ceded in European treaties early in the 19th century. French claims to sovereignty over the hinterland were regularly disputed by the leaders (referred to as "amirs" or "commanders" by the French) of the regions of Trarza

and, to the east, Brakna—named for the two Ḥassānī lineages that dominated the Sénégal River valley—who claimed territory on both sides of the Sénégal River. The French governor of the region, Col. Louis Faidherbe, entered into treaty relations with the amirs in 1858, but France made little effort to exert control over southern Mauritania until the opening years of the 20th century. The "pacification" of Mauritania, as it was styled by the French military, continued until 1912, and the final battle to subdue a Reguibat band took place in 1934. The French nickname for the colony was "*Le Grand Vide*" ("the great void"); so long as the population was quiet there was little evidence of a French presence. Moorish lineages were engaged on both sides of the colonial occupation, some assisting the French and others opposing their presence. Some who benefited from the French presence were well positioned to take on prominent political roles in 1958 when the first elected government under Moktar Ould Daddah negotiated membership in the French Community. The Islamic Republic of Mauritania was declared an independent state on Nov. 28, 1960; it became a member of the United Nations in October 1961.

## STRUGGLE FOR POSTINDEPENDENCE STABILITY

The small political elite that guided the independence movement was divided over whether the country should be

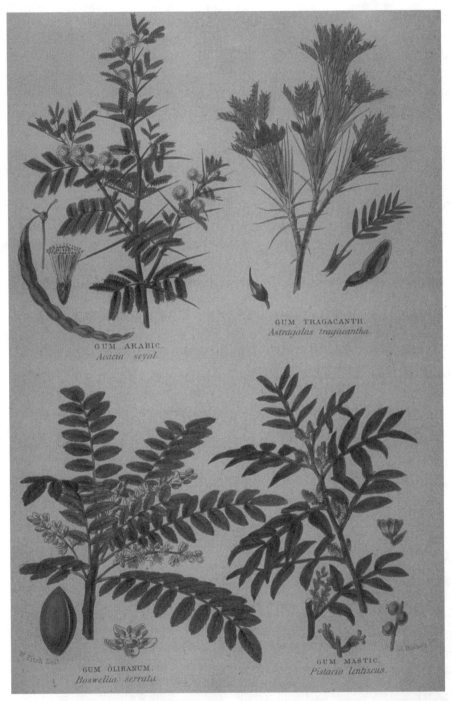

*The gum arabic plant (top left), significant for its use in textile manufacturing, drew Spanish and Dutch traders to the Mauritanian coast in the 17th century.* Time & Life Pictures/Getty Images

oriented toward Senegal and black, French-speaking Africa or toward nearby Arab Morocco and the rest of the Arab world. This was complicated by the fact that Morocco, under King Hassan II, waged an irredentist campaign—including temporary occupation of parts of the Mauritania—during the 1960s. The political direction under Ould Daddah was one of cautious balance between the country's African and Arab roots; independence came with close ties to France and full participation in the Organization of African Unity (later the African Union [AU]) but also with membership in the Arab League in 1973. The political conflict of those early years continued to manifest itself decades later.

As Mauritania's first postindependence president, Ould Daddah appeared securely established in spite of occasional strikes by miners and demonstrations by students, because his policies seemed attuned to a population that was largely oriented by ethnic group and engaged in agriculture or pastoralism. In 1969 Morocco's King Hassan II had reversed his policy and recognized Mauritanian independence as part of his plan to gain control of what was then Spanish Sahara (now Western Sahara), and Morocco and Mauritania divided that country in 1976. The difficulties of suppressing the Saharawi independence movement led by the Polisario Front guerrillas in Mauritania's portion of Western Sahara contributed to Ould Daddah's downfall. In July 1978 he was deposed and exiled in a military coup led by the chief of staff, Col. Mustapha Ould Salek.

Ould Salek resigned his position in June 1979, and under his successor, Lieut. Col. Mohamed Mahmoud Ould Louly, Mauritania signed a treaty with the Polisario Front in August in an effort to disentangle itself from Western Sahara. This worsened relations with Morocco. Ould Louly was in turn replaced in January 1980 by the prime minister, Lieut. Col. Mohamed Khouna Ould Haidalla. In December 1984 Col. Maaouya Ould Sidi Ahmed Taya took over the presidency and the office of prime minister from Ould Haidalla in a bloodless coup, and Mauritania renewed diplomatic ties with Morocco in 1985, seeking again to resolve the dispute in Western Sahara.

Conflict with Senegal was another concern. Sparked by ethnic tension, economic competition, the struggle for herding rights along the Sénégal River, and long-smouldering resentment on both sides at the roles played by one another's citizens in local economies, in 1989 Mauritania and Senegal both expelled tens of thousands of each other's citizens, cancelled diplomatic relations, and teetered on the brink of war. Diplomatic ties were not reestablished until April 1992, and although efforts to repatriate the large refugee populations that had fled to their respective home countries were undertaken, by the early 2000s not all had yet returned.

Domestically, Ould Taya pursued an aggressive Arabization policy within the government as well as the educational system considered by many black Mauritanians as prejudicial. Some of the president's other initiatives were more widely accepted: he presided over a return to civilian government and the development of a multiparty system, opened the country to a relatively free press, and inaugurated a new constitution (1991) while cooperating closely with the World Bank and the International Monetary Fund in making structural adjustments and privatizing the economy. Ould Taya was subsequently victorious in the country's first multiparty presidential elections in 1992 and was reelected in 1997 and 2003. The elections, however, drew allegations of fraud.

In August 2005, while Ould Taya was out of the country, army officers staged a successful coup. Col. Ely Ould Mohamed Vall, a former close ally of Ould Taya, emerged as the leader of the ruling Military Council for Justice and Democracy. He pledged that democracy would be restored, and in 2006 he presented a referendum on constitutional reforms. Voters overwhelmingly approved the changes, which included limiting presidents to two consecutive terms of five rather than six years. In March 2007 presidential elections were held, and Sidi Ould Cheikh Abdallahi became Mauritania's first democratically elected president.

Criticism against President Abdallahi simmered in the months following his election, and tensions escalated in May 2008 when Abdallahi appointed a number of ministers who had held important posts in Ould Taya's government, some of whom had been accused of corruption. In July the parliament passed a vote of no confidence, which was followed by the departure of almost 50 ruling-party members of parliament in early August. On Aug. 6, 2008, President Abdallahi dismissed a number of high-ranking army officials rumoured to have been involved in the parliamentary crisis; in response the military promptly staged a coup and removed him from power. In December 2008 Abdallahi was released after several months' house arrest. With the continued failure of the military government to reinstate civilian rule, early the following year the AU imposed sanctions on Mauritania that included financial measures and a ban on travel. External pressures mounted on the military regime and led to a new round of elections in July 2009, when the coup leader, Gen. Mohamed Ould Abdel Aziz—now a populist advocate for the poor—was affirmed in office.

# CHAPTER 19

## NIGER

Niger is a landlocked country in western Africa. A former French colony, it gained independence in 1960. The capital is Niamey.

### EARLY HISTORY

One of the central themes of the history of Niger is the interaction between the Tuareg (and also Tubu) nomads of the vast Saharan north and the sedentary agriculturalists of the south—that is, the interaction between opposed yet complementary ways of life and civilizations. Among the agriculturalists the main ethnic groups are the Songhai-Zarma in the west, the Hausa in the centre, and the Kanuri in the east. The Hausa have always been the most numerous. They constitute nearly half of the total population of Niger.

In the 14th century (possibly also earlier and later) the Tuareg-controlled kingdom of Takedda, west of the Aïr Massif, played a prominent role in long-distance trade, notably owing to the importance of its copper mines. Copper was then used as a currency throughout western Africa. Archaeological evidence attests to the existence of communities of agriculturalists, probably Songhai-speaking, in this region, which is now desert, at the time of the kingdom of Takedda. Takedda was succeeded at an unknown date by the sultanate of Agadez.

For many centuries the southeastern third of present-day Niger constituted one of the most important provinces of the Kanuri empire of Bornu. The might of Bornu was based on the control of a number of salt-producing sites and of long-distance trade, notably along the string of oases between Lake Chad and the Fezzan via Kawar.

The great drought of about 1735–56—the prelude to the present dry cycle, which set in about 1880—had an adverse effect upon the natural environment. This may explain why both the communities of agriculturalists west of Aïr and the oases between Lake Chad and Kawar disappeared. It may perhaps also explain in part why the Tuareg were able to extend their control over a fair portion of the sedentary south.

At the time of the colonial conquest, the disparate regions the French molded into an entity known as Niger may be best described as an assemblage of peripheral borderlands. As borderlands, however, these regions had played a significant role as zones of refuge—the west after 1591 and the Moroccan conquest of the Songhai empire and the Hausa region much later, after the 1804 Fulani jihad in central Hausaland (i.e., present-day northern Nigeria). In both cases the refugees were people who had lost in the military conflicts, as well as the religious struggles, of their respective homelands. Thus both regions became bastions of "traditionalism" in the face of partly alien conquerors attempting to impose Islam.

## COLONIAL ADMINISTRATION

The French conquest began in earnest only in 1899. It nearly met with disaster owing to the local population's determined resistance against the notorious expedition in 1899 led by the French officers Capt. Paul Voulet and Capt. Charles Chanoine. It was only in 1922, after the severe drought and famine of 1913–15 and the Tuareg uprising of 1916–17, that the French felt safe enough to establish a regular administration under civilian control. By then the power of the Tuareg had been broken.

As elsewhere, the peace in French West Africa (pax gallica) meant, among other things, the rapid spread of Islam, a steep demographic increase, and, although exclusively among the Hausa, the extension of cash crop cultivation. The Songhai-Zarma, on the other hand, responded to the French tax demands by engaging themselves as seasonal labourers in the coastal regions.

Through the reforms of 1946, France's African subjects were in theory granted full citizenship. Thus Niger, along with the other colonies (renamed "overseas territories") in black Africa, was represented in the French parliament. Consultative-legislative assemblies were also set up locally. These reforms secured the ascent of a tiny new elite, the so-called évolués—i.e., those who had been trained in French schools. Many were descendants of former slaves, and most were Songhai-Zarma. Indeed, the people of the west had proved to be far more open to European influence than, for instance, the Hausa.

At least until 1954–55 the French administration (headed for 12 years by Gov. Jean Toby) remained firmly in control of the political situation. The first local executive was established in 1957. Its head, the left-wing trade unionist Djibo Bakary, advocated a no vote in the referendum of 1958, but 72 percent of the votes cast were in favour of a continued link with France. Nevertheless, under Bakary's successor, his cousin and fellow Songhai-Zarma Hamani Diori, independence was proclaimed on Aug. 3, 1960.

## INDEPENDENCE AND CONFLICT

After independence was proclaimed, Diori set up a single-party dictatorship and ruled until he was toppled in a coup in 1974. There followed a military dictatorship headed first by Seyni Kountché (until his death in 1987) and then by Ali Seibou. Mahamane Ousmane of the Social Democratic Convention became president in the country's first multiparty presidential elections in 1993. Meanwhile, a Tuareg rebellion that had begun in the northern part of the country in the early 1990s gained momentum until a ceasefire agreement in 1995 ended much of the fighting. Ousmane was ousted in 1996 during a military coup led by Col. Ibrahim Baré Maïnassara. After a brief period of military rule, Maïnassara was elected president in elections marred

by anomalies. Maïnassara's administration was not well-received, and in 1999 he was assassinated during a coup that was followed by a nine-month transitional government led by Maj. Daouda Malam Wanké and the National Reconciliation Council (Conseil de Reconciliation Nationale; CRN).

Later that year a new constitution was promulgated and elections were held, leading to the subsequent return to democratic government under Pres. Mamadou Tandja of the National Movement for a Developing Society (Mouvement National pour une Société de Développement; MNSD).

At the beginning of the 21st century, increasing demand for the adoption of Islamic Sharī'ah law was the root of much conflict between Islamic activists and Nigeriens who were not in favour of the strict religious code. Niger struggled to maintain its fragile peace as well as to improve its dismal economic situation. Tandja's leadership was widely credited with bringing political stability to Niger, and he was reelected in 2004.

The issue of slavery—still prevalent in Niger and other West African countries despite the fact that it is illegal—was brought to the forefront in 2008 when the Economic Community of West African States (ECOWAS) Court of Justice found the Nigerien government guilty of failing to protect a woman from slavery by not enforcing the country's antislavery laws. Activists hailed the verdict as a historic human rights victory and hoped that the ruling would encourage the enforcement

*Mamadou Tandja, president of Niger (1999–2010).* Francois Mori/AFP/Getty Images

of antislavery laws not only in Niger but also in other West African countries bound by the ECOWAS ruling.

## 2009 CONSTITUTIONAL CRISIS

Under the two-term limit prescribed in the constitution, Tandja was scheduled to step down from office in December 2009. However, in the period leading up to the 2009 presidential election, the issue of a third term for Tandja was a source of contention between the president and the other branches of government. Tandja's goal was to extend his rule for another three years, during which time a new constitution would be drafted that would move the country from a semi-presidential republic to a full presidential republic; he also cited the need for his continued leadership because of various economic development projects that were not yet complete. To extend his rule, Tandja requested that a referendum be held to change the constitution to allow for the three-year extension of his term, which the National Assembly refused to approve. He then took his request for the referendum to the country's Constitutional Court, but on May 26 the court issued a non-binding ruling that the referendum would be unconstitutional without the approval of the National Assembly; later that day Tandja dissolved the legislative body. In early June Tandja created a committee to draft a new constitution, which would provide for the three-year extension of his rule

and would remove presidential term limits. On June 5 a presidential decree called for a referendum on this new constitution to be held on August 4.

Tandja's actions elicited widespread discontent in the country as well as in the international community. Strikes and demonstrations were held to protest against the upcoming referendum. A coalition of many political parties and civil groups, calling themselves the Front for Defence of Democracy (FDD), challenged the presidential decree before the Constitutional Court, and the resulting court ruling on June 12 annulled the presidential decree, declaring that the referendum could not be held without the approval of the now-dissolved National Assembly; this ruling, unlike the court's previous one, was legally binding. Tandja requested that the Constitutional Court rescind its ruling, but it was upheld by the court on June 26. Tandja responded later that day by announcing that he had assumed emergency powers and declaring his intent to rule by decree. Three days later he dissolved the Constitutional Court.

Tandja was not swayed by the increasing criticism of his actions, the accusations that he was circumventing the democratic process, or the pressure from international donors (some of whom threatened to withhold economic aid unless the democratic process was restored). The referendum was held as scheduled on August 4, although opposition leaders urged voters to boycott it. Official results indicated that more than 92 percent of the voters approved the referendum, and Tandja would thus be able to remain in power for an additional three years after the scheduled end of his term in December 2009.

On October 20 an election was held to replace the National Assembly that Tandja had dissolved in May. The election was boycotted by the opposition and was the target of international criticism. In the days prior, ECOWAS exhorted Tandja to postpone the election until talks could be held with the opposition; when its call went unheeded and the election took place as scheduled, ECOWAS suspended Niger's membership in the organization. Election results were announced several days later and indicated that Tandja's party, the MNSD, won a majority of the seats.

Despite the apparent referendum and election victories, Tandja and his actions remained unpopular with many, and on Feb. 18, 2010, there were indications that a coup attempt was under way in the capital. Although reports on the incident were initially varied and conflicting, it was eventually announced that Tandja and other members of his government had been seized by soldiers and were being detained. Later that evening the coup participants announced the formation of a military junta, the Supreme Council for the Restoration of Democracy, and said that they had suspended the country's constitution, dissolved all state institutions, and intended to restore democracy.

# CHAPTER 20

## NIGERIA

Nigeria is located on the Atlantic coast of western Africa, along the Gulf of Guinea. Comprised of former British colonial holdings, it gained independence in 1960. The capital is Abuja.

### EARLY HISTORY

Evidence of human occupation in Nigeria dates back thousands of years. The oldest fossil remains found by archaeologists in the southwestern area of Iwo Eleru, near Akure, have been dated to about 9000 BCE.

### THE NOK CULTURE

There are isolated collections of ancient tools and artifacts of different periods of the Stone Age, but the oldest recognizable evidence of an organized society belongs to the Nok culture (c. 500 BCE–c. 200 CE). Named for the village of Nok, site of some of the finds, the ancient culture produced fine terra-cotta figurines, which were accidentally discovered by tin miners on the Jos Plateau in the 1930s. Initially Neolithic (New Stone Age), the Nok culture made the transition to the Iron Age. Its people raised crops and cattle and seem to have paid particular attention to personal adornment, especially of the hair. Distinctive features of Nok art include naturalism, stylized treatment of the mouth and

*This terra-cotta female figure from the Jos Plateau is one remnant of the ancient Nok culture of Nigeria.* Museum of Fine Arts, Houston, Texas, USA/Funds from the Brown Foundation Accessions Endowment Fund/The Bridgeman Art Library

eyes, relative proportions of the human head, body, and feet, distortions of the human facial features, and treatment of animal forms. The spread of Nok-type figures in a wide area south of the Jos Plateau, covering southern Kaduna state southeastward to Katsina Ala, south of the Benue River, suggests a well-established culture that left traces still identifiable in the lives of the peoples of the area today. Many of the distinctive features of Nok art can also be traced in later developments of Nigerian art produced in such places as Igbo Ukwu, Ife, Esie, and Benin City.

## IGBO UKWU

Bronzes, which have been dated to about the 9th century CE, were discovered in the 1930s and '40s at Igbo Ukwu, near the southwestern city of Onitsha. They reveal not only a high artistic tradition but also a well-structured society with wide-ranging economic relationships. Of particular interest is the source of the copper and lead used to make the bronzes, which may have been Tadmekka in the Sahara, and of the coloured glass beads, some of which may have come from Venice and India, the latter via trade routes through Egypt, the Nile valley, and the Chad basin. It is believed that the bronzes were part of the furniture in the burial chamber of a high personage, possibly a forerunner of the *eze nri*, a priest-king, who held religious but not political power over large parts of the Igbo-inhabited region well into the 20th century.

# KINGDOMS AND EMPIRES OF PRECOLONIAL NIGERIA

Many indigenous polities emerged in Nigeria before the British took control in the late 19th century. In the north there were several large and developed systems, including the Hausa states of Kano, Katsina, Zaria, and Gobir; Kanem-Borno; and the Jukun states of Kwararafa, Kona, Pinduga, and Wukari. Smaller kingdoms included those of the Igala, Nupe, and Ebira. Notable in the south were the Yoruba states of Ife and Oyo, the Edo state of Benin, the Itsekiri state of Warri, the Efik state of Calabar, and the Ijo city-states of Nembe, Elem Kalabari, Bonny, and Okrika.

## KANEM-BORNO

The history of Borno antedates the 9th century, when Arabic writers in North Africa first noted the kingdom of Kanem, east of Lake Chad. The lake was then much larger than the present-day body of water, and its basin attracted settlements and encouraged exchange. A pastoral group, ancestors of the Kanuri, established a centralized state over those referred to collectively as the Sao. Initially, trading links extended to the Nile valley of Egypt. There is some evidence that Kanem had made contact with the Christian kingdoms of Nubia before it was overrun by Muslims, who gained a foothold in the ruling family of Kanem in the 11th century. From Kanem the rulers tried to dominate the areas south and west of the lake as well. By the 12th century they had been compelled by attacks from the Sao to move their capital to the region west of Lake Chad, and they gradually lost control of most of the original Kanem.

For a long time, Borno was the dominant power in the central Sudan, including much of Hausaland. The Bayajidda legend, concerning a mythical Middle Eastern ancestor of the Hausa, seems to suggest that the rise of a centralized political system in Hausaland was influenced from Borno. Though the rulers of Borno embraced Islam, the structure of the monarchy remained traditional, with the queen mother and other female officials exercising considerable power. The selection of the monarch, the coronation rites, and other bases of royal authority were dictated by pre-Islamic beliefs. The princes and other members of the royal family were granted fiefs and posted away from the capital to govern frontier zones, while people of slave origin were preferred for the royal guard and palace officials.

## HAUSALAND

For centuries the Hausa have occupied the northern plains beyond the Jos Plateau, which were a crossroads open not only to Borno but also to the states of Mali and Songhai in the western Sudan, the trans-Saharan routes to northern Africa, and various trade routes to the forest areas of Borgu, Oyo, and Benin.

Perhaps because of this strategic location, the Hausa developed a number of centralized states—such as Daura, Katsina, Kano, Zaria, Gobir, and, later, Kebbi—each with a walled city, a market centre, and a monarchical system of government. Islam, which was introduced from the Mali empire in the 14th century, strengthened both the monarchical system and the commercial contacts, but it remained predominantly an urban religion until the beginning of the 19th century. Even within the walled cities, however, some pre-Islamic rites remained part of the ceremonies that sustained monarchical authority. A considerable rivalry existed between the different states over agricultural land and the control of trade and trade routes, and Hausaland was periodically conquered by powerful neighbours such as Borno and Songhai.

## YORUBALAND AND BENIN

Ife, which flourished between the 11th and 15th centuries, emerged as a major power in the forested areas west of the Niger and south of Hausaland. Some of the characteristic features of Yoruba culture emerged during that time: a monarchical system based on city-states and nucleated villages; a pantheon of gods, a few of which were recognized widely but with several local variations; and divination centred on the deity Ifa, with its corpus of sacred chants. Ife is best known for its potsherd pavements and for the great artistry of its terra-cottas and bronzes, especially the naturalism of many of its bronze figures. Ife's influence on surrounding states is evident in the fact that all the monarchies of Yoruba states claim descent from Ife as a way of establishing legitimacy, sometimes borrowing regalia from Ife to use in coronation rites and sometimes sending remains of deceased rulers to Ife for burial.

Oyo, founded in the 14th century and located in the savanna to the north of the forest, gradually supplanted the older kingdom of Ife. After more than a century of struggle with nearby Borgu and Nupe, it established itself strategically as the emporium for exchanging goods from the north—rock salt, copper, textiles, leather goods, and horses—with products from the south—kola nuts, indigo, parrots, and cowries. By the 17th century it had built up a cavalry force with which it dominated people in western Yorubaland and in the dry gap to the coast; to the south, infestations of tsetse flies prevented kingdoms there from effectively utilizing horses.

When the Portuguese arrived in the kingdom of Benin in the 15th century, they found a monarchy, dating back many centuries, with a complex structure of chiefs and palace officials presiding over a kingdom that was expanding in all directions. In time, Benin dominated not only the Edo-speaking peoples to the north and south but also the area eastward to the Niger and, along the coast, to Lagos (which the Edo now claim to have founded) and even into present-day Ghana. It also exerted considerable influence on eastern Yorubaland and

maintained trading connections with Oyo. Benin art, which began to flourish in the 15th century, was characterized by naturalistic bronze sculptures and bronze door panels that covered the outside of the royal palace.

## IGBOLAND AND THE DELTA CITY-STATES

Many Nigerian peoples did not develop centralized monarchical states. Of these, the Igbo were probably the most remarkable because of the size of their territory and the density of population. The Igbo characteristic decentralized society seems to have been a deliberate departure from the earlier traditions of Nri; monarchical institutions in such outlying cities as Asaba, Onitsha, and Aboh probably arose through the influence of the kingdoms of Igala and Benin. Igbo lineages were organized in self-contained villages or federations of village communities, with societies of elders and age grade associations sharing various governmental functions. The same was true of the Ijo of the Niger delta and peoples of the Cross River area, where secret societies also played a prominent role in administration. Monarchical structures began to emerge by the 18th century in response to the needs of the overseas trade.

Initially, Portuguese contacts focused on Benin and Warri. By the 17th and 18th centuries, at the height of the slave trade, the delta city-states had become the principal outlets of that activity. Various coastal communities organized themselves as entrepôts of the slave trade, so that they would not also become its victims. Similarly, the Igbo, like the Benin and Yoruba kingdoms, supplied slaves to the coast, although Benin had largely ended its involvement in the Atlantic slave trade by the 18th century. The deleterious effect of the slave trade on the society and the economy was felt everywhere, but, in terms of loss of population, those who suffered most appear to have been the noncentralized peoples of the middle belt. The trade also caused severe economic and political dislocations, intercommunal rivalries, and the forced migrations of millions of people out of Nigeria.

## THE SOKOTO JIHAD

At the beginning of the 19th century, Islam was well established at all the major centres of the Hausa states and Borno. The *etsu* (ruler) of Nupe had accepted Islam, and a few teachers and itinerant preachers were also known in parts of the Oyo empire. A group of Muslim intellectuals, most of them Fulani led by Usman dan Fodio, were unhappy that in all these places the rulers allowed the practice of Islam to be mixed with aspects of traditional religion and that nowhere was Islamic law (the Sharī'ah) observed in full. After 20 years of writing, teaching, and preaching in Gobir and surrounding states, Shehu (meaning "chief" or "senior") Usman (as he was now called) withdrew his followers to Gudu, where they formally proclaimed him *amīr*

*al-mu'minīn* ("commander of the faithful"), pledged their loyalty, and prepared for war. In 1804 he called on his followers and all lovers of true Islam to rise up and overthrow the unjust rulers. He appealed to the masses of slaves and to the pastoral Fulani as oppressed people to join the revolt.

The high degree of communication that existed at this time among the different peoples in the area that would become Nigeria was evidenced when the call to jihad—made in Gudu, in the northwest— had repercussions throughout the entire area comprising the present-day country. As a result of the considerable interaction along trade routes and rivers draining the northern plains to the Niger-Benue valley, through the delta, and across the coastal lagoons, the call to jihad was answered not only in the Hausa states, such as Kano, Katsina, and Zaria, but also in Borno, Bauchi, Gombe, and Adamawa and eventually in Nupe, Ilorin, and other places where there were pockets of Fulani scholars.

Thus was created a caliphate, with its seat at the newly established town of Sokoto. Each emirate enjoyed autonomy but pledged loyalty to the *amīr al-mu'minīn* and made contributions for the upkeep of Sokoto. Disputes within or between emirates were referred to Sokoto for settlement by officials who traveled as often as possible to oversee developments. Usman himself retired in 1811 to concentrate on the intellectual direction of the movement, which followed the teachings of the Qadiri brother-hood and strict adherence to the Maliki code of laws. His brother Abdullahi and his son Muhammad Bello carried on the jihad and laid the basis of admin-istration. When Usman died in 1817, Muhammad Bello succeeded him as *amīr al-mu'minīn*, while Abdullahi, as emir of Gwandu, was given charge of the west-ern emirates, notably Nupe and Ilorin. In this way, all the Hausa states, parts of Borno, Nupe, Ilorin, and Fulani outposts in Bauchi and Adamawa were drawn into a single politico-religious system. The rulers of Borno invited Shehu (Sheikh) Muḥammad al-Amīn al-Kānemī, a dis-tinguished scholar and statesman who disagreed with the Fulani view that jihad was an acceptable tool against backslid-ing Muslims, to lead their defense of Borno against the Fulani jihad. In the process Islam was revived in Borno, and the old Seyfawa dynasty was eventually replaced by that of Shehu Muḥammad al-Kānemī.

## THE COLLAPSE OF OYO

Although the Fulani intrusion into Ilorin largely contributed to the collapse of the Oyo empire, it was not the only cause. Deep-seated conflicts arose between the *alafin*, or ruler, and his chiefs, including both provincial rulers and lineage chiefs and councillors at the capital. In spite of the external threat from the Fulani and others, the conflicts could not be resolved. Fulani ascendancy at Ilorin cut off the supply of horses to Oyo and made the defense of the capital untenable. Large groups of people from Oyo had to migrate southward, where they estab-lished a new capital (at present-day Oyo) and other centres such as Ibadan and Ijaye. This pressure, in turn, pushed the Egba farther south, where they founded the town of Abeokuta about 1830. The collapse of the Oyo empire unleashed a major redistribution of the Yoruba people and precipitated a series of Yoruba wars that lasted until 1886.

## YORUBA

*The Yoruba are one of the three largest ethnic groups of Nigeria and are concentrated in the southwestern part of that country. Much smaller, scattered groups live in Benin and northern Togo. The Yoruba numbered more than 20 million at the turn of the 21st century. They speak a language of the Benue-Congo branch of the Niger-Congo language family.*

*Most Yoruba men are farmers, growing yams, corn (maize), and millet as staples and plan-tains, peanuts (groundnuts), beans, and peas as subsidiary crops; cocoa is a major cash crop. Others are traders or craftsmen. Women do little farm work but control much of the complex mar-ket system—their status depends more on their own position in the marketplace than on their husbands' status. The Yoruba have traditionally been among the most skilled and productive craftsmen of Africa. They worked at such trades as blacksmithing, weaving, leatherworking,* glassmaking, and ivory and wood carving. In the 13th and 14th centuries Yoruba bronze casting using the lost-wax (cire perdue) method reached a peak of technical excellence never subsequently equaled in western Africa. Yoruba women engage in cotton spinning, basketry, and dyeing.

The Yoruba have shared a common language and culture for centuries but were probably never a single political unit. They seem to have migrated from the east to their present lands west of the lower Niger River more than a millennium ago. They eventually became the most urbanized Africans of precolonial times. They formed numerous kingdoms of various sizes, each of which was centred on a capital city or town and ruled by a hereditary king, or oba. Their towns became densely populated and eventually grew into the present-day cities of Oyo, Ile-Ife, Ilesha, Ibadan, Ilorin, Ijebu-Ode, Ikere-Ekiti, and others. Oyo developed in the 17th century into the largest of the Yoruba kingdoms, while Ile-Ife remained a town of potent religious significance as the site of the earth's creation according to Yoruba mythology. Oyo and the other kingdoms declined in the late 18th and 19th centuries owing to disputes among minor Yoruba rulers and invasions by the Fon of Dahomey (now Benin) and the Muslim Fulani. The traditional Yoruba kingships still survive, but with only a hint of their former political power.

In a traditional Yoruba town the large and elaborate palace of the oba lies at the centre, and grouped around it are the compounds of the patrilineages. The palace and the compounds are now often modern structures.

There is much diversity in social and political organization among the Yoruba, but they share many basic features. Inheritance and succession are based on patrilineal descent; members of the patrilineage live together under the authority of a headman, share certain names and taboos, worship their own deity, and have rights in lineage lands. The Yoruba also have several kinds of voluntary associations, including the egbe, a male recreational association; the aro, a mutual-aid association of farmers; and the esusu, whose members contribute a fixed amount of money and from which they can receive loans. Political authority is vested in the oba and a council of chiefs; constituent towns each have their own ruler, who is subordinate to the oba. The oba is also a ritual leader and is considered sacred.

Many Yoruba are now Christians or Muslims, but aspects of their traditional religion survive. The traditional Yoruba religion has an elaborate hierarchy of deities, including a supreme creator and some 400 lesser gods and spirits, most of whom are associated with their own cults and priests. The Yoruba language has an extensive literature of poetry, short stories, myths, and proverbs.

## THE ARRIVAL OF THE BRITISH

The Sokoto jihad and the Yoruba wars stimulated the slave trade at a time when the British were actively trying to stop it. Slaves formerly had been traded for European goods, especially guns and gunpowder, but now the British encouraged trade in palm oil in the Niger delta states, ostensibly to replace the trade in slaves. They later discovered that the demand for palm oil was in fact stimulating an internal slave trade, because slaves were largely responsible for collecting palm fruits, manufacturing palm oil, and transporting it to the coast, whether by canoe or by human porterage. The palm oil trade was also linked to the Sokoto jihad and the Yoruba wars, because many warriors recognized the importance of slaves not only as soldiers and producers of food to feed soldiers but additionally as producers of palm oil to trade for European dane guns and other goods.

Many of the slaves exported in the 1820s and '30s were intercepted by the ships of the Royal Navy, emancipated, and deposited in Sierra Leone under missionary tutelage. Some of them began to migrate back from Sierra Leone in search of home and trade. They invited missionaries to follow them and, in the 1840s, made themselves available as agents who allowed missionaries and British traders to gain access to such places as Lagos, Abeokuta, Calabar, Lokoja, Onitsha, Brass, and Bonny. In 1841 the British tried to settle some Egba on a model farm in Lokoja, but the plan was aborted because the mortality rate among European officials was so high. It was also partly to protect the Egba that the British shelled Lagos in 1851, expelled Kosoko, the reigning *oba*, and restored his uncle, Akitoye, who appeared more willing to join in a campaign to abolish the slave trade. The British annexed Lagos in 1861 in order to protect Akitoye's son and successor, foil Kosoko's bid to return, and secure a base for further activities.

The British were not yet willing to assume the expense of maintaining an administration in Nigeria. To reduce costs, Lagos was administered first from Freetown in Sierra Leone, along with Gold Coast forts such as Elmina, and later from Accra (in present-day Ghana); only in 1886 did Lagos became a separate colony. A consul was maintained at Fernando Po to oversee the lucrative palm oil trade in the region called the Oil Rivers. Missionaries were active: Presbyterians in Calabar and the Church Missionary Society (CMS), Methodists, and Baptists in Lagos, Abeokuta, Ibadan, Oyo, and Ogbomoso. The CMS pioneered trade on the Niger by encouraging Scottish explorer and merchant Macgregor Laird to run a monthly steamboat, which provided transportation for missionary agents and Sierra Leonean traders going up the Niger. In this way Bishop Samuel Ajayi Crowther—born in the Yoruba-inhabited area of Oshogbo and the first African ordained by the CMS—was able to establish mission stations at Onitsha, Lokoja, and Eggan and later at Brass and Bonny.

By the 1870s the Niger trade was becoming profitable, and a few French companies took notice. French Roman Catholic missionaries, established in Ouidah (Whydah), arrived in Lagos and considered missionary work on the Niger. The British responded to such evidence of rivalry by defending their right to free navigation on the river at the Berlin West Africa Conference of 1884–85. At the same time, George Dashwood Goldie, a British businessman, bought out all French rivals and created the Royal Niger Company (chartered 1886) in order to control trade on the Niger and administer the immense territories of the Sokoto caliphate and Borno. In addition, two other protectorates were declared, one over the Oil Rivers and the other over the hinterland of Lagos, to establish a claim that these areas were also British "spheres of interest."

The boundaries of the two protectorates and the territories of the Royal Niger Company were difficult to define, but the tension was eased in 1894 when both entities were merged into the Niger Coast Protectorate. Rivalry between the Royal Niger Company and the Lagos Protectorate over the boundary between the emirate of Ilorin and the empire of Ibadan was resolved with the abrogation of the charter of the Royal Niger Company on Jan. 1, 1900, in return for wide mineral concessions.

In the north Frederick Lugard, the first high commissioner of Northern Nigeria, was instrumental in subjugating the Fulani emirs. Some were deposed, some were defeated in battle, and others collaborated. By 1903 the conquest of the emirates was complete. The mud-walled city of Kano was captured in February, and, after a vigorous skirmish at Kotorkwashi, the sultan's capital, Sokoto, fell the next month. All the territories were now under British control, and the search for an identity began, first as Northern and Southern Nigeria and then with eventual amalgamation.

The British penetration of Nigeria met with various forms of resistance throughout the country. In the south

the British had to fight many wars, in particular the wars against the Ijebu (a Yoruba group) in 1892, the Aro of eastern Igboland, and, until 1914, the Aniocha of western Igboland. In the north many emirates did not take military action, but the deposed caliph, Atahiru I, rebelled in 1903. Many Muslims resorted to migration as a form of resistance, a tactic known as the *hejira*, in which those perceived as infidels are avoided.

Resistance was strong in western Igboland, where a series of wars were waged against the British. The Ekumeku, who were well organized and whose leaders were joined in secrecy oaths, effectively utilized guerrilla tactics to attack the British. Their forces, which were drawn from hundreds of Igbo youth from all parts of the region, created many problems for the British, but the British used forceful tactics and heavy armaments (destroying homes, farms, and roads) to prevail. The Ekumeku, however, became a great source of Igbo nationalism.

## NIGERIA AS A COLONY

After the British government assumed direct control of the Royal Niger Company's territories, the northern areas were renamed the Protectorate of Northern Nigeria, and the land in the Niger delta and along the lower reaches of the river was added to the Niger Coast Protectorate, which was renamed the Protectorate of Southern Nigeria. Lagos remained the capital of the south, with

Zungeru the new capital of the north. On Jan. 1, 1914, following the recommendations of Sir Frederick Lugard, the two protectorates were amalgamated to form the Colony and Protectorate of Nigeria under a single governor-general resident in Lagos. Between 1919 and 1954 the title reverted to governor.

Following Lugard's success in the north, he set out the principles of the administrative system subsequently institutionalized as "indirect rule." Essentially, local government was to be left in the hands of the traditional chiefs, subject to the guidance of European officers. Native institutions were utilized and interference with local customs kept to a minimum, although the British did not always understand the local customs. While this system had built-in contradictions, over the years the Nigerian system developed into a sophisticated form of local government, especially in the emirates and under the banner of "native administration," which became the hallmark of British colonial rule in Africa.

Many changes accompanied British rule: Western education, the English language, and Christianity spread during the period; new forms of money, transportation, and communication were developed; and the Nigerian economy became based on the export of cash crops. Areas with lucrative crops such as cacao and peanuts (groundnuts) profited, while many people in different parts of the country had to migrate to work elsewhere as tenant farmers or use their newly acquired education and skills to work in cities as wage earners, traders, and artisans. Two tiers of government emerged, central and local. The central government, presided over by the governor-general and accountable to the secretary for the colonies in London, was more powerful but distant from the people. Local administration, where the colonial citizens typically experienced colonial authority, was based on the policy of indirect rule first developed in the north.

To prevent any united opposition to its authority, the British adopted a divide-and-rule policy, keeping Nigerian groups separate from one another as much as possible. Traditional authorities were co-opted in the north, where the spread of Western education by Christian missionaries was strongly resisted by Muslim leaders. In the south the British occasionally created a political hierarchy where there had been none before; in most cases they ruled through those who were most malleable, whether these people had held traditional positions of authority or not. Because Western education and Christianity spread rapidly in the south and not in the north, development was much slower in the north, and the growing disparity between north and south later caused political tensions.

Further dislocation accompanied the outbreak of World War I. Locally this involved the immediate invasion of the German-held Kamerun (Cameroon) by Nigerian forces, followed by a costly campaign that lasted until 1916. Later Nigerian troops were sent to East Africa. (During World War II they again served

*Nnamdi Azikiwe , the first president of independent Nigeria (1963–66).* Encyclopædia Britannica, Inc.

in East Africa, as well as in Burma [now Myanmar].) In 1922 Kamerun was divided under a League of Nations mandate between France and Britain, Britain administering its area within the government of Nigeria; after 1946 the mandated areas were redesignated as a United Nations (UN) trust territory.

Although colonial rule appeared secure in the first two decades of the 20th century, the British struggled to keep control of their Nigerian colony and continued to do so until Nigeria became independent in 1960. The British, when faced with dissent, tended to grant political reforms in an effort to dispel the attractiveness of more-radical suggestions. Early on in colonial rule, for example, Nigerians protested the manner in which water rates and head taxes were collected. Nigerians also requested more political representation. The Nigerian Legislative Council was established in 1914 and was given limited jurisdiction; it was replaced in 1922 by a larger one that included elected members from Lagos and Calabar, although its powers also were limited and the northern provinces remained outside its control. A more representative system did not appear until 1946, when each geographic group of provinces had its own House of Assembly, with a majority of nonofficial (though not yet all elected) members; there were also a House of Chiefs and, in Lagos, a central Legislative Council. By 1919 the National Council of British West Africa, an organization consisting of elites across West Africa, was demanding that half the members of the Legislative Council be Africans; they also wanted a university in West Africa and more senior positions for Africans in the colonial civil service.

Beginning in the 1920s, a number of Nigerians joined other blacks in various parts of the world to embark on the wider project of Pan-Africanism, which sought to liberate black people from racism and European domination. In 1923 Herbert Macaulay, the grandson of Samuel Ajayi Crowther, established the first Nigerian political party, the Nigerian National Democratic Party, which successfully contested three Lagos seats in the Legislative Council. Macaulay was despised by the British, but he came to be regarded as the "father of modern Nigerian nationalism."

After the 1930s, political activities focused primarily on ways to end British rule. A national party, the Nigerian Youth Movement, emerged in 1934, and its members won elections to the Legislative Council. After 1940, political activities were broadened to include more people. In 1944 Macaulay and Nnamdi Azikiwe, an Igbo who had been educated in the United States, united more than 40 different groups to establish the National Council of Nigeria and the Cameroons (NCNC). The forces unleashed against the British were now diverse, including soldiers who had served in World War II, the media, restless youth, market women, educated people, and farmers, all of whom became committed to the anticolonial movement. Political leaders resorted to the use of political parties and the media

*Nigerian politician Obafemi Awolowo.* Encyclopædia Britannica, Inc.

to mobilize millions of Nigerians against the continuation of British rule.

The British answered this activity by attempting to create a more representational colonial system. The Macpherson constitution, promulgated in 1951, provided for a central House of Representatives, but friction between the central and regional legislatures, related to the question of where supreme party authority lay, soon caused a breakdown. In response to Azikiwe and other nationalists, the Lyttelton constitution of 1954 created a fully federal system, comprising the three geographic regions of Nigeria, the Southern Cameroons, and the Federal Territory of Lagos. Each region had a governor, premier, cabinet, legislature, and civil service, with the significantly weaker federal government represented in Lagos by a governor-general, bureaucracy, House of Representatives, and Senate.

The southern protectorate was divided into two provinces in 1939—Western and Eastern—and in 1954 they, along with the northern protectorate, were renamed the Western, Eastern, and Northern regions as part of Nigeria's reconstruction into a federal state. Internal self-government was granted to the Western and Eastern regions in 1957. The Eastern region was dominated by Azikiwe and the Western one by Chief Obafemi Awolowo, a Yoruba lawyer who in 1950 founded the Action Group. Demanding immediate self-government, the Action Group was opposed by the Northern People's Congress (NPC), which was composed largely of northerners and headed by several leaders, including Abubakar Tafawa Balewa. At its own request the Northern region was not given internal self-government until 1959, because northerners feared that their region might lose its claim to an equal share in the operation and opportunities of the federal government if it was not given time to catch up with the educationally advanced south. Among the problems needing attention before the British would grant full independence was the minorities' fear of discrimination by a future government based on majority ethnic groups. After the Willink Commission examined and reported on this issue in 1958, independence was granted.

## INDEPENDENT NIGERIA

Nigeria was granted independence on Oct. 1, 1960. A new constitution established a federal system with an elected prime minister and a ceremonial head of state. The NCNC, now headed by Azikiwe (who had taken control after Macaulay's death in 1946), formed a coalition with Balewa's NPC after neither party won a majority in the 1959 elections. Balewa continued to serve as the prime minister, a position he had held since 1957, while Azikiwe took the largely ceremonial position of president of the Senate. Following a UN-supervised referendum, the northern part of the Trust Territory of the Cameroons joined the Northern region in June 1961, while in October the Southern Cameroons united with

Cameroun to form the Federal Republic of Cameroon. On Oct. 1, 1963, Nigeria became a republic. Azikiwe became president of the country, although as prime minister Balewa was still more powerful.

After a brief honeymoon period, Nigeria's long-standing regional stresses, caused by ethnic competitiveness, educational inequality, and economic imbalance, again came to the fore in the controversial census of 1962–63. In an attempt to stave off ethnic conflict, the Mid-West region was created in August 1963 by dividing the Western region. Despite this division, the country still was segmented into three large geographic regions, each of which was essentially controlled by an ethnic group: the west by the Yoruba, the east by the Igbo, and the north by the Hausa-Fulani. Conflicts were endemic, as regional leaders protected their privileges; the south complained of northern domination, and the north feared that the southern elite was bent on capturing power. In the west the government had fallen apart in 1962, and a boycott of the federal election of December 1964 brought the country to the brink of breakdown. The point of no return was reached in January 1966, when, after the collapse of order in the west following the fraudulent election of October 1965, a group of army officers attempted to overthrow the federal government, and Prime Minister Balewa and two of the regional premiers were murdered. A military administration was set up under Maj. Gen. Johnson Aguiyi-Ironsi, but his plan to abolish the regions and impose a unitary government met with anti-Igbo riots in the north. The military intervention worsened the political situation, as the army itself split along ethnic lines, its officers clashed over power, and the instigators and leaders of the January coup were accused of favouring Igbo domination. In July 1966 northern officers staged a countercoup, Aguiyi-Ironsi was assassinated, and Lieut. Col. (later Gen.) Yakubu Gowon came to power. The crisis was compounded by intercommunal clashes in the north and threats of secession in the south.

Gowon's attempt to hold a conference to settle the constitutional future of Nigeria was abandoned after a series of ethnic massacres in October. A last-ditch effort to save the country was made in January 1967, when the Eastern delegation, led by Lieut. Col. (later Gen.) Odumegwu Ojukwu, agreed to meet the others on neutral ground at Aburi, Ghana, but the situation deteriorated after differences developed over the interpretation of the accord. In May the Eastern region's consultative assembly authorized Ojukwu to establish a sovereign republic, while, at the same time, the federal military government promulgated a decree dividing the four regions into 12 states, including 6 in the north and 3 in the east, in an attempt to break the power of the regions.

## THE CIVIL WAR

On May 30, 1967, Ojukwu declared the secession of the three states of the Eastern region under the name of the

Republic of Biafra, which the federal government interpreted as an act of rebellion. Fighting broke out in early July and within weeks had escalated into a full-scale civil war. In August Biafran troops crossed the Niger, seized Benin City, and were well on their way to Lagos before they were checked at Ore, a small town in Western state (now Ondo state). Shortly thereafter, federal troops entered Enugu, the provisional capital of Biafra, and penetrated the Igbo heartland. The next two years were marked by stiff resistance in the shrinking Biafran enclave and by heavy casualties among civilians as well as in both armies, all set within what threatened to be a military stalemate. Peacemaking attempts by the Organization of African Unity (now the African Union) remained ineffective, while Biafra began earning recognition from African states and securing aid from international organizations for what was by then a starving population.

The final Biafran collapse began on Dec. 24, 1969, when federal troops launched a massive effort at a time when Biafra was short on ammunition, its people were desperate for food, and its leaders controlled only one-sixth of the territory that had formed the Biafran republic in 1967. Ojukwu fled to Côte d'Ivoire on Jan. 11, 1970, and a Biafran deputation formally surrendered in Lagos four days later.

General Gowon was able, through his own personal magnetism, to reconcile the two sides so that the former Biafran states were integrated into the country once again and were not blamed for the war. The oil boom that followed the war allowed the federal government to finance development programs and consolidate its power. In 1974 Gowon postponed until 1976 the target date for a return to civilian rule, but he was overthrown in July 1975 and fled to Great Britain. The new head of state, Brig. Gen. Murtala Ramat Mohammed, initiated many changes during his brief time in office: he began the process of moving the federal capital to Abuja, addressed the issue of government inefficiency, and, most important, initiated the process for a return to civilian rule. He was assassinated in February 1976 during an unsuccessful coup attempt, and his top aide, Lieut. Gen. Olusegun Obasanjo, became head of the government.

## THE SECOND REPUBLIC

Obasanjo pursued Mohammed's desire to return the country to civilian rule. As a first step, a new constitution was promulgated that replaced the British-style parliamentary system with a presidential one. The president was invested with greater power but could assume office only after winning one-fourth of the votes in two-thirds of the states in the federation.

Many political parties emerged, but only five were registered: the National Party of Nigeria (NPN), the Unity Party of Nigeria, the People's Redemption Party (PRP), the Great Nigeria People's Party, and the Nigeria People's Party. All promised to improve education and social services, provide welfare, rebuild the economy and support private industry, and pursue a radical, anti-imperialist foreign policy. The PRP was notable for expressing socialist ideas and rhetoric. Shehu Shagari, the candidate of the dominant party, the right-wing NPN, narrowly won the 1979 presidential election, defeating Chief Obafemi Awolowo.

The NPN's party leaders used political power as an opportunity to gain access to public treasuries and distribute privileges to their followers. Members of the public were angry, and many openly challenged the relevance of a democracy that could not produce leaders who would improve their lives and provide moral authority. Even in this climate, however, Shagari was reelected president in August–September 1983, although his landslide victory was attributed to gross voting irregularities. Shagari was not able to manage the political crisis that followed or to end Nigeria's continuing economic decline, and the military seized the opportunity to stage a coup on Dec. 31, 1983, that brought Maj. Gen. Muhammad Buhari to power.

## MILITARY REGIMES

Buhari justified his coup and subsequent actions by citing the troubles of the Second Republic and the declining economy. The regime declared a "War Against Indiscipline" (WAI), which resulted in the arrest, detention, and jailing of a number of politicians. When the WAI was extended to journalists and others

not responsible for the social decay and economic problems, the government's popularity began to wane. Gen. Ibrahim Babangida assumed power following a bloodless coup in August 1985.

Babangida at first presented to the public and the media the image of an affectionate and considerate leader. He released political detainees and promised that public opinion would influence his decisions and those of the Armed Forces Ruling Council, the supreme governing body. The public, however, demanded an end to military rule. Babangida outwardly supported a return to civilian government but worked to undermine the process in order to retain power.

A transition program was announced in 1986 that was to terminate in 1990 (later extended to 1993), and the military controlled the process. The government created two political parties, the Social Democratic Party (SDP) and the National Republican Party (NRP), and produced their agendas for them; freely formed parties were not registered, and many politicians were banned from politics. The 1979 constitution was modified by a Constituent Assembly, and a series of elections were then held for local government councillors, state governors, and legislatures.

Although Babangida voided presidential primary elections held in 1992, and all the candidates were banned from politics, a presidential election was slated for June 1993 between two pro-government candidates: Chief M.K.O. Abiola of the SDP and Alhaji Bashir Tofa of the NRP. The Babangida government believed that the elections would never take place and felt that, even if they did, the north-south divide would lead to a stalemate, as Abiola came from the south and Tofa from the north. Contrary to government expectation, however, the election was held on schedule, and it was free, fair, and peaceful. Chief Abiola won, but Babangida annulled the results before they became official. This turned out to be a serious miscalculation that forced him out of power in August 1993, and an Interim National Government (ING) was instituted, led by Yoruba businessman Ernest Shonekan. The ING faced opposition from all sides, and Gen. Sani Abacha, the defense minister under Babangida, overthrew it in November, reinstating military rule. Like Babangida, he promised a transition to civilian rule while pursuing the means to maintain power, but, unlike Babangida, he used excessive force to attain his ambition.

If the political future of Nigeria appeared bright with the victory of Chief Abiola in June 1993, Abacha's seizure of power and subsequent rule reversed most of the gains that the country had made since 1960. At no time since the mid-1960s did so many question the existence of Nigeria as a political entity. When leading politicians did not call for the breakup of the country, they advocated a confederacy with a weakened centre and even a divided army and police force. Opposition forces called for a national conference to renegotiate the basis of Nigerian unity. The country's international image was damaged, as it suffered serious condemnation and isolation.

The Abacha regime ignored due process of law, press freedom, individual liberty, and human rights. The government used violence as a weapon against its opponents and critics; when Abiola proclaimed himself president, he was arrested in June 1994 and died in jail in 1998. Trade union movements were suspended and protesters were killed, yet opposition to the government, particularly outside of the country, did not abate. Abacha and his loyalists again used the state as an instrument of personal gain.

The decisive turning point in military disengagement came with Abacha's sudden death in June 1998. Gen. Abdulsalam Abubakar, appointed to replace him, promised to transfer power to civilians. He freed political prisoners, ended the harassment of political opponents, and set forth a timetable for the transition to civilian rule. The country's international image improved, but economic performance remained sluggish.

## RETURN TO CIVILIAN RULE

After Abacha's death, political activity blossomed as numerous parties were formed. Of these, three emerged that were able to contest elections: the People's Democratic Party (PDP), the Alliance for Democracy, and the All People's Party. A series of elections were held in January–March 1999 in which councillors for local governments, legislatures for state and federal assemblies, and state governors were selected. The presidential election took place in February and was carefully monitored by an international team of observers that included former U.S. president Jimmy Carter. Olusegun Obasanjo of the PDP, who as head of state in 1976–79 had overseen the last transition from military rule, was declared the winner and was sworn in on May 29. A new constitution was also promulgated that month. Nigerians, tired of prolonged and crisis-prone military regimes, welcomed the change of government, as did the international community. In the first civilian-administered elections since the country achieved independence in 1960, Obasanjo was reelected in 2003, although there were widespread reports of voting irregularities.

Although conditions in Nigeria were generally improved under Obasanjo, there was still considerable strife within the country. Ethnic conflict—previously kept in check during the periods of military rule—now erupted in various parts of Nigeria, and friction increased between Muslims and Christians when some of the northern and central states chose to adopt Islamic law (the Sharī'ah). Demonstrations were held to protest the government's oil policies and high fuel prices. Residents of the Niger delta also protested the operations of petroleum companies in their area, asserting that the companies exploited their land while not providing a reasonable share of the petroleum profits in return. Their protests evolved into coordinated

militant action in 2006; the Movement for the Emancipation of the Niger Delta (MEND) was among the most active of such militant groups. Petroleum companies were targeted: their employees were kidnapped and refineries and pipelines were damaged as militants attempted to disrupt oil production and inflict economic loss.

Obasanjo was also faced with resolving an ongoing border dispute with neighbouring Cameroon over rights to the Bakassi Peninsula, an oil-rich area to which both countries had strong cultural ties. Under the terms of a 2002 International Court of Justice ruling, the region was awarded to Cameroon, and Obasanjo was criticized by the international community when Nigeria did not immediately comply by withdrawing its troops from the area in the subsequent years. He also received much domestic criticism for contemplating withdrawal from the peninsula by those who questioned the fate of the large number of Nigerians living in the region and cited the long-standing cultural ties between the Bakassi Peninsula and Nigeria. Nevertheless, Obasanjo eventually honoured the terms of the ruling in 2006 when Nigeria relinquished its claim to the peninsula and withdrew its forces.

The transfer of the peninsula to Cameroon was not without its problems, including the ongoing issue of resettling Nigerians displaced by the transfer and the dissatisfaction of those who remained but were now under Cameroonian rule. Still, the region experienced a relative peace until November 2007, when Cameroonian troops stationed in the area were killed by assailants who reportedly wore Nigerian military uniforms. Nigeria quickly asserted that its military was not involved in the incident and cited recent criminal activity in the Niger delta region, where military supplies—including uniforms—had been stolen; the actual identities of the assailants were not immediately known. Later that month Nigeria's Senate voted to void the agreement that had ceded the Bakassi Peninsula to Cameroon. However, this action did not affect the actual status of the peninsula, and a ceremony held on Aug. 14, 2008, marked the completion of the peninsula's transfer from Nigeria to Cameroon.

Meanwhile, Obasanjo was the subject of domestic and international criticism for his attempt to amend the constitution to allow him to stand for a third term as president; the proposed amendment was rejected by the Senate in 2006. With Obasanjo unable to contest the election, Umaru Yar'Adua was selected to stand as the PDP's candidate in the April 2007 presidential poll. He was declared the winner, but international observers strongly condemned the election as being marred by voting irregularities and fraud. Nonetheless, Yar'Adua was sworn in as president on May 29, 2007.

Yar'Adua's health was the subject of rumours, as he had traveled abroad for medical treatment several times in the years prior to his presidency and continued to do so after the election. His ability to serve as president while dealing with health issues was called into question after he went to Saudi Arabia in late November 2009 for treatment of heart problems and kidney problems. After he had been absent from Nigeria for several weeks, critics complained of a power vacuum in the country, and there were calls for Yar'Adua to formally transfer power to the vice president, Goodluck Jonathan. Although a ruling by a Nigerian court on Jan. 29, 2010, indicated that Yar'Adua was not obligated to hand over power to the vice president while he was out of the country for medical treatment, the controversy surrounding his prolonged absence remained. On Feb. 9, 2010, the National Assembly voted to have Jonathan assume full power and serve as acting president until Yar'Adua was able to resume his duties. Jonathan agreed and assumed power later that day, but it was unclear whether or not the assumption of power was constitutional. When Yar'Adua returned to Nigeria on Feb. 24, 2010, it was announced that Jonathan would remain as acting president while Yar'Adua continued to recuperate. Yar'Adua never fully recovered, however, and he died on May 5, 2010; Jonathan was sworn in as president the following day.

# CHAPTER 21

# SENEGAL

S enegal is located in western Africa, on the Atlantic coast. The former French colony gained independence in 1960. The capital is Dakar.

## EARLY HISTORY

Senegal has been inhabited since ancient times. Paleolithic and Neolithic axes and arrows have been found near Dakar, and stone circles, as well as copper and iron objects, have been found in central Senegal. The stone circles, thought to date from the 3rd century BCE to the 16th century CE, were designated a UNESCO World Heritage site in 2006.

The Fulani and Tukulor occupied the lower Sénégal River valley in the 11th century. The name Senegal appears to be derived from that of the Zenaga Imazighen of Mauritania and northern Senegal. About 1040, Zenaga Imazighen established a Muslim *ribāṭ* (fortified religious retreat), perhaps on an island in the river; this became the base for the Almoravids, who converted the Tukulor, conquered Morocco, and crossed into Spain. The Almoravid attacks on the Soninke empire of Ghana contributed to the empire's eventual decline. Between 1150 and 1350 the legendary leader Njajan Njay founded the Jolof kingdom, which in the 16th century split into the competing Wolof states of Walo, Kajor, Baol, Sine, and Salum. Islamic influence spread throughout the region in variable strength; it gained new impetus in the late 17th century, and after 1776 Tukulor Muslims established a theocratic confederacy in Fouta.

Portuguese navigators reached the Cape Verde peninsula about 1444; they established trading factories at the mouth of the Sénégal, on Gorée Island, at Rufisque, and along the coast to the south. In the 17th century their power was superseded by that of the Dutch and then the French.

## WOLOF

*A Wolof woman in traditional Wolof attire and ornamentation. Ariadne Van Zandbergen/Photolibrary/Getty Images*

*The Wolof (also spelled Ouolofa) are a Muslim people of Senegal and The Gambia who speak the Wolof language of the Atlantic branch of the Niger-Congo language family. The typical rural community is small (about 100 persons).*

*Most Wolof are farmers, growing peanuts (groundnuts) as a cash crop and millet and sorghum as staples; many, however, live and work in Dakar and Banjul as traders, goldsmiths, tailors, carpenters, teachers, and civil servants. Traditional groups were characterized by a markedly hierarchical social stratification, including royalty, an aristocracy, a warrior class, commoners, slaves, and members of low-status artisan castes; at their head was a paramount chief.*

*In the past the Wolof observed double descent; i.e., descent was traced through both the male and female lines. Islamic influence, however, has tended to make the male line dominant. A household unit may consist of a nuclear family (husband, wife, and minor children) or a polygynous family (a husband, his several wives, and their children); other close kin, however, may sometimes be found together with the nuclear family. Wolof women are renowned for their elaborate hairstyles, abundant gold ornaments, and voluminous dresses.*

## THE FRENCH PERIOD

A French factory at the mouth of the Sénégal River was rebuilt in 1659 at N'Dar, an island in the river that became the town of Saint-Louis, and in 1677 France took over Gorée from the Dutch. These two communities became bases for French trading companies that bought slaves, gold, and gum arabic in the region and became homes for free Christian Africans and Eurafricans.

After two periods of British occupation, Saint-Louis and Gorée were returned to France in 1816. When attempts to grow cotton near Saint-Louis proved unprofitable, trade for gum in the Sénégal valley was substituted. In 1848 the marginal colonial economy was further disrupted when the Second Republic outlawed slavery on French soil.

In 1854 Napoleon III granted the request of local merchants for a greater French military presence and appointed Commandant Louis-Léon-César Faidherbe governor. At the same time, al-Ḥājj 'Umar Tal, a Tukulor, conquered the Bambara kingdom of Kaarta as well as the states of Segu and Macina, but he was unable to control his home territory of Fouta because the French occupied the land. A military stalemate after 1857 led to a truce of coexistence between the two powers, although the French exploited the internal conflicts in the region after 'Umar Tal's death in 1864. When Faidherbe retired in 1865, French power

was paramount over most of the territory of modern Senegal, with peanut cultivation and export reaping great economic benefits for the colonists.

In 1879 the French government approved a large program of railway construction (built 1882–86). One line linked Saint-Louis with Dakar through the main peanut area in Kajor. Another rail line, the Dakar-Niger line, was not completed until 1923 and facilitated access to the territory formerly controlled by 'Umar Tal. Meanwhile, France was consolidating direct control over the rest of Senegal and its other African colonies. In 1895 Jean-Baptiste Chaudié became first governor-general of French West Africa, and in 1902 its capital moved from Saint-Louis to Dakar.

Before this new autocratic empire established its rigid administrative control over such traditional chiefs as it still tolerated, the Third Republic had recognized the inhabitants of Saint-Louis, Gorée, Dakar, and Rufisque, regardless of ethnicity, as French citizens. In 1914 the African electors succeeded in sending Blaise Diagne, an African former colonial official, as their deputy to the National Assembly in Paris. In return for assistance in recruiting African soldiers in World War I (some 200,000 in all from French West Africa), Diagne obtained confirmation of full French citizenship rights for this urban minority, even if they chose to retain their status under Muslim law. These privileges were lost between 1940 and 1942, when French West Africa

# LÉOPOLD SENGHOR

(b. Oct. 9, 1906, Joal, Senegal, French West Africa [now in Senegal]—
d. Dec. 20, 2001, Verson, France)

*Léopold Senghor was a poet, teacher, and statesman. He was the first president of Senegal.*

*After attending schools in Senegal, Senghor went to Paris in 1928 on a partial scholarship and continued his formal studies at the Lycée Louis-le-Grand and at the Sorbonne. During these years Senghor discovered the unmistakable imprint of African art on modern painting, sculpture, and music, which confirmed his belief in Africa's potential contribution to modern culture.*

*Senghor was one of the originators in the 1930s and '40s of the concept of Negritude, which is often defined as the literary and artistic expression of the black African experience, and he became Negritude's foremost spokesman. He was also a distinguished poet in his own right and had many published works of his own.*

*In 1935 Senghor became the first African agrégé, the highest rank of qualified teacher in the French school system, which allowed him to teach at both the lycée and university levels. He was drafted in 1939 at the beginning of World War II and captured in 1940. He spent two years in Nazi concentration camps, where he wrote some of his finest poems. On his release he joined the Resistance in France.*

*After the war Senghor became a member of the French Constituent Assembly. In 1946 he was sent as one of Senegal's two deputies to the National Assembly in Paris and was reelected by a wide margin in the 1951 elections. Five years later he became mayor of Thiès, Senegal's railroad centre, and was again reelected deputy.*

*Senghor helped establish an alliance between French Equatorial Africa and French West Africa that led to the creation in 1959 of the short-lived Mali Federation, of which Senegal was a member (along with French Sudan [Mali], Dahomey [Benin], and Upper Volta [Burkina Faso]). The Mali Federation lasted only until the following August, when its last two members, Senegal and French Sudan, separated. Senegal then became an independent republic, and Senghor was unanimously elected president.*

*As chief executive, Senghor tried to modernize Senegal's agriculture, instill a sense of enlightened citizenship, combat corruption and inefficiency, forge closer ties with his African neighbours, and continue cooperation with the French. He advocated a form of socialism that was based on African realities and was often called "African socialism." Senghor's socialism was democratic and humanistic, and it shunned such slogans as "dictatorship of the proletariat."*

*Senghor stepped down on Dec. 31, 1980, the first African president to leave office voluntarily, and retired to France. He was inducted into the French Academy in 1984, becoming the first African member in that body's history.*

passed under control of the wartime Vichy government, but were restored under the Fourth Republic (1947–58).

Two socialist deputies elected in 1946, Lamine Guèye and Léopold Senghor, at first concentrated on restoring the original French citizenship rights and then extending them to the whole Senegalese population. But political life was increasingly influenced by nationalist movements elsewhere in Africa and Asia, as well as by strong internal tensions, notably those revealed by a sustained railway strike in 1947–48. Senghor, a poet and philosopher who sought some synthesis between an authentic African identity and French civilization, built a strong political position on partnership with the leaders of the Mourides (Murīdiyyah) and other socially conservative Muslim orders, but he was increasingly driven toward claiming political independence. In 1958 the Senegalese electorate accepted his advice to vote in favour of membership in Charles de Gaulle's proposed French Community, but two years later Senegal claimed and received independence (initially within the short-lived Mali Federation).

## INDEPENDENT SENEGAL

As president, Senghor maintained collaboration internally with Muslim religious leaders and externally with France, which continued to provide economic, technical, and military support. The economy, however, remained vulnerable both to fluctuations in world prices for peanuts and phosphates and to the Sahelian droughts, and the government found it increasingly difficult to satisfy the expectations of the working class and of a rapidly growing student body. Although Senegal remained more tolerant and pluralist than many African states, there were encroachments on political freedoms. In 1976, however, Senghor authorized the formation of two opposition parties; Abdou Diouf, to whom he transmitted presidential power in January 1981, tentatively extended these freedoms.

Under Diouf the Socialist Party (PS) maintained Senghor's alliance with the Muslim hierarchies. When the PS secured more than 80 percent of the votes in the 1983 elections, there were complaints of unfair practice, and the eight deputies returned by the Senegalese Democratic Party (PDS) of Abdoulaye Wade initially refused to take their seats. Nevertheless, the framework of parliamentary democracy survived the continuing economic stringency of the 1980s. In 1988 Diouf's presidential majority dropped to 73 percent, and the PDS won 17 of the 120 parliamentary seats. Charges of inequity and fraud, and considerable violence, were followed by the declaration of a state of emergency. Wade was imprisoned but was subsequently pardoned.

Diouf found it increasingly difficult to meet prescriptions for economic adjustment while trying to contain social and ethnic pressures caused by falling export values, rising costs of living, and mounting unemployment. The proclamation in 1981 of the Senegambian confederation, established after Senegalese troops marched into The Gambia to crush a military coup, was abrogated in 1989. That same year a long-standing border dispute between Senegal and Mauritania erupted into serious ethnic violence; several hundred Senegalese were massacred in Mauritania, and both countries expelled tens of thousands of expatriates. Senegalese merchants took over many of the businesses previously owned and operated by Mauritanians in Senegal. Tensions have remained high ever since, despite an agreement in April 1992 between the two countries to restore diplomatic relations. In 2000 tensions were further heightened over the issue of Sénégal River usage rights; violence was averted when the Senegalese government abandoned a controversial irrigation plan.

Generally peaceful elections in 1993 resulted in victory for Diouf and the PS. The French decision in 1994 to devalue the African franc by 50 percent negatively affected the Senegalese economy and sparked the most-serious uprisings in the country in years, led by dissatisfied urban youths. The government quickly crushed the demonstrations and arrested hundreds. The difficult economic conditions continued, exacerbated by periodic droughts and inflation. Despite the economic problems, however, the Diouf regime retained the support of the powerful Muslim leadership in the country, and the PS won legislative elections again in 1998, although opposition parties did make some gains, especially in the urban Dakar region. Wade finally won the presidency in March 2000, marking the first time since the country's independence that a presidential candidate was elected from a party other than the PS. Wade's victory also ushered in a peaceful and democratic transfer of power, a significant event on the African continent. He was reelected in 2007.

The greatest challenge still facing the Senegalese government was the long-standing conflict in Casamance, the southern area physically isolated from the rest of the country by The Gambia. Since 1982 a rebel group, primarily based in the Diola areas, has been fighting for independence, and many people have died as a result of the fighting. The Senegalese government refused to negotiate with the rebels, and a 1998 attempted military coup in neighbouring Guinea-Bissau, which involved guerrillas from Casamance, was repressed by government troops and led to renewed violence in the area. The leader of the main rebel forces declared the war over in 2003, and a peace agreement was signed in 2004, but some rebel factions continued to fight.

# CHAPTER 22

# SIERRA LEONE

S ierra Leone is located in western Africa, on the Atlantic coast. The former British colony gained independence in 1961. The capital is Freetown.

## EARLY HISTORY

Archaeological findings show that Sierra Leone has been inhabited for thousands of years. Traditional historiography has customarily presented it as peopled by successive waves of invaders, but the language pattern suggests that the coastal Bulom (Sherbro), Temne, and Limba have been in continuous settled occupation for a long time, with subsequent sporadic immigration from inland by Mande-speaking peoples, including Vai, Loko, and Mende. They organized themselves in small political units—independent kingdoms or chiefdoms—whose rulers' powers were checked by councils. Secret societies, notably the Poro society, also exercised political power, as well as instructing initiates in the customs of the country.

Muslim traders brought Islam, which became firmly established in the north and subsequently spread through the rest of the country.

Portuguese voyagers gave the name Serra Lyoa ("Lion Mountains"), later corrupted to Sierra Leone, to the mountainous peninsula at the mouth of the Rokel (Seli) River where, from the 15th century onward, European traders congregated near the site of present-day Freetown under the protection of African rulers, who welcomed them for the commercial opportunities they provided—namely, the exchange of imported manufactured goods for ivory and slaves to be employed across the Atlantic.

A group of freed slaves arrived in Sierra Leone from England in 1787 to form a settlement. It failed but was revived by the Sierra Leone Company, a commercial company sponsored by English opponents of the slave trade. Black settlers who had liberated themselves from American slavery were brought over from Nova Scotia and built a new settlement, named Freetown. In 1800 "Maroons," free blacks from Jamaica, were also brought in. These settlers were English-speaking, and many were literate and Christian.

After the British Parliament made the slave trade illegal in 1807, the British government took over the settlement (Jan. 1, 1808) as a naval base against the slave trade and as a centre to which slaves, captured in transit across the Atlantic, could be brought and freed. Between 1807 and 1864, when the last slave ship case was adjudicated in the Freetown courts, the British navy brought in more than 50,000 "recaptives," also known as "liberated Africans." Drawn from all over western Africa, these heterogeneous people lacked any common language or culture. The government therefore introduced a deliberate policy of turning them into a homogeneous Christian community. Protestant missionaries, along with the black pastors of Freetown churches, worked with such

success that within a generation the policy was virtually fulfilled. The (Anglican) Church Missionary Society founded an institution to train teachers and missionaries, Fourah Bay College, which was affiliated to the University of Durham in England in 1876. The society also opened boys' and girls' secondary schools.

The recaptives and their children, known as Creoles (today usually rendered Krios), prospered as traders, and some entered the professions, qualifying in Britain as doctors and lawyers. Thus, they formed an educated West African elite. Notable examples include James Africanus Beale Horton, who qualified as a doctor and served as an officer in the British army and published books on medical and political subjects, and Sir Samuel Lewis, a distinguished barrister. Many Creoles sought employment opportunities in other parts of West Africa. At their suggestion, Anglican missions were founded in what is now Nigeria, where one of them, Samuel Adjai Crowther, became a bishop.

## COLONY AND PROTECTORATE

During the 19th century the area around the coastal settlements was drawn increasingly into the British economic sphere. There was a market in Britain for shipbuilding timber, and most of the accessible forest trees in the coastal country were felled, altering the environment irrevocably. There was also a European market for vegetable oils, and unprocessed palm produce and peanuts were supplied in return for imported manufactures. Rulers fought for control of the trading centres and built up larger territories for themselves.

The colonial government made treaties of friendship with neighbouring rulers and gradually acquired jurisdiction over the coastline. At the period of the European partition of Africa, frontiers were delimited with the neighbouring French and Liberian governments, and a British protectorate was proclaimed in 1896 over the area within the frontier lines, though the original colony retained its status. To raise revenue to pay for administration of the protectorate, a hut tax was imposed. The ruling chiefs, who had not been consulted about the protectorate, objected, and a revolt broke out in 1898 under Bai Bureh. It was suppressed by the end of the year. There were no further large-scale armed risings against the British.

In the protectorate the chiefs ruled under the supervision of British district commissioners. Innovation was discouraged, and little was done to extend education. In the colony many Creoles had held senior official posts in the 19th century and looked forward to governing themselves ultimately. After the protectorate was assumed, however, they were gradually removed from office, and the colony and protectorate were governed by British administrators.

## INDEPENDENCE

After World War II the British government gave in to nationalist demands in Sierra Leone, as elsewhere in West Africa. Democratic institutions were hurriedly constituted. The small Creole minority hoped to entrench their rights politically, but the 1951 constitution gave control to the majority. The government elected under it was led by Milton (later Sir Milton) Margai of the Sierra Leone People's Party, a predominantly protectorate party.

During the 1950s, parliamentary institutions on the British pattern were introduced in stages. The last stage was reached on April 27, 1961, when Sierra Leone became an independent state within the Commonwealth.

The first years of independence were prosperous. Mineral resources (iron ore and diamonds) brought in substantial revenue, much of which was used for development, particularly education. Njala University College was founded in the early 1960s and amalgamated in 1967 with Fourah Bay College as the University of Sierra Leone.

Sir Milton Margai died in 1964 and was succeeded by his brother, Sir Albert Margai. The opposition All-Peoples' Congress (APC), led by Siaka Stevens, won the 1967 general election. But the army intervened and set up a military government, the National Reformation Council, under Lieut. Col. Andrew Juxon-Smith. After a year the privates and noncommissioned officers mutinied, imprisoned their officers, and restored parliamentary rule under Stevens and the APC.

The subsequent years were stormy, the government regularly imposing states of emergency and executing its political opponents. In 1971 Sierra Leone became a republic, with Stevens as executive president. Meanwhile, the economy deteriorated; the supply of iron ore was exhausted, and most of the diamonds were smuggled, thus depriving the government of revenue. Stevens's style of government encouraged his supporters to enrich themselves at public expense. Public dissatisfaction grew, led by student protests. Stevens's answer was to introduce one-party rule in 1978. In 1985

Stevens retired, having chosen the head of the army, Joseph Saidu Momoh, as his successor. Widespread corruption continued, and the economy further deteriorated.

## CIVIL WAR

The difficulties in the country were compounded in March 1991 when conflict in neighbouring Liberia spilled over the border into Sierra Leone. Momoh responded by deploying troops to the border region

*Soldiers of the Sierra Leone army.* Christophe Simon/AFP/Getty Images

to repel the incursion of Liberian rebels known as the National Patriotic Front of Liberia (NPFL), led by Charles Taylor. Sierra Leone's army came under attack not only from the NPFL but also from the Revolutionary United Front (RUF), led by former Sierra Leone army corporal Foday Sankoh, who was collaborating with the Liberian rebels; this was the beginning of what would be a long and brutal civil war.

In April 1992 Momoh was deposed in a coup led by Capt. Valentine E.M. Strasser, who cited the poor conditions endured by the troops engaged in fighting the rebels as one of the reasons for ousting Momoh. A National Provisional Ruling Council (NPRC) was established with Strasser as the head of state. During Strasser's administration the civil war escalated, with the RUF increasing the amount of territory under its control, including lucrative diamond mines—the source of the "blood" or "conflict" diamonds used to fund its activities. There were disturbing reports of atrocities committed against the civilian population not only by rebel forces but also by some government troops. Civilians were subject to horrific acts of mutilation, including having their limbs, ears, and lips cut off. Incidents of rape and forced labour were widespread, and many civilians were used as unwilling human shields or held in captivity and subjected to repeated acts of sexual violence by the combatants. Forced conscription was pervasive and made many civilians, including children, unwilling participants in the conflict.

Strasser was ousted in another military coup in January 1996 after it was feared that he would not transfer power to a civilian government, as originally promised. Brig. Gen. Julius Maada Bio briefly assumed control of the government with the pledge that elections would soon be held. The RUF, however, requested that elections be postponed until it could reach a peace agreement with the government; this request was rebuffed, and the RUF intensified its violent campaign. Nonetheless, elections were still held: Ahmad Tejan Kabbah of the Sierra Leone People's Party won the presidential election and took office on March 29, 1996. A peace agreement between Kabbah and RUF leader Sankoh, known as the Abidjan Agreement, was reached later that year in November, but it was not successfully implemented.

In May 1997 the country experienced yet another coup as Maj. Johnny Paul Koroma seized power. Koroma, who attributed the previous government's failure to implement the Abidjan Agreement as the reason for the coup, formed the Armed Forces Revolutionary Council (AFRC), which included members of the RUF, to rule the country; President Kabbah was sent into exile. The AFRC met with increasing resistance on all fronts: domestically, its troops were engaged in battle with militia forces loyal to Kabbah's government; internationally, the Commonwealth suspended Sierra Leone, and the United Nations Security Council imposed sanctions on the country.

## DIAMONDS

*In Sierra Leone diamonds are mined by a few private companies and by vast numbers of private prospectors. The National Diamond Mining Company (Diminco) also mined diamonds until 1995. Mining methods range from mechanical grab lines with washing and separator plants to crude hand digging and panning. Many diamonds are found in river gravels, especially along the Sewa-Bafi river system. Official exports of diamonds have declined dramatically since the 1960s due to extensive smuggling and the depletion of reserves. Foreign investment beginning in the mid-1990s helped develop the deep-mining of diamonds, which was officially suspended after 1999 and then slowly reinstated after the war's end in 2002. Internal instability left much of the diamond region in the hands of rebel forces throughout the 1990s and early 21st century, thereby providing them with a lucrative source of funding for their rebellion. The trading of these so-called "blood" or "conflict" diamonds—a problem not only in Sierra Leone but also in other African countries—became a source of worldwide controversy. The United Nations Security Council passed a resolution in July 2000 that banned the import of uncertified rough diamonds from Sierra Leone; the embargo was lifted in June 2003.*

The AFRC was overthrown in February 1998 by Economic Community of West African States Monitoring Group (ECOMOG) troops, who intervened with the support of the international community. President Kabbah's government was restored in March, but ECOMOG and government troops continued to battle rebel forces until July 1999, when another peace accord—the Lomé Agreement—was signed. The Lomé Agreement proposed a power-sharing plan that included Sankoh and other rebels in the government and required the RUF and the AFRC forces to surrender their weapons.

The newfound peace was soon threatened by divisions among the rebels. In August, forces aligned with the AFRC—resentful of their exclusion from the power-sharing arrangements defined in the peace accord—took several hostages, including ECOMOG troops, UN military observers, aid workers, and journalists. Although these hostages were eventually released, the AFRC fighters continued with abductions and later captured several RUF leaders. Meanwhile, it became clear that, although Sankoh had agreed to the terms of the peace accord, RUF rebels had no intention of complying, as they continued their brutal attacks on civilians and refused to surrender their weapons; they also attacked and abducted UN Mission to Sierra Leone (UNAMSIL) peacekeeping troops, who had entered the country in November 1999.

With Sankoh doing little to rein in the rebels, a fierce battle around Freetown erupted in May 2000, during which Sankoh was captured by government forces, and the RUF was driven away from the capital by the Sierra Leonean army, with the help of British troops and progovernment militias. After Sankoh's capture, the RUF continued to operate under Gen. Issa Sesay; other heavily armed militias also held power in the country.

Throughout 2001 UNAMSIL worked to implement a compromise based on the Lomé Agreement, and it had success with disarming many RUF rebels and the progovernment militia. The RUF also released some territory that had been under its control, and UN peacekeeping troops began securing more of the country. Gradually, peace began to seem more obtainable.

An official end to the civil war was declared on Jan. 5, 2002. By that time, it was estimated that at least 50,000 people had died, with hundreds of thousands more affected by the violence and some two million people displaced by the conflict.

## POST-CIVIL WAR

The first post-civil war elections were held in May 2002, with Kabbah winning reelection with a majority of the vote. Kabbah's administration focused on fostering reconciliation, maintaining internal security, and promoting economic recovery and reform. To that end, both a Truth and Reconciliation Committee and a UN-sponsored war-crimes tribunal (the Special Court for Sierra Leone) were established that summer, and UN peacekeeping troops remained in the country until December 2005. Economic recovery in the postwar years was somewhat aided by significant debt relief and the reopening of bauxite and rutile mines. Still, in the years after the war, Sierra Leone was consistently rated as one of the world's poorest countries.

In June 2007 the Special Court for Sierra Leone began trying former Liberian rebel and president Charles Taylor, who in 2003 had been indicted for his involvement in Sierra Leone's civil war and charged with war crimes and crimes against humanity; due to security concerns, his trial was conducted at The Hague. Sierra Leone held presidential and parliamentary elections later that summer; Ernest Bai Koroma of the opposition party All People's Congress was elected president, and his party was successful in winning a majority of parliamentary seats. Koroma's administration tackled the ongoing issues of rebuilding the economy, eliminating corruption, and improving the quality of life in the country.

# CHAPTER 23

## TOGO

Togo is located on the coast of western Africa, along the Gulf of Guinea. Initially a German protectorate, administration was divided between the French and British after World War I. The British territory joined with the Gold Coast (now Ghana) and the French territory gained independence in 1960. The capital is Lomé.

### EARLY HISTORY

Until 1884 Togoland was an indeterminate buffer zone between the warring states of Asante and Dahomey. The only port was Petit Popo (Anécho, or Aného). Throughout the 18th century the Togo portion of the Slave Coast was held by the Danes.

### GERMAN OCCUPATION

German missionaries arrived in Ewe territory in 1847, and German traders were soon established at Anécho. In 1884 Gustav Nachtigal, sent by the German government, induced a number of coastal chiefs to accept German protection. The protectorate was recognized in 1885, and its coastal frontiers with Dahomey and the Gold Coast were defined by treaties with France and Great Britain. German military expeditions (1888–97) met with little resistance, securing a hinterland the boundaries of which also were determined by treaties with France (1897) and Great Britain (1899).

Lomé, at the western end of the coast, was selected as the colonial capital in 1897, a modern town was laid out, and in 1904 a jetty was built. Three railways were constructed to open up the interior. Exploitation was confined to the coastal and central areas and was exclusively agricultural. Plantations were established both by the government and by private German corporations, but crop development was left mainly to the Togolese, assisted by agriculturists trained at a college in Nuatja (Notsé). Upwardly mobile Ewe were recruited into what was supposed to be Germany's *Musterkolonie* (model colony). Trade was chiefly in palm products, rubber, cotton, and cocoa beans. German administration was efficient but marred by its harsh treatment of Africans and use of forced labour.

On Aug. 7, 1914, at the outset of World War I, British and French colonial troops from the Gold Coast and Dahomey invaded Togoland and on August 26 secured the unconditional surrender of the Germans. Thereafter the western part of the colony was administered by Britain, the eastern part by France. By an Anglo-French agreement of July 10, 1919, France secured the railway system and the whole coastline. After Germany renounced its sovereignty in the Treaty of Versailles, the League of Nations in 1922 issued mandates to Britain and France for the administration of their spheres.

## LEAGUE OF NATIONS MANDATE

The northern part of the British-mandated territory was administered with the Northern Territories of the Gold Coast, the southern part with the Gold Coast Colony. Although the British administration built roads connecting its sphere with the road system of the Gold Coast, the bulk of the territory's external trade passed over the railways of French Togo.

French Togo was administered by a commissioner assisted by a consultative executive council. When British Togo was attached to the Gold Coast, French Togo was formed into a distinct unit until 1934, when a kind of economic union was established with Dahomey; this was replaced in 1936 by a qualified integration with French West Africa that lasted 10 years. Agricultural development was pursued, and a planned settlement of the interior by the Kabre and other peoples was carried out. Peanut (groundnut) cultivation was introduced in the northern areas, and energetic action was taken against trypanosomiasis (sleeping sickness).

After World War II French Togo sent a deputy to the French National Assembly, a counselor to the Assembly of the French Union, and two senators to the Council of the Republic. A representative assembly was concerned with internal affairs.

## UNITED NATIONS TRUSTEESHIP

In 1946 the British and French governments placed their spheres of Togoland under United Nations (UN) trusteeship. After 1947 the Ewe people in southern Togoland represented to the Trusteeship Council that either their territories or the whole of Togoland should be brought under a common administration. These proposals were difficult to implement because Ewe also inhabited the southeastern part of the Gold Coast Colony and because not all the people of southern Togoland were Ewe. The British colony was also rapidly advancing toward self-government, and the incorporation of the northern part of the British sphere with the Northern Territories of the Gold Coast had reunited the Dagomba and Mamprusi kingdoms, both of which had been cut in two by the pre-1914 boundary. Following a plebiscite held under UN auspices on May 9, 1956, the British trust territory of Togoland was on December 13 incorporated into the Gold Coast (although in the southern districts of Ho and Kpandu the Ewe vote showed a two-to-one majority in favour of continued British trusteeship). The Gold Coast and Togoland together were renamed Ghana and achieved independence in 1957.

## INDEPENDENCE

French Togoland became an autonomous republic within the French Union on Aug. 30, 1956. This status was confirmed (despite Ewe opposition) by a plebiscite held in October under French auspices. Nicolas Grunitzky was appointed premier. Following UN representations, elections in April 1958 favoured complete independence and rejected Grunitzky's Togolese Progress Party in favour of Sylvanus Olympio's Togolese National Unity Party. Togo became independent on April 27, 1960.

After the 1961 elections, which established a presidential form of government, Olympio became the first president. He maintained economic cooperation with France. Togo became a member of the Organization of African Unity (OAU, now the African Union) in 1963 and in 1965 subscribed to the renewed Joint African and Malagasy Organization, which provided for economic, political, and social cooperation among French-speaking African states.

Ghanaian pressure for the integration of Togo with Ghana was resisted by the Togolese and led to strained relations between the two republics, including a trade embargo imposed by Ghana. Olympio's increasingly harsh rule and policy of fiscal austerity came to an end on Jan. 13, 1963. Having rejected petitions to integrate into the national army Togolese noncommissioned officers recently demobilized from France's colonial armies, Olympio was shot at the gates of the U.S. embassy (while seeking sanctuary) by Sgt. Étienne Gnassingbé Eyadéma (later called Gnassingbé

*Togo's first president, Sylvanus Olympio, was in power from 1961 until 1963.* AFP/Getty Images

Eyadéma). Grunitzky was invited to return from exile and assume the presidency, and he was confirmed in office in subsequent elections that also created a new constitution and legislature. Most of the noncommissioned officers were integrated into an expanded army—many as commissioned officers.

Cabinet infighting, aggravated in the south by Ewe feelings that with Olympio's assassination they had lost power to Grunitzky's largely pro-northern administration, led to chronic instability. On Jan. 13, 1967, Eyadéma, then a lieutenant colonel and chief of staff, once again seized power and dissolved all political parties. Though relying primarily on the support of his kinsmen in the north and the largely northern-staffed army, Eyadéma's rule was stabilized by a number of other factors. Phosphate exports dramatically improved the economic picture, allowing the regime to satisfy regional and ethnic interests and to begin the first serious effort at transforming the countryside. Meticulous ethnic balancing of the cabinet and an open-door economic policy further attracted support from prospering traders (and smugglers into Ghana), and by 1972 Eyadéma felt secure enough to seek popular legitimation via a presidential plebiscite. In 1974 the phosphate industry was nationalized, generating increased state revenues. On Dec. 30, 1979, the first legislative elections since 1967 were held under a new constitution that formally placed Togo under civilian, one-party rule headed by President Eyadéma and the Rally of the Togolese

People. Legislative elections were held again in 1985.

Eyadéma's power was overtly challenged on Sept. 23, 1986, when a group of armed dissidents entered the country from Ghana. The ensuing violent confrontation between the dissidents and Togolese authorities, largely centred in Lomé, ended after several hours and resulted in the deaths or arrests of most dissidents. Later that year, Eyadéma was elected to a second seven-year term with almost 100 percent of the vote. A commission was established in 1990 to draft a new constitution, which prompted the legalization of political parties in 1991 and the adoption of a democratic constitution in 1992. However, in the first multiparty elections in August 1993, Eyadéma was reelected president amid allegations of electoral fraud, and the same charges were leveled in 1998. Protests over the 1998 elections continued into 1999, affecting the legislative elections held that year, and instigated an independent inquiry by the UN and the OAU. Their joint report, issued in 2001, found that the government had systematically violated human rights during the 1998 presidential election. Eyadéma's reelection in 2003 was again clouded by accusations of fraud; however, these claims were refuted by international observers.

Despite his long tenure, Eyadéma's regime was not without its opponents. Most of these were Ewe from the south (including the self-exiled sons of Olympio) rebelling against the northerner Eyadéma and the cult of personality that progressively surrounded him. The opposition sponsored conspiracies to topple Eyadéma and was held responsible for a number of bombings in Lomé. Civil unrest, in the form of strikes and sometimes-violent demonstrations, plagued Eyadéma as well. The regime's patronage base—and, by extension, its stability—was also undermined in the 1980s and '90s by an economic downturn. Falling global prices for phosphates led to sharply lower state revenues, while growing corruption and massive expenditures on the bloated civil service and inefficient public enterprises strained the fiscal resources of the state. Togo's costly government-owned industries were dismantled or privatized, and the country's heavy national debt was often rescheduled. In 2004 the European Union agreed to resume the flow of monetary aid to Togo, which had been halted in 1993 as a protest against the poor governance and lack of democracy in the country, if Togo met specified criteria addressing such issues as election reform and the repeal of controversial press laws.

After Eyadéma's unexpected death in February 2005, his son, Faure Gnassingbé, was hastily installed as president by the military—an action critics characterized as a coup. After weeks of international condemnation, Gnassingbé stepped down and a presidential election was held in April. He was declared the winner of that election, which was initially certified by some international observers as free and fair but later marred as reports of considerable fraud emerged. The opposition refused to immediately concede defeat, and hundreds of people were killed and thousands fled from the country in the violent post-election aftermath.

Dialogue between the government and the opposition—which had lapsed following the death of Eyadéma the previous year—resumed in 2006 and led, with opposition participation, to the formation of a transitional government. Legislative elections late the following year, in which the ruling party was victorious, were characterized as free and fair by international observers. Presidential elections held on March 4, 2010, were also deemed largely free and fair by international observers, although some procedural problems were noted. Gnassingbé was said to be the winner by a large margin over his closest opponent, but the main opposition group disputed the outcome.

# CONCLUSION

The history of western Africa is long and varied. Evidence indicates that the region has been inhabited since prehistoric time. Most documented accounts of the region's history begin about 1000 CE, and from this time the region's development can be traced with greater detail. The development of powerful African states such as Ghana, Mali, Songhai, Hausa, and Kanem-Bornu that flourished at various times during the 7th–19th centuries CE and their impact on the region is evident. The historical importance of such places as the famed city of Timbuktu—thought to have been founded about the 11th century and still in existence today—is also clear from documentation regarding its role as a trading post on the trans-Saharan caravan route and as a centre of Islamic culture *c.* 1400–1600. One can also see how western Africa was affected by the Atlantic slave trade, which began in the 15th century, reached its peak in the 18th century, and largely ended in the 19th century. The impact of the spread of Islam throughout the region across the centuries, particularly during the 19th century, remains prevalent in western Africa today.

Colonial partitioning and administration, which lasted well into the 20th century, also had a huge and lasting impact on the region. Indeed, most of the countries of western Africa today owe their borders to somewhat arbitrary divisions created by colonialism. The colonial experience differed for the many countries of the region. The majority of western African colonies were under British and French administration, and most gained independence under largely peaceful circumstances and enjoyed smooth transitions as they adjusted to their new status. The few colonies that were under Portuguese or Spanish administration were not so fortunate: Portugal's colonies of Cape Verde and Guinea Bissau achieved independence only after years of conflict, and Spain's lone colony of Equatorial Guinea was ill-prepared for its newfound status. Since decolonization, the region—like many other parts of the world—has had its share of peace, economic growth, and political stability as well as economic woes and conflict across ethnic, religious, and political lines. Nonetheless, many of the countries in the region have demonstrated their ability to aptly meet such challenges as they arise, and their ongoing success in doing so will shape western Africa's growth, prosperity, and stability in the 21st century.

# GLOSSARY

**animism** Belief in the existence of spirits separable from bodies.

**autochthonous** Formed or originating in the place where found.

**barracoon** An enclosure or barracks formerly used for temporary confinement of slaves or convicts.

**capricious** Impulsive and unpredictable.

**caravansary** An inn or public building (usually constructed outside the walls of a town or village) used for sheltering caravans and other travelers.

**coffle** Slaves or animals bound or chained together in a train.

**de facto** Existing as a matter of course, without lawful authority.

**de jure** Existing by right, according to the law.

**depredation** Ravaging or pillaging of an area or people.

**entrepôt** A warehouse, depot, or commercial centre.

**internecine** Pertaining to conflict that occurs between members of a group.

**irredentist** Concerned with regaining control of land that once belonged to one group or nation but later became subject to the rule of a foreign body.

**jihad** Arabic term literally meaning "struggle" or "battle." The term has come to denote any conflict waged for principle or belief and is often translated to mean "holy war," although it also signifies any internal struggle related to the practice of Islam and spiritual discipline.

**lacustrine** Pertaining to, formed in, living in, or growing in a lake.

**levirate** The sometimes compulsory marriage of a widow to a brother of her deceased husband.

**littoral** A coastal region.

**mission civilisatrice** French term literally meaning "civilizing mission." The idea served as justification for France's colonial policies and its effort to replace indigenous traditions with those it deemed more advanced or "civilized."

**overweening** Arrogant or presumptuous.

**paramountcy** Supremacy or dominance over others.

**parastatal** An organization that the government operates in either an official or unofficial capacity.

**plebiscite** A vote by the electorate expressing an opinion for or against a proposal, especially on a choice of government or ruler.

**potsherd** A pottery fragment usually unearthed as an archaeological relic.

**primus inter pares** First among equals.

**remunerative** Profitable.

**riverine** Pertaining to or located near a river.

**sororate** The marriage of one man to two or more sisters, usually successively and after the first wife has been found to be barren, or after her death.

**suzerainty** A relationship between states in which the international affairs of a subservient state are controlled by a more powerful one.

**tariqa** Arabic term literally meaning "road," "path," or "way." After the 12th century, the term came to designate a community or mystic order that followed a sheikh and his ritual system.

**tributary** A state or group that pays another ruler in exchange for protection or services.

**triumvirate** A ruling body composed of three jointly operated units.

# BIBLIOGRAPHY

The standard work on western Africa is J.F. Ade Ajayi and Michael Crowder (eds.), *History of West Africa*, 3rd ed., 2 vol. (1976–87). Treatment of the pre-jihad history of the western and central Sudan can be found in the classic by E.W. Bovill, *The Golden Trade of the Moors*, 2nd ed. rev. by Robin Hallett (1995). Robert Smith, *Kingdoms of the Yoruba*, 3rd ed. (1988), provides an early history of the Guinea region. Philip D. Curtin, *The Atlantic Slave Trade* (1969), provided an innovative analysis, but the basic data have been reworked in a useful general history, Paul E. Lovejoy, *Transformations in Slavery*, 2nd ed. (2000).

For the European partition of western Africa, one of the standard works is *West Africa Partitioned*, 2 vol. (1974–85); but see also A.S. Kanya-Forstner, *The Conquest of the Western Sudan* (1969, reprinted 2009). Coverage of the colonial period can be found in Anne Phillips, *The Enigma of Colonialism: British Policy in West Africa* (1989); and Martin Klein, *Slavery and Colonial Rule in French West Africa* (1998). Works dealing with the transition to independence include John D. Hargreaves, *Decolonization in Africa*, 2nd ed. (1996, reprinted 2001); and Prosser Gifford and Wm. Roger Louis (eds.), *The Transfer of Power in Africa: Decolonization, 1940–1960* (1982).

Coverage of western Africa since independence is included in Richard J. Reid, *A History of Modern Africa: 1800 to the Present* (2009). Political treatment of the postindependence period can be found in Patrick Chabal (ed.), *Political Domination in Africa* (1986); and R.A. Akindele, *Civil Society, Good Governance, and the Challenge of Regional Security in West Africa* (2003). For the Francophone states, good general surveys include Patrick Manning, *Francophone Sub-Saharan Africa, 1880–1985* (1988); and Charles Forsdick and David Murphy, *Francophone Postcolonial Studies: A Critical Introduction* (2003). No comparable survey exists for the Anglophone states, but see Peter Duignan and Robert H. Jackson (eds.), *Politics and Government in African States, 1960–1985* (1986). An introduction to the Lusophone states is Basil Davidson, *No Fist Is Big Enough to Hide the Sky*, new ed. (1983), on Guinea and Cape Verde. A useful source that contains historical overviews of each western African country and updated essays on political, social, and economic developments is Europa Regional Surveys of the World, *Africa South of the Sahara* (annual).

# INDEX